Hot Topics

Instructor's Manual for Books 1 2 3

Cheryl Pavlik
Rebecca Tarver Chase

THOMSON
HEINLE

Austrialia • Canada • Mexico • Singapore • United Kingdom • United States

THOMSON

HEINLE

HOT TOPICS INSTRUCTOR'S MANUAL
by *Cheryl Pavlik*
and *Rebecca Tarver Chase*

Publisher, Academic ESL: *James W. Brown*
Publisher, Adult ESL: *Sherrise Roehr*
Director of Product Development: *Anita Raducanu*
Development Editor: *Sarah Barnicle*
Editorial Assistants: *Katherine Reilly;
Bridget McLaughlin*
Marketing Manager: *Laura Needham*

Senior Production Editor: *Maryellen Killeen*
Senior Print Buyer: *Mary Beth Hennebury*
Project Manager: *Tunde A. Dewey*
Compositor: *Parkwood Composition*
Text Printer/Binder: *Thomson/West*
Cover and Interior Designer: *Lori Stuart*

Copyright © 2006 Thomson/Heinle, a part of the Thomson Corporation. Thomson Learning™ is a trademark used herein under license.

Printed in the United States
2 3 4 5 6 7 8 9 10   08 07 06

For more information, contact Thomson/Heinle, 25 Thomson Place, Boston, MA 002210 USA, or you can visit our Internet site at http://www.heinle.com

ALL RIGHTS RESERVED. No part of this work covered by the copyright hereon may be reproduced or used in any form or by any means—graphic, electronic, or mechanical, including photocopying, recording, taping, Web distribution or information storage and retrieval systems—without the written permission of the publisher.

For permission to use material from this text or product, contact us:
Tel   1-800-730-2214
Fax   1-800-730-2215
Web   www.thomsonrights.com

Library of Congress Control Number
2005921079

ISBN: 1-4130-0714-7

CONTENTS: Hot Topics 1

Contents: Hot Topics 1		iii
Contents: Hot Topics 2		iv
Contents: Hot Topics 3		v
To the Teacher (with additional notes about the Instructor's Manual)		vii
Chapter 1	Pampered Pets: Love me? Love my dog!	1
Chapter 2	Silly Sports: Can you really call this a sport?	4
Chapter 3	Modern Marriage: Until death do us part?	7
Chapter 4	Shopping: The New Drug of Choice	10
Chapter 5	Las Vegas: Sin City	14
Chapter 6	Shoplifting: Why is the price tag still on your hat?	17
Chapter 7	Gluttony: You are what you eat!	20
Chapter 8	Get-Rich-Quick Scams: Have I got a deal for *YOU!*	24
Chapter 9	Sports Doping: Does it matter if you win or lose?	27
Chapter 10	White-Collar Crime: When *A LOT* just isn't enough!	30
Chapter 11	The Homeless: It's Not Their Choice	33
Chapter 12	Beauty Contests: The Business of Beauty	36
Chapter 13	Drug Trends: Legal but Lethal	39
Chapter 14	Nature: Paradise Lost—Can we get it back?	42

CONTENTS: Hot Topics 2

◊◊◊	**Chapter 1**	Reality TV: Would you be a survivor?	**47**
◊◊◊	**Chapter 2**	Violence in Sports: When is a game not a game?	**50**
◊◊◊	**Chapter 3**	Advertising: We know what you want *before* you do!	**53**
◊◊◊	**Chapter 4**	Fashion: You mean you're wearing *THAT*?	**56**
◊	**Chapter 5**	Work: Is it interfering with your life?	**59**
◊◊◊◊	**Chapter 6**	Internet Dating: Is this really *YOUR* photo?	**63**
◊◊◊	**Chapter 7**	Anger: I'm not angry! You're angry!	**66**
◊◊	**Chapter 8**	Psychics: What do they know that we don't?	**69**
◊◊	**Chapter 9**	Beauty: Mirror, Mirror, on the Wall . . .	**72**
◊◊◊	**Chapter 10**	Lying: What's *THAT* on your resume?	**75**
◊	**Chapter 11**	Intelligence: How important is it?	**78**
◊◊	**Chapter 12**	Graffiti: You call this *ART*?	**81**
◊◊◊◊	**Chapter 13**	Child Labor: Who made your sneakers?	**84**
◊◊◊◊◊	**Chapter 14**	Infidelity: Our Cheating Hearts	**87**

CONTENTS: Hot Topics 3

Chapter 1	The Cruelty of Strangers: Who can you trust?	91
Chapter 2	Crime and Punishment: Justice for all?	94
Chapter 3	Fertility Now: Babies by Design	97
Chapter 4	Gambling: Wanna' bet?	100
Chapter 5	The Disabled: Handicapped? Not us!	103
Chapter 6	Marriage: Why marry just one?	108
Chapter 7	Prostitution: Looking for a good time?	111
Chapter 8	Education: Is *everyone* cheating?	114
Chapter 9	Gender: Are women weak? Are men necessary?	118
Chapter 10	Immigration: Is it time to shut the door?	121
Chapter 11	Business: Globalization or cultural imperialism?	125
Chapter 12	Sex Education: How much do we need to know?	128
Chapter 13	Cults: Path to God or somewhere else?	132
Chapter 14	Strange Brains: Unlocking the Secrets	136

TO THE TEACHER

In the 30 years that I have been in English language training (ELT), I have despaired of the lack of stimulating reading texts, accompanied by activities written specifically to energize and inspire the mature English learner. Why aren't many reading texts sufficient? Although English language learners may not yet have mastered English syntax, they still have interests beyond the mundane, and they certainly have ample reasoning ability. And while many reading texts are written about subjects of broad appeal, virtually all of them avoid topics that are deemed "too controversial" for the classroom setting. Unfortunately, many of those neglected topics are of great interest and relevance to adult lives. By steering course themes away from controversy, the instructor also steers students away from motivating and stimulating topics.

The *Hot Topics* series is different from other reading and discussion texts because it dares to deal with demanding subjects such as *crime, gender difference,* and *religion.* These topics have not been chosen to shock students, but merely to give them a chance to talk about matters that people discuss every day in their first languages. That said, not every topic will be appropriate for every classroom. Some themes such as *the disabled* will probably be acceptable in any classroom. Others such as *mental illness* or *prostitution* might prove problematic in some teaching situations. To assist, each chapter in the Brief Contents is rated by the amount of controversy it is likely to cause. Of course, teachers should read the articles in each chapter carefully and decide if their students would feel comfortable having a discussion on a particular topic. Another way to determine which chapters to use in class might be to have students look through the book and then vote on specific topics they are interested in reading and discussing. And finally, even though the chapters at the beginning of each book are generally easier than the chapters at the end, the text has been designed so that chapters can be omitted entirely or covered in a different order.

Series Overview

Hot Topics is a three-level reading discussion series written for inquisitive, mature English language learners. Each chapter contains several high-interest readings on a specific controversial and thought-provoking topic. *Hot Topics 1* and *2* are composed of highly adapted readings or pieces composed by the author. *Hot Topics 3* differs from the preceding two levels in that the majority of readings are authentic or only slightly adapted from sources such as the New York Times, CNN, and the BBC.

Reading Selections

Each level of *Hot Topics* consists of 14 chapters. The readings in *Hot Topics* are crafted to present students with challenging reading material including some vocabulary that one might not expect to find in a pre-college text. The reason for this is twofold. First, it is almost impossible to deal with these "hot" topics in a meaningful way without more sophisticated vocabulary. Second, and more importantly, it is ineffective to teach reading strategies using materials that provide no challenge. In the same way that one would not use a hammer to push in a thumbtack, readers do not need reading strategies when the meaning of a text is evident. Reading strategies are best learned when one *has to* employ them to aid comprehension.

Each chapter in each book is composed of two parts. Part I will contain two or three short readings on a topic. These readings are preceded by activities that help students make guesses about the genre, level, and content of the material, activating student schemata or background knowledge bases before reading the text. The readings are followed by extensive exercises that help students thoroughly analyze the content and the structure of the readings.

Part II consists of a single, more challenging reading. Although more difficult, the readings in Part II have direct topical and lexical connection to the readings in Part I. Research shows that the amount of background knowledge one has on a subject directly affects reading comprehension. Therefore, these readings will move the students to an even higher reading level by building on the concepts, information, and vocabulary that they have acquired in Part I. Complete comprehension of the text will not be expected, however. For some students this will prove a difficult task in itself. However, learning to cope with a less than full understanding is an important reading strategy—probably one of the most useful ones that nonnative readers will learn.

Chapter Outline and Teaching Suggestions

PART I

Preview

This section contains prereading questions, photographs, and activities that introduce the topic and some of the vocabulary. This section is best completed as group work or class discussion.

Predict

In this section, students are directed to look at certain features of the text(s) and then make predictions. These predictions include areas such as content, genre, level of difficulty, and reliability of the information.

Read It

This section is generally composed of two or three readings centered on a particular "hot" topic. In each reading, the topic is approached in a different style, chosen so that students will be able to experience a variety of genres such as newspaper, magazine and Internet articles, interviews, pamphlets, charts, and advertisements. Photographs occasionally serve as prompts to assist comprehension, or to stimulate curiosity and conversation about the topics.

Reading Comprehension

The reading comprehension section is composed of three sections.

- **Check Your Predictions**—Students are asked to evaluate their predicting ability.

- **Check the Facts**—Students answer factual questions. This is meant to be fairly simple and the exercise can be completed individually or in groups.

- **Analyze**—This section will include more sophisticated questions that will have students make inferences, as well as analyze and synthesize the information they have read.

Vocabulary Work

Vocabulary Work has two sections.

- **Guess Meaning from Context**—Exercises highlight probable unknown vocabulary words that students should be able to guess using different types of contextual clues. Some of the most common clues students should be looking for include: internal definitions, *restatement* or synonyms that precede or follow the new word, and examples. However, one of the most powerful ways to guess is to use *real world* knowledge. Students must learn to trust their own ability to make educated guesses about meaning based on their own experience.

- **Guess Meaning from Related Words**—This section focuses on words that can be guessed through morphological analysis. Although morphology is a "context clue," it is so important that it requires a chapter section of its own. The more students learn to recognize related words, the faster their vocabularies will grow. Students who speak languages such as Spanish—a language that has a large number of cognates or words that look similar to their English counterparts—should also be encouraged to use their native language knowledge as well.

Reading Skills

This section focuses on helpful reading skills and strategies, such as identifying cohesive elements, analyzing organization, understanding appositives and elipsis, and identifying the author's purpose.

Discussion

Questions in this section are designed to encourage class or group discussion. For instructors wishing to follow-up the readings with writing responses, it would be helpful for students to first discuss and then write their individual opinions and/or summarize those of their peers. Asking students to summarize is an effective way to examine their understanding of main ideas and themes from a reading.

PART II

Readings in Part II have been chosen so they are more challenging than those in Part I. Students are asked to read only for the most important ideas. The readings are chosen for:

- important ideas stated more than once,
- important ideas not obscured by difficult vocabulary and high-level structures,
- vocabulary from Part I readings,
- and forms of vocabulary words already seen in Part I.

Two activity sections follow the Part II reading. The first consists of questions that will help students gain the skill of identifying essential vocabulary and disregarding vocabulary they can ignore. The second part instructs and examines higher level reading skills such as understanding organization and metaphor.

Idea Exchange

Each chapter ends with a comprehensive discussion activity called Idea Exchange. This activity has two steps.

- **Think about Your Ideas**—This section is a structured exercise that helps students clarify their thoughts before they are asked to speak. By filling out charts, answering questions, or putting items in order, students clarify their ideas on the topic.
- **Talk about Your Ideas**—The language in this activity is directly applicable to the discussion questions in the step above.

CNN® Video Activities

The CNN video news clip activities at the back of the student text are thematically related to each chapter. Activities are designed to recycle themes and vocabulary from each chapter, and to encourage further class discussion and written responses to these real life news items.

A Word on Methodology and Classroom Management

Class Work, Group Work, Pair Work, and Individual Work

One of the most basic questions a teacher must decide before beginning an activity is whether it is best done as class work, group work, or individual work. Each has its place in the language classroom. For some activities, the answer is obvious. Reading should always be an individual activity. Reading aloud to the class can be pronunciation practice for the reader or listening practice for the listeners, but it is not reading for comprehension.

On the other hand, many activities in this text can be done successfully in pairs, groups, or with the entire class working together. If possible, a mix of individual, pair, group, and class work is probably best. For example, two students may work together and then share their work with a larger group that then shares its ideas with the entire class.

Some rules of thumb are:

- Pair work is often most successful in activities that have one right answer. Pairs should be able to check their answers or at least share them with the class.
- Groups work best when one group member records the discussion, so that the group can then report to the class. In this way, everyone gets the maximum benefit.
- Think of yourself as the manager of a whole class activity rather than the focal point. Make sure that students talk to each other, not just to you. For example, you might appoint yourself secretary and write students' ideas on the board as they are talking.

Error Correction

Language errors are bound to occur in discussions at this level. However, the purpose of the discussions in this text is fluency not accuracy. Therefore, errors should not be dealt with unless they make comprehension difficult or impossible. Make unobtrusive notes about persistent errors that you want to deal with later. In those cases where it is difficult to understand what a student is trying to say, first give the student a chance to clarify. If they cannot do this, restate what you think they are trying to say.

Dictionaries

Frequent dictionary use makes reading a slow, laborious affair. Students should be taught first to try to guess the meaning of a word using context and word form clues before they resort to a dictionary. In addition, although a good learner's English-English dictionary is helpful, bilingual dictionaries should be discouraged as they are often inaccurate. Students should use a dictionary that supplies simple and clear definitions, context sentences, and synonyms. We recommend *Heinle's Newbury House Dictionary with CD-ROM, 4th Edition*.

About the Instructor's Manual

The *Hot Topics Instructor's Manual for Books 1-3* provides chapter by chapter background information and teaching points, answer keys, and video scripts for each level of the series. The following are features of the instructor's notes.

- **Summary**—The notes include chapter summaries that briefly review each reading and its theme. Each reading has been recorded on audio CD and cassette tape, and the audio locations are found here in the *Instructor's Manual*.

- **Background**—Following the summary is background information providing historical details and the social context behind how the topics came to be so controversial or relevant to the contemporary cultural landscape.

- **Teaching Notes**—Teaching ideas for each chapter are included in this section. These ideas include ways to focus on particular exercises using different teaching methods. Ideas for group and pair work, as well as for writing assignments may be included.

- **Internet Activities**—To encourage students to read and research more about particular topics, Web sites are provided with suggestions for follow-up activities. However, because this publisher cannot guarantee the content at these Web addresses, these activities are easily adapted to key word searches using a reliable search engine. Whenever possible instructors should first investigate search results for appropriate material before assigning such searches to students. Remind students to never share personal or financial information with unreliable Web sites.

- **CNN Video Clip Summary**—Along with the video clip summaries, this section also provides video script locations in the *Instructor's Manual* and student book locations for the accompanying video activities.

Finally, thanks to all instructors who, by selecting the *Hot Topics* series, recognize that ESL students are mature learners who have the right to read about unconventional and provocative topics in the news. By offering your students challenging reading topics that encourage curiosity and debate, their ideas and opinions will become essential and fruitful parts of their classroom experience.

CHERYL PAVLIK

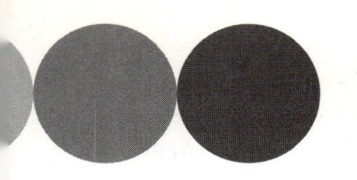

HOT TOPICS 1: Instructor's Manual

CHAPTER 1 — Pampered Pets: Love me? Love my dog!
Pages 1–12

Summary For people who believe that nothing is too good for their pets, this chapter presents a restaurant in Chicago that caters to dogs rather than people, a kennel that resembles a vacation resort, and in Part II, the next best thing to immortality for pets—cloning. Less extravagant viewpoints on pets are also offered.

Audio The readings in this chapter can be heard on the *Hot Topics 1* Audio CD 1 Tracks 1-3 or Audio Tape 1 Side A.

Background Inspired by the hard tack sea biscuits that sustained sailors, companies were manufacturing pet food as early as 1890. These days, pet food and treats may be in the form of dry kibble, canned food, or the semi-moist contents of foil pouches, and ingredients range from ordinary to organically grown. Besides food, pet stores offer toys, grooming tools, bedding and books, and services for pets include everything from the annual veterinary check-up to psychic readings and elaborate funerals.

Teaching Note Reinforce the ideas in the *Understanding Summaries* section and give students the opportunity to express their opinions about pets by having the students write paragraphs with summaries and quotations. First, students need to prepare a few questions related to the readings such as "Would you spend extra money to leave your dog at Camp Hideaway, or would you pay less for a standard kennel?" Then interview two or three classmates to find out their opinions, being sure to write down exact quotations. Students should use Part A on page 8 as a model to write their own paragraphs. If possible, combine all of the paragraphs in a document for the class to read and enjoy.

Internet Activity Have the class compile a chart showing how much money is spent on pets in a number of countries around the world. Students should enter the terms *spending pets China*, for example, to find out statistics for China. Be sure to locate information for all the students' countries, and if necessary, show them how to use an online currency exchange calculator such as http://www.xe.com/ucc/ in order to present the amounts in a consistent way.

Video Clip Summary Jen Rogers reports on a variety of ways that some pet owners splurge on their pets, from organic pet food to acupuncture and expensive surgery.

Video Script Go to page 3 in this Instructor's Manual for the "Pampering Your Pet" video script and recommended video vocabulary for review.

Video Activity Go to page 169 in the student book for activities to accompany the CNN video clip.

ANSWER KEY—Chapter 1: Pampered Pets: Love me? Love my dog!

PREVIEW (Page 1): Answers will vary.

PART I

Predict (Page 2)
A.
1. Reading 2
2. Reading 1
3. Reading 1
4. Reading 1

Reading Comprehension

Check Your Predictions (Page 4): Answers will vary.

Check the Facts

Reading 1 (Page 5)
A.
1. True (but only Candy)   5. False
2. False   6. False
3. False   7. True
4. True

Chapter 1 • Hot Topics 1   1

B.

1. **Vera Carter (restaurant owner)** She does not think a restaurant for dogs is strange. She thinks that food is a way for pet owners to return the loyalty and love their animals give them.
Carl Gregory (pet industry expert) He agrees with Carter, and notes that Americans spent twice as much money on pets in 2004 as they did in 1994.
Jack Simpson (web blogger) He thinks dog restaurants are absurd.
Sherry Evans (pet owner) She disagrees with Simpson.

2. hotels—rooms for pets and room service for pets
restaurants—pet food
bakeries—pet treats

Reading 2 (Page 6)
A.

1. True	2. False
3. False	4. False
5. True	6. False

B.

1. They have pool time and play time.
2. Cats have private rooms with windows. Dogs have indoor heated dog runs, and an outdoor exercise area for social dogs.

Analyze (Page 6) (Answers may vary.)
Suggested answers:

1. Yes, because he is interested in the pet industry.
2. Yes, because hotels offer rooms for people and their pets.
3. No, because she says her dog Lulu is her baby.
4. Yes, because it has special facilities.
5. They refer to common pet names. He uses them because it makes the article more interesting.

Vocabulary Work
Guess Meaning from Context: Using World Knowledge (Page 7)
(Answers may vary.)

eating stands—knowledge about restaurants and food vendors
pet treats—knowledge about bakeries
dog runs—knowledge about dogs

Understanding Summaries (Page 8)

A. *Some people don't like the idea of a restaurant for dogs* is a summary of Jack Simpson's ideas, so *absurd* probably has a negative meaning. *Dog owner Sherry Evans doesn't agree* is also a summary, so we can guess that *ridiculous* has a negative meaning and *sweet* and *precious* are positive.

B. The amount 34 million dollars is two times as much as 17 million dollars.

Guess Meaning from Related Words (Page 8)

Phrase	Meaning
peanut butter-flavored ice cream	ice cream that tastes like peanut butter
pet-industry expert	an expert in the business of products for pets
pet-friendly rooms	rooms where you can have pets
mail-order steak	steak you can order by mail
sit-down restaurant	a restaurant with tables and chairs

Reading Skills
Identifying the Author's Purpose (Page 9)

1. Reading 1 informs readers. The writer wants readers to know about all the new services for pets, which indicate how much people pamper their pets.
2. Reading 2 persuades readers. The writer wants readers to take their pets to Camp Hideaway.
3. a. The writer uses quotes in Reading 1 to show how people feel about the different services for pets.
b. We do not know the writer's opinion.
4. a. The writer uses exclamation points for emphasis.
b. confidence; high-class place; enjoy; respected; private; happy
c. The author says only positive things about Camp Hideaway, so she / he must think it's a good place for animals.

Discussion (Page 9): Answers will vary.

PART II (Page 10)

1. Exact genetic copies.
2. It clones cats and soon will clone dogs.
3. They guarantee that the clone will be healthy and that it will look a lot like the original animal.
4. No. Some pet owners would rather have another pet.

Vocabulary Work

Guess Meaning from Context (Page 11)

(Answers may vary.)

1. a. Something related to genes. It also has to do with cloning, so it is probably something about making clones.
   b. *Billion* looks like *million,* so it is probably a number. *Multi-* may mean many. It probably means many million.
   c. They guarantee that the clone will be healthy. It probably means something like promise.
   d. It contains the word love and describes a pet. Therefore, it is probably a pet that loves a person or a person that loves a pet.
   e. An animal shelter is a place that you can go to get a new pet. It is probably a place that takes care of unwanted pets or something like a pet store.

2. a. This doesn't mean "lose" like "can't find." It refers to cats dying. Probably it is another word for dying.
   b. Late usually means "not on time." However, that doesn't make sense in this sentence. It describes her cat that died.

Reading Skills

Analyzing Quotations (Page 11)

1. Lou Hawthorne — *for*
2. Marsha Brooks — *for*
3. Karen Lawrence — *against*

CNN Video Activities: Pampering Your Pet

Understand It (Page 169)

1. c   2. b   3. a   4. d

VIDEO TRANSCRIPT—Chapter 1: Pampering Your Pet

DVD Title 2   Running time: 01:58

Video Vocabulary

beck and call — ready to obey
booming — time of rapid growth in business
dog day — a period of stagnation or inactivity
lap of luxury — to be in a position of great wealth
pamper — to take more care of something than is necessary
watch your figure — to be careful not to gain weight

Video Script

Reporter: Sushi? Acupuncture? 24-hour room service? Pampering the family pet has taken on new proportions.

Karen Stein: Sushi, poochie sushi, treats. And all the food here is organic. There's no sugar. It's the right amount of fiber. And this one has been purchased by Minnie Driver, Salma Hayak, Leeza Gibbons.

Reporter: It's not just celebrities spending big to keep their lapdogs in the lap of luxury.

Sandra Rosker-Kelly: There isn't anything that I can't believe. We've seen everything.

Reporter: At this cat hotel, you can watch TV from the privacy of your own room while also watching your figure.

Sandra Rosker-Kelly: We have a lot of, um, extraordinary diets, like raw food diets.

Reporter: Whatever your cat's tastes, naturally having a staff of five at your feline's beck and call will cost you. A room with a TV runs $35 a day. But that's nothing compared to the booming business of animal hospitals.

Dr. David Bruyette: We do a lot of orthopedic surgeries, knee surgeries, hip surgeries, and a lot of cancer surgeries. Total hip replacement surgeries run around $4 to 4,500 and then cancer surgeries, depending on the type of surgery and the type of aftercare afterwards, can run, you know, 5, 6, 7 thousand dollars.

Reporter: Of course some owners have pet insurance, but others give their credit cards a workout. Spending freely on the latest treatments - high tech or alternative.

Dr. William Farber: I practice a lot of acupuncture, chiropractic. I use herbs, nutraceuticals, homeopathic agents, Bach flower remedies to try and compliment what we're doing in terms of Western therapeutic measures.

Reporter: New Age music, a skilled pair of hands, a dog day most people would take any day of the week.

Jen Rogers, CNN Financial News, Los Angeles.

CHAPTER 2 — Silly Sports: Can you really call this a sport?

Pages 13–24

Summary So you haven't heard of extreme ironing? Find out all the details in Reading 1 of this chapter. Reading 2 discusses competitive eating, and the reading in Part II draws the line between sports, athletic competitions, and other activities.

Audio The readings in this chapter can be heard on the *Hot Topics 1* Audio CD 1 Tracks 4-6 or Audio Tape 1 Side A.

Background In Reading 1 we meet Phil Shaw, who invented extreme ironing, and who would like to see the offbeat sport included in the Olympics someday. His dream may be a long shot, but recently baseball and softball were voted out of the games. Supporters of more conventional sports like golf, karate, and rugby are making bids to replace the ousted sports, but perhaps the International Olympic Committee is ready for something a little more outlandish. Phil Shaw hopes so.

Teaching Note Recycle the vocabulary from the chart on page 20 by giving students the chance to invent their own silly sport. Encourage them to use as many of the words as possible, for example by explaining what equipment *competitors* need and where they *compete*. They can describe the *championship*, and say who the *corporate* sponsors are. This activity could be written or oral, and visual aids might be helpful as well as fun.

Internet Activity Invite students to visit the official homepage of extreme ironing at www.extremeironing.com, where they'll find information about competitions and other extreme ironing news. One of the features of the site is the galleries, where students can enjoy photos of competitors ironing underwater or clinging to cliffs. Instruct them to scan for all the place names they can find, then report back to the class, pointing out on a world map all the places they saw in the photos.

Video Clip Summary The occasion is the Thanksgiving Invitational, where contestants win by eating the largest number of turkey dinners in twelve minutes. Competitive eaters describe some of their accomplishments, including reindeer eating and glazed doughnut eating. Footage of contestants' food-covered faces ranks "moderate" on the "gross-out" scale.

Video Script Go to page 6 in this Instructor's Manual for the "The Sport of Eating" video script and recommended video vocabulary for review.

Video Activity Go to page 170 in the student book for activities to accompany the CNN video clip.

ANSWER KEY — Chapter 2: Silly Sports: Can you really call this a sport?

PREVIEW (Page 13): Answers will vary.

PART I

Predict (Page 14)

A.

1. Readings 1 & 2
2. Readings 1 & 2
3. Reading 2
4. Readings 1 & 2

B. Answers will vary.

Reading Comprehension

Check Your Predictions (Page 16): Answers will vary.

Check the Facts

Reading 1 (Page 17)

A.

1. True
2. False
3. False
4. True
5. True
6. True

B.

1. iron / ironing board / clothes   2. c   3. b

Reading 2 (Page 18)

A.

1. False   3. True   5. False   7. True
2. True   4. False 6. False

B.

1. a & c
2. (Answers will vary.)

lobster eating   rice ball eating
bean eating   cow brain eating
hard-boiled egg eating   chicken wing eating
taco eating   matzo ball eating
hot dog eating   pickle eating

Hot Topics 1 • Chapter 2

Analyze (Page 18)

1. Yes, because it is a physical activity and it is competitive.
2. The writer doesn't want to say that the competitors vomit after they eat, but he implies it. He says that they aren't fat and they use metal buckets.

Vocabulary Work

Guess Meaning from Context (Page 19)

It can help because everything in the list is something that you need to iron. Since the list includes an iron and an ironing board, "laundry" must be clothes.

All the items in the list are food competitions so chicken-wings, pickles, and matzo balls must be kinds of food.

(Answers may vary.)

1. Both of these things must be things you can use to heat an iron.
2. The first sentence says that the ironing is important. The phrase contains the word well. I think pressed may mean the same as iron.
3. A sponsor is someone who pays your bills.
4. A kayak is probably a kind of boat that is difficult to iron on.

Guess Meaning from Related Words (Page 20)

1.

Reading 1

compete / competition / competitor
corporation / corporate
champion / championship

Reading 2

competition / competitive
champion / championship

2.

Noun (person): competitor, champion
Noun (thing): competition, corporation, championship
Verb: compete
Adjective: competitive, corporate
Adverb:

3. (Answers may vary.)

a. An ironing board is something that you use to iron clothes on.
b. An electric generator is something that makes electricity.
c. A gas stove is something that uses gas to make heat for cooking.
d. Underwater means below the surface of the water.
e. Ballroom dancing is a kind of formal dancing.
f. Synchronized swimming is a kind of group swimming.

Reading Skills

Finding Main Ideas and Supporting Details (Page 21)

(Answers may vary.)

Paragraph 1: *Main Idea*—Although not all activities are sports, extreme ironing is a sport since it combines physical activity with competition.
Detail—Gardening is definitely not a sport.
Paragraph 2: *Main Idea*—The definition of extreme ironing is pressing clothes in very difficult places.
Detail—Some ironists take electric generators to the competition site.
Paragraph 3: *Main Idea*—Extreme ironists compete in some amazing places.
Detail—Contestants iron in canoes.
Paragraph 4: *Main Idea*—Extreme ironists are serious about their sport.
Detail—Phil Shaw is the inventor of extreme ironing.

PART II (Page 22)

1. golf / baseball
2. The competition itself, not a judge or judges, should decide the result.
3. No, because some athletes such as gymnasts are judged.
4. No. The author says that bowlers and golfers are not athletes.

Vocabulary Work

Guess Meaning from Context (Page 23)

1. result—decision
2. determine—decide
3. influence—affect
4. umpires/referees—people who makes sure that competitors follow the rules
5. athleticism—physical ability
6. curling—a game
7. participate—take part in

Reading Skills

Understanding the Writer's Tone (Page 24)

1. No. The writer begins by saying "In my opinion", and ends in the same way, saying that NASCAR is

not even good entertainment. It seems reasonable, but it doesn't give both sides of the argument.

2. Readers may not agree that bowling is a sport, or that figure skating is not a sport. They may not agree that NASCAR isn't good entertainment.

CNN Video Activities: The Sport of Eating
Understand It (Page 170)

A. 1. c   2. b   3. d   4. d
B. 1. c   2. a   3. b

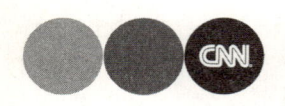

VIDEO TRANSCRIPT—Chapter 2: The Sport of Eating
DVD Title 3   Running time: 02:32

Video Vocabulary

Khyber Pass   a 33-mile mountain pass connecting the mountains of Pakistan and Afghanistan

stuff   to fill, usually tightly or completely, by pushing something into something else

shovel   to pick up or move something with a shoveling motion

utensil   a tool or implement, especially for eating food

Video Script

Reporter: Most people stuff the turkey. These turkeys stuff themselves.
Announcer: He's got a throat that makes the Khyber Pass look like the eye of the needle.
Reporter: They call it the Thanksgiving Invitational, though it didn't look so inviting to us.
Announcer: It looks as if he has just bitten off the head of a turkey.
Reporter: And you thought the hot dog eating contest was gross. Now we've got to watch these guys gobble, gobble, gobble.
George Shea: Let's get the Thanksgiving meal over and done with in 12 minutes and get to the TV for football.
Reporter: The goal to eat as many one pound plates of food as possible in 12 minutes.
Announcer: You may use your hand to help with the eating process. But you may not shovel the food into your mouth with your hand.
Reporter: For some it was BYOU, bring your own utensils.
Man: It's the ultimate weapon in eating.
Reporter: Though the utensils seem to trip up some of the contestants, as did the green beans.
Announcer: In France, Richard, we call green beans "haricot vert".
Reporter: These guys make kids seem like Miss Manners. Competitors belong to the International Federation of Competitive Eating.
George Shea: The IFOCE is the world body that governs all stomach centric sports.
Reporter: They don't stop at turkey or hot dogs. Take Dale Boone.
Dale Boone: I'm also the reindeer world eating champion.
Reporter: Or contest judge George Lerman.
George Lerman: I hold two jalapeño pepper titles. I'm the current hamburger champ out of Duluth, Minnesota.
Reporter: Or Eric "Badlands" Booker.
Eric Booker: And also 49 glazed donuts in 8 minutes.
Reporter: Booker prepared for the turkey contest by eating up to 10 pounds of cabbage a day.
Eric Booker: It gives the stomach a nice stretch.
Reporter: Bill Leiderman attributes his skills to what he calls the bonus lamb chop from childhood. Get out your calculator.
Bill Leiderman: There were four of us in the family. You know lamb chops come in packages of 3. So they'd always come back with nine lamb chops. So there'd be two each plus one extra lamb chop. Whoever ate those first two lamb chops first got that bonus chop.
Announcer: You may stand if you like. 3, 2, 1.
Reporter: The winner is a 440 pound subway conductor.
Announcer: With five and a half pounds of Thanksgiving meal: Eric "Badlands" Booker.
Reporter: Five and a half plates makes going back for seconds seem like a diet.
Eric Booker: Oh yeah, yeah. I'm not even full. I'm not even half full.
Announcer: They are not eating like turkeys. No, they are eating like swine.
Reporter: Watching these guys eat is enough to make you go cold turkey.

Jeannie Mose, CNN, New York.

Hot Topics 1 • Chapter 2

CHAPTER 3 — Modern Marriage: Until death do us part?
Pages 25–36

Summary In the form of an advice column, Reading 1 raises the very modern question of whether it's acceptable for women to propose marriage to men. In Reading 2, a pair of researchers uses a point system and videotaped conversations between married people in order to predict the likelihood of couples getting divorced. The Reading in Part II explains that the governments of the United States and Singapore are trying to encourage marriage, but for very different reasons.

Audio The readings in this chapter can be heard on the *Hot Topics* 1 Audio CD 1 Tracks 7-9 or Audio Tape 1 Side A.

Background Marriage, that time-honored institution, may not at first glance seem like a controversial topic. On closer inspection, there is plenty to talk about: people questioning the traditional gender roles associated with marriage, people of different races or nationalities getting married, people deciding to live together without ever getting married, and gay marriage being legalized in some places. And if marriage itself isn't interesting enough, the topic of divorce raises an additional set of issues.

Teaching Note The *Reading Skills* section in Part I draws the students' attention to transition words and phrases, which are very helpful for comprehension, but only if the reader notices them. After discussing the article in Part II, have students re-read it, searching for any transition words or phrases. Ask them to explain the function of those they find.

Internet Activity Search the Internet for an interactive marriage quiz that is appropriate for your group of students — something along the lines of *Are you ready for marriage?* or *Will your marriage last?* or *Is he/she the one?* After everyone takes the quiz, discuss the results, then let small groups create their own quizzes for classmates to take. Maintain an atmosphere of fun so that students don't base important life decisions on quizzes such as these!

Video Clip Summary The State of Oklahoma hopes to reduce poverty by reducing the divorce rate. Governor Frank Keating says that investing state money in marriage counseling will save money in the long run. The clip opens and closes with scenes from a wedding, and couples involved in a marriage workshop are also shown.

Video Script Go to page 9 in this Instructor's Manual for the "State-sponsored Marriage in Oklahoma" video script and recommended video vocabulary for review.

Video Activity Go to page 171 in the student book for activities to accompany the CNN video clip.

ANSWER KEY — Chapter 3: Modern Marriage: Until death do us part?

PREVIEW (Page 25): Answers will vary.

PART I

Predict (Page 26)

A.
1. Readings 1 & 2
2. Readings 1 & 2
3. Reading 1
4. Reading 2

B. Answers will vary.

Reading Comprehension

Check Your Predictions (Page 29): Answers will vary.

Check the Facts

Reading 1 (Page 29)

A.
1. False   3. False   5. False   7. True
2. False   4. True   6. False

B.
1. educated / strong / self-confident
2. The proposal shouldn't be a surprise. She should write it down and practice it.

Reading 2 (Page 30)

A.
1. True   4. True   7. False
2. False   5. False   8. True
3. False   6. True

B.
1. physical information
   conversation
   body language / facial reactions
2. rolls her eyes
   smiles

Analyze (Page 31)

1. Halle Berry. The sentence says, "In real life . . ."
2. (Answers may vary.) Because a lot of people drink champagne at weddings.

Vocabulary Work

Guess Meaning from Context (Page 31)

A. 1. c   2. a   3. b   4. e   5. d

B. (Answers may vary.)
1. these days; at this time
2. information about the body

Guess Meaning from Related Words

1.

Reading 1 (Page 31)

1. propose / proposal
2. self-confident / self-confidence
3. advice / advisor / advise
4. columnist

Reading 2 (Page 32)

1. married / marriage
2. mathematical / mathematician
3. predicts / prediction
4. necessary / necessarily
5. psychology / psychologist
6. agree / disagree

2.

Noun (person): advisor, columnist, mathematician, psychologist
Noun (thing): proposal, self-confidence, advice, column, marriage, prediction, psychology
Verb: propose, advise, predict, agree / disagree
Adjective: self-confident, married, mathematical, necessary
Adverb: necessarily

Reading Skills (Page 33)

Understanding Transition Words and Phrases

1. add ideas
2. add ideas
3. time order
4. time order
5. time order

PART II (Page 33)

1. Singapore / the U.S.
2. Singapore has a marriage service. The U.S. is teaching people about marriage.
3. The U.S. program is for poor people. The Singapore program is for young single people.
4. In the U.S. some people think that marriage is a private decision. In Singapore, some people think that the program is good. Others think that it is not the government's business.

Vocabulary Work

Guess Meaning from Context (Page 35)

1. matchmakers — people who introduce single people to each other
2. computer-dating service — an Internet company that matches single people with common interests and likes
3. promote — support
4. organize — arrange; control

Reading Skills

Identifying Referents (Page 35)

1. the government's
2. the programs
3. women with children
4. some people
5. some people
6. poor women

CNN Video Activities: State-sponsored Marriage in Oklahoma

Understand It (Page 171)

1. divorce
2. initiative
3. five
4. poor
5. workshops
6. marry
7. tax payers
8. experiment

VIDEO TRANSCRIPT—Chapter 3: State-sponsored Marriage in Oklahoma

DVD Title 4   Running time: 03:23

Video Vocabulary

backwards   in the opposite or wrong order
initiative   the first step
movement   a political or social cause
workshop   a small group of students or professionals who study together

Video Script

Reporter: It's an April wedding in Oklahoma, a state that has a lot riding on marriage.

Man 1: And pledge my life and love to you.

Man 2: And pledge my life and love to you.

Reporter: Oklahoma has the second highest divorce rate in the country. State officials say in half the counties divorce petitions outnumber marriage licenses. So the governor has launched a marriage initiative. Why a marriage initiative?

Governor: Strictly for the purpose of lifting this state up economically.

Reporter: Governor Frank Keating has put his state at the forefront of the marriage movement, vowing to cut the state's divorce rate by a third in ten years. Marriage is so personal and intimate, should it be government's business to promote marriage?

Governor: If the marriage doesn't work out, guess what? A judge that you've never met in your life, you don't know that person from Adam, determines where your paycheck goes and where do the kids live. If that's not government being intrusive, I don't know what government could do any worse.

Reporter: The idea behind the marriage movement is that marriage is an antidote to poverty. The poverty rate for single mothers is five times that of married couples with children. Promoting weddings may make politicians feel good, but a number of critics say the marriage movement is a simplistic fix that won't necessarily lift people out of poverty. Being unmarried, they say, is usually a symptom of poverty, not the cause.

Woman 1: Oklahoma really has it backwards. It's true that divorce causes poverty in some cases, but what's even more true is that poverty causes divorce. Poor people are less likely to get married and they're less likely to stay married.

Reporter: But Oklahoma is betting on marriage. Governor Keating has set aside ten million dollars in welfare money to promote marriage.

Woman 2: Me and him, we hardly ever talk.

Woman 3: Today what we're trying to do is to approach a new way to be heard.

Reporter: Some of that money has gone to training volunteers around the state to run marriage workshops. Available free to any couple, married or thinking about it.

Man: I can feel that, though, Fay is trying to push more on me than I can handle. It may not be real; it may not be accurate. But that's the way I feel.

Reporter: Keating has also corralled 800 ministers around the state into signing a marriage covenant.

Man 2: Hey Heather. How are you?

Reporter: That means they'll only marry couples that go through premarital counseling first.

Man 3: You know, I'm not one of the best listeners around and especially when you get emotion, you know, running through it.

Reporter: Heather and Chris plan to marry in May.

Man 2: We have had a lot of couples that decide, even without my initiating it, not to get married. They just decided that they agreed to part company.

Reporter: Governor Keating believes supporting marriage with tax dollars pays off. He says tax payers pay the price when marriages fall apart in welfare, broken homes, and damaged children.

Governor: We think to take a little drop at the front end to avoid a flood at the tail end makes good sense.

Reporter: Keating admits the marriage initiative is an experiment, but with one in two marriages ending in divorce he says we can't afford not to try it.

Kathy Slobogin, CNN, Oklahoma City.

CHAPTER 4 — SHOPPING: THE NEW DRUG OF CHOICE
Pages 37–48

Summary Chapter 4 examines our love of shopping. Reading 1 describes the psychological effects of shopping on recreational shoppers, and Reading 2 is an enticing advertisement for a California shopping mall. The author of Part II takes a stand against consumerism, and suggests that we can have more satisfying lives by spending less.

Audio The readings in this chapter can be heard on the *Hot Topics 1* Audio CD 1 Tracks 10-12 or Audio Tape 1 Side A.

Background At one end of the spectrum are compulsive shoppers, or "shopaholics", who seem to have no control over their impulse to spend. At the other end are people who argue that consumerism is bad for communities and the environment, not to mention personal finances. Somewhere between are the recreational shoppers, who enjoy the shopping experience as a pleasant form of entertainment.

Teaching Note We sometimes say that numbers don't lie, and numbers and statistics as supporting details can indeed be very convincing. To illustrate this, ask the students to find all of the numbers in Reading 2, and have a discussion about the purpose of those numbers. For example, 53 movies is a larger number than any normal cinema complex can offer, so there must be a great variety of movies—something for everyone. Go back to Chapter 3 and do the same with Readings 1 and 2, which contain research statistics involving proposals and married couples.

Internet Activity Visit http://www.media-awareness.ca/english/parents/marketing/index.cfm or http://frugalliving.about.com/od/consumerism/, which contain articles on marketing, consumerism, and anti-consumerism. Create a worksheet with directions to an appropriate article, along with several questions for the students to answer while reading the article. Other articles can be found by entering the word *consumerism* in an Internet search engine. (Many of these will have a more editorial tone than the articles at the sites above.)

Video Clip Summary Reporter Michelle Han takes a look at financial responsibility for older children, or "'tweens". The clip features Rosie, a 'tween whose mother is determined to teach her daughter how to handle money. Then-mayor Arnold Schwarzenegger makes an appearance, comparing the lessons about money he teaches his children with the lessons he plans to teach Sacramento, and the instructor of a financial awareness class in Hong Kong and author Nathan Dungan offer their expert opinions.

Video Script Go to page 12 in this Instructor's Manual for the "'Tween Addiction to Shopping" video script and recommended video vocabulary for review.

Video Activity Go to page 172 in the student book for activities to accompany the CNN video clip.

ANSWER KEY—Chapter 4: SHOPPING: THE NEW DRUG OF CHOICE

PREVIEW (Page 37): Answers will vary.

PART I

Predict (Page 38)
A.
1. Readings 1 & 2
2. Reading 2
3. Reading 2
4. Reading 1

B. Answers will vary.

Reading Comprehension

Check Your Predictions (Page 40): Answers will vary.

Check the Facts

Reading 1 (Page 41)
A.
1. False
2. True
3. False
4. False
5. True
6. True
7. False
8. False

Hot Topics 1 • Chapter 4

B.

1.

	more materialistic	older	more self-confident	less self-control
recreational shoppers	✔			✔
ordinary shoppers		✔	✔	

2. b & c

Reading 2 (Page 42)
A.

1. True
3. False
5. True

2. True
4. False
6. False

B.

1. at the Food Court
2. You can shop, eat, and go to the movies. You can also go to concerts, fashion shows, parties, and parades.

Analyze (Page 42)

1. Yes, because there are a lot of stores. There are also many other things to do.
2. The writer probably disagrees with recreational shopping because at the end of the article the writer compares it to other addictions. *"However, in the future will we think of recreational shopping as an addiction like smoking or drinking?"*

Vocabulary Work
Guess Meaning from Context (Page 42)

1.

a. identify / verb / to recognize something
b. ordinary / adjective / normal or regular
c. material / adjective / physical
d. negative / adjective / bad
e. pretended / verb / behaved like actors in an imaginary situation
f. contemporary / adjective / modern

2.

1. Venue is a kind of place.
2. Carts & kiosks are a kind of place.
3. A roof is probably a thing or place.
4. Fashion show is a kind of activity.
5. Baby back ribs are a kind of food.

3.

I know happiness is good. "And" is the connector, so fulfillment is probably good, too.
Worried and angry are bad. "Or" is the connector, so depressed is probably bad, too.

Guess Meaning From Related Words

1.

Reading 1 (Page 43)

1. addicted / addiction / addicts
2. recreation / recreational
3. happy / happiness

Reading 2 (Page 44)

1. special / specialty
2. informal / formal

2.

Noun (person):
Noun (thing): addiction, recreation, speciality, happiness
Verb:
Adjective: addicted, recreational, special / speciality, informal / formal, happy
Adverb:

3.

shoppertainment: shopper and entertainment (entertainment for shoppers)
moviegoers: movie and go and —er suffix for person (people who go to movies)
seafood: sea and food (food from the sea)
pocketbook: pocket and book (Pocketbook is misleading. It is not a book that you keep in your pocket. It is a purse.)

Reading Skills

Identifying the Author's Purpose (Page 44)

What is the author's purpose in each article? Why do you think so? (Answers may vary. Suggested responses below.)

1.
A. To teach readers how to do something.
B. To inform readers about something. (Reading 1 & 2)
C. To describe something to readers. (Reading 2)
D. To persuade readers to do something. (Reading 2)

2.
Reading 1 is to inform. Reading 2 is to persuade.

PART II (Page 45)

1. yes
2. They buy food and other things. They eat in restaurants. They go to movies and amusement parks.
3. Non-consuming experiences are more important because we create the experience.
4. We can consume less.

Vocabulary Work

Guess Meaning from Related Words (Page 46)

1. consume / consumer / consuming / non-consuming / consumerist
2. action / interaction
3. create / recreated
4. package / packaged

Guess Meaning from Context (Page 47):
(Answers may vary.)

1. An amusement park is a place to spend money. It is a kind of park, so it is probably for recreation. (Amuse means to enjoy, so it is a place to enjoy yourself.)
2. A drive-thru is a place to spend money. Thru sounds like through, so it is probably a place you can drive your car into. Perhaps it is like a fast food restaurant.
3. A convenience store is a place to spend money. It is a kind of store. (Convenient means easy, so it is an easy place to shop.)
4. Pump is a noun, with gas as an adjective. Perhaps it is a place to buy gasoline.

Reading Skills

Read for Main Ideas (Page 47)

Paragraph 1: Introduction—we consume most of the time
Paragraph 2: Explanation of why consuming activities aren't special
Paragraph 3: Explanation of why non-consuming activities are special
Paragraph 4: Call to action

CNN Video Activities: 'Tween Addiction to Shopping

Understand It (Page 172)

A.
1. False   2. True   3. False
4. True   5. True   6. False

B. 1. b   2. c   3. a

VIDEO TRANSCRIPT—Chapter 4: 'TWEEN ADDICTION TO SHOPPING
DVD Title 5   Running time: 03:53

Video Vocabulary

allowance   money for everyday expenses
budget   to make financial predictions
discipline   control of the mind and body
gratitude   thankfulness
sensitize   to make sensitive or hypersensitive
temptation   a desire for something
'tween   a child between middle childhood and adolescence, usually between 8 and 12 years old

Video Script

Arnold Schwarzenegger: Maria and I, we teach our kids the basic principles. We teach them don't spend more money than you have, that's what I teach my six year old. And I promise you, that is what I will teach Sacramento.

Kid: I want to buy this for my mobile.

Reporter: But teaching kids to save could be more difficult than saving Sacramento because most children today have very unhealthy financial habits.

Rosie: I don't even save money.

Kid 2: I just go into a shop and then I just buy everything.

Rosie: I'm really bad so my mum has to keep my money otherwise, like, I go really crazy and I don't look after it.

Reporter: Eleven-year-old Rosie has a weekly allowance. Out of it comes bus rides and food, anything left she can use herself. But the temptation to spend and spend it quickly is greater than Rosie's willpower. She's been known to call home for help when stranded on the wrong end of the ferry.

Rosie: My mum always wonders where my money goes and stuff. She keeps thinking I, like, flush it down the toilet.

Reporter: Do you think it's important to try and save?

Rosie: No.

Reporter: Rosie is what marketing people label a "tween." A generation worth hundreds of billions of spending dollars a year and twice that when influencing parental purchases. They're tempted by DVDs, CDs, computer games, fashion and sports goods. No wonder consumer experts like Annette Nazaroff develop sophisticated ways to reach the Rosies of the world, as well as their parents' hard earned cash.

Annette Nazaroff: One of our clients, Nike, for instance, goes to a lot of trouble to think about where children are at, how they talk amongst themselves and what they aspire to and reaches them in their place. They come into their world using their language and I believe that's very successful.

Reporter: Successful, yes, if you're selling to kids. But not if you're Rosie's mother trying to teach her simple principles like budgeting and saving. But where are most parents getting guidance?

Tracey Duggan: Here. I don't think I'm doing a very good job. I get irate when she's spent it all by Wednesday and, I don't know, I'm going on what other people do and trial and error.

Woman: How much did it cost?

Reporter: Others go for the tutorial approach, such as this financial awareness class in Hong Kong. With kids as young as twelve in her class, teacher Vivien Eakin believes it's never too soon to learn about money management.

Vivien Eakin: It's really because the habits you pick up as a child often last a lifetime. And so if you get into bad spending habits when you're little chances are you'll still be spending that way when you're a hundred and five.

Reporter: Something that financial guru Nathan Dungan agrees on. His book highlights mass marketing and materialism. Why kids fall foul to it and what parents can do to stop them. Share, save, and spend is his recipe to success.

Nathan Dungan: When you start with sharing, you're sensitizing kids to the needs of others. Thereby, you're teaching them gratitude for the things they already have. Second thing is saving, which is, you know, teaching them to save for a goal. So if they want something, let them save their money for it. Thereby it teaches patience and discipline that will serve them invaluably as they purchase the big ticket items later on in life like cars or homes. And then the third word is spend, which is the difference between needs and wants.

Reporter: Try telling that to Rosie, which is exactly what her mum is struggling to do.

Tracey Duggan: We're at week six of this regime and it's not going . . . I'm on her back all of the time and I'm not sure that's the idea.

Reporter: But you're not going to give up?

Tracey Duggan: Oh, no way, no way. I'm going to . . . she will be good with money. For sure.

Michelle Han, CNN.

CHAPTER 5 — Las Vegas: Sin City
Pages 49–60

Summary Chapter 5 takes readers to America's gambling capital—Las Vegas. Reading 1 exposes Las Vegas' mob roots, and describes the changes that have made it a somewhat more respectable tourist destination today. Reading 2 is an advertisement for a chapel that makes Las Vegas wedding dreams a reality, and in Part II, a journalist interviews four Las Vegas strippers.

Audio The readings in this chapter can be heard on the *Hot Topics 1* Audio CD 1 Tracks 13-15 or Audio Tape 1 Side A.

Background To the more than 35 million tourists who visit Las Vegas each year, it might be surprising to learn that from 1910 until 1931, gambling was illegal in Las Vegas. They also might not know that the city began in 1905 with the auctioning of 110 acres of land, or that it is one of the fastest growing metropolitan areas in the United States, with 5,000 people relocating every month. On the other hand, those tourists know what Las Vegas is famous for, and they flock to the city of excesses for the colorful lights, the gambling, the spectacular shows and the tacky shows, and of course, the sometimes spontaneous weddings.

Teaching Note Chapter 5 is a rich source of new vocabulary. Recycle it in any of the following ways:
- Have students write a reaction to the chapter using several of the new words.
- Play a memory game in which an even number of words and their definitions are written on separate cards, then arranged face down in a grid. Students turn over two cards at a time, replacing them if there's not a match, and keeping them if there is.
- Ask questions containing the vocabulary, such as "How do *casinos* make a *profit*?" or "What makes a person seem *sophisticated*?"
- Have students replace underlined words in sentences with synonyms from the chapter.

Internet Activity Send students online to find out about the three people mentioned in Reading 2. Assign Elvis Presley to one third of the students, King Tut to another third, and King Arthur to the rest. Instruct the students to answer the questions *Who?*, *When?*, *Where?*, and *What?* (Who was he? When and where did he live? What was he famous for?) Let the three groups assemble to compare notes, then create an information gap activity by forming groups of three, with one student who is knowledgeable about each historical figure, so that everyone can get all the information.

CNN Video Clip Summary The CNN clip features scenes from inside casinos and comments from serious gamblers. The reporter presents statistics about gamblers which casinos have compiled.

Video Script Go to page 16 in this Instructor's Manual for the "The Gambling Lifestyle" video script and recommended video vocabulary for review.

Video Activity Go to page 173 in the student book for activities to accompany the CNN video clip.

ANSWER KEY—Chapter 5: Las Vegas: Sin City

PREVIEW (Page 49) Answers will vary.

PART I

Predict (Page 50)
1. Reading 1
2. Readings 1 & 2
3. Reading 2
4. Readings 1 & 2

Reading Comprehension

Check Your Predictions (Page 52): Answers will vary.

Check the Facts

Reading 1 (Page 53)

A.
1. True
2. False
3. True
4. False
5. True
6. True
7. True
8. False

B.

1. (Answers will vary.) The mafia doesn't control it anymore. It isn't as cheap. Gambling is not the only profitable business in Las Vegas. There are many expensive restaurants, hotels and services.
2. You can still gamble there. You can still get married quickly.

Reading 2 (Page 53)

A.

1. True   3. False   5. False
2. True   4. True   6. True

B.

1. Elvis Presley; King Tut; King Arthur; outer space
2. costumes; theater sets; smoke machine; lighting

Analyze (Page 54)

1. Both readings are about Las Vegas & what actives are legal in the city. Reading 1 is about the history of Las Vegas. Reading 2 is about weddings in Las Vegas.
2. Because you can get married quickly.
3. Probably, since the Elvis Presley wedding is very popular at the chapel.

Vocabulary Work

Guess Meaning from Context (Page 54)

1. mafia; mob; organized crime (refer to a group of criminals) gangster; mobster; Mafioso (names for criminals)
2. They all refer to things that are expensive and high-class.
3. *Launder* means *to wash*. Dirty money probably means money from illegal activities. If you wash dirty money, you must make it clean. So it refers to making illegal profit appear legal.
4. Reading 1: 1. c, 2. e, 3. g, 4. b, 5. h, 6. a, 7. f, 8. d
   Reading 2: 1. b, 2. c, 3. d, 4. a.

Guess Meaning From Related Words (Page 55)

1.

Reading 1

yearly / year; luxury / luxurious; profit / profitable

Reading 2

remember / memorable; possible / possibilities

2.

Noun (person):
Noun (thing): year, luxury, profit, possibilities
Verb: remember
Adjective: yearly, luxurious, profitable, memorable, possible
Adverb:

3.

long and time	something that lasts for a long time
no and wait	something you don't have to wait for
non and stop	something that doesn't stop
candle and light	lit with candles

Reading Skills

Understanding Organization (Page 56)

1. Part 1 is a description of old Las Vegas; Part II is a description of Las Vegas today.
2. Part 1 is mostly in the past tense; Part II is mostly in the present tense.
3. Paragraph 1 describes the history of Las Vegas; Paragraph 2 describes the change from mafia ownership to capitalist ownership of the casinos; Paragraph 3 says that many tourists from all over the world visit Las Vegas, and that gambling is profitable; Paragraph 4 talks about other ways that Las Vegas is profitable.

PART II (Page 57)

	Married? Children?	Advantages of the job	Disadvantages of the job	Future plans
Dina	divorced, 2 children	salary	she can't tell her kids	find another job
Sherona	not married	enjoys dancing	men bother her sometimes	become a real estate agent, get married, have children
Yolanda	married, no children	salary	X	buy a house, have children

Vocabulary Work
Guess Meaning from Context (Page 59)

stripper
waitress
croupier
real estate agent
veterinarian
security guard
bouncer

Reading Skills
Understanding Informal Language (Page 59)

1. left
2. two times
3. people
4. a good salary
5. involved with
6. friends; jealous
7. children
8. man
9. don't touch
10. obey the rules
11. makes them leave

CNN Video Activities: The Gambling Lifestyle
Understand It (Page 173)

1. twenty-six
2. groceries
3. woman
4. income
5. coupon
6. attend

VIDEO TRANSCRIPT—Chapter 5: *The Gambling Lifestyle*
DVD Title 6   Running time: 01:40

Video Vocabulary

buck   a U.S. dollar
characteristics   a special quality
lifeblood   basic to sustain and give strength to a business, economy, culture, etc.
stack the odds   make it more likely that someone will win
stingy   unwilling to share or spend

Video Script

Woman: Usually once a week, sometimes twice.
Man: Thirty to forty weekends a year.
Woman 2: Every weekend.
Reporter: Regular gamblers like these are the lifeblood of casinos. Figuring out who they are and what they like can translate into big bucks. Each year some 50 million Americans gamble away 26 billion dollars at casinos.
Man 2: I like the rush, you know? I like when my heart beats fast.
Reporter: According to a congressional commission, we spend more money each year on gambling than we do on groceries. Who are these gamblers? Casinos spend a lot of time and money trying to answer that question. Through surveys and studies, they've identified certain characteristics that make up a gambling personality. Results may surprise you.

The typical casino gambler is a middle-aged woman. Her household income is about $50,000, 20% higher than the overall U.S. population. The gamblers may throw money away at casinos, but elsewhere they're stingy with their cash. 56% are coupon clippers, 62% bargain shop. And as for faith, that blessing of the dice before a big roll is more likely a nod to lady luck. Divine intervention. Gamblers are 11% less likely to attend a place of worship than non-gamblers. Why would casinos collect such seemingly random bits of information? Well, to put it in gambling terms, it helps the house stack the odds against you.

Anderson Cooper, CNN, New York.

CHAPTER 6
Pages 61–72

Shoplifting: Why is the price tag still on your hat?

Summary Chapter 6 looks at the strange appeal of shoplifting. Reading 1 categorizes shoplifters according to the reasons they steal, and Reading 2 addresses the problem of teenage shoplifting. The founder of a support group for kleptomaniacs explains in Part II why the holiday shopping season is especially stressful for addictive-compulsive shoplifters.

Audio The readings in this chapter can be heard on the *Hot Topics 1* Audio CD 1 Tracks 16-18 or Audio Tape 1 Side B.

Background The "professional" shoplifter, someone who steals merchandise in order to sell it, is often very clever, dropping small items into an umbrella hanging from an arm, placing clothing under a baby in a stroller, or wearing more clothes when leaving the store than when entering. But that type of shoplifter is also relatively rare. Most shoplifters steal for no reason they can explain, simply because there is an opportunity. Consequences of shoplifting include higher prices to make up for losses and security costs, shame and possible criminal charges when shoplifters are caught.

Teaching Note Reading 2 presents advice on what a teenager should do if a friend shoplifts. Encourage careful reading of this section and give students an opportunity to speak by having partners prepare and perform role-plays that illustrate the situation. The conversations should follow the suggestions in the reading. If possible, find out what services for shoplifters are available in your community so students have that information on hand.

Internet Activity The CNN video clip was taped before the sentencing of Winona Ryder, but mentions options including jail time, probation, community service, and restitution. After watching the clip, ask students to go online and find out what Ryder's sentence on December 6, 2002 actually was. Students can find the information by entering *winona ryder sentence* in an Internet search engine.

Video Clip Summary The video clip begins with a jury delivering a guilty verdict in the Winona Ryder shoplifting trial. According to the prosecution, Ryder stole merchandise from Saks for the thrill of it, and was caught with the help of observant store employees and a surveillance tape.

Video Script Go to page 19 in this Instructor's Manual for the "Actress Nabbed in Shoplifting Scandal" video script and recommended video vocabulary for review.

Video Activity Go to page 174 in the student book for activities to accompany the CNN video clip.

ANSWER KEY—Chapter 6: Shoplifting: Why is the price tag still on your hat?

PREVIEW (Page 61)
1. 23
2. 25; 75
3. 48
4. 70
5. thirteen

PART I

Predict (Page 62)
1. 1 & 2
2. 2
3. 1
4. 1 & 2

Reading Comprehension

Check Your Predictions (Page 64): Answers will vary.

Check the Facts

Reading 1 (Page 65)
A.
1. False
2. False
3. True
4. False
5. True
6. True

B.

Type of Shoplifter	Percentage of shoplifters that are this type	Reasons they steal	Items they steal	What they do if they are caught	Feelings they have if they are caught
Addictive-Compulsive	85%	can't stop	inexpensive things, gifts	might cry	feel guilty
Professionals	2%	for money	expensive things	run away	not guilty
The Poor	5%	for money	necessary things	—	sorry or angry
Thrill-Seekers	5%	for excitement	CD's, clothes, computer games	—	—
Drug Addicts	2%	for money	expensive things	run away	—
Kleptomaniacs	1%	can't stop	anything	make excuses	not guilty

Reading 2 (Page 65)
A.
1. False   2. True   3. True
4. False   5. True   6. True

B.
1. a b c   2. c d

Analyze (Page 66)

1. Probably not because they are careless and they don't feel guilty or ashamed.
2. Professionals are like drug addicts because they make up 2% of shoplifters, they steal expensive items, and if they're caught, they try to run away.
3. In Reading 1, teenagers are mentioned as Thrill Seekers, who make up 5% of shoplifters, but Reading 2 says that 25% of people caught shoplifting are teenagers.

Vocabulary Work

Guess Meaning from Context (Page 66)

1. compulsive behaviors: such as overeating, shopping, drugs or gambling
   emotional: They might cry.
   necessities: food, baby diapers, toiletries, or children's clothing

2. collected: something like cool and calm
   makeup: something that a teenager might like to have
   hot line: a program that offers help to people in the community
3. high: explained by *Because they feel good*; Being high must mean feeling good.
   this guilt by association: Refers back to *If the police catch your friend, they will think that you are a shoplifter too.*

Guess Meaning from Related Words (Page 67)

1.
a. shoplift / shoplifter / shoplifting
b. compulsive / compulsion
c. inexpensive / expensive
d. emotion / emotional
e. guilt / guilty
f. shame / ashamed
g. exciting / excitement
h. necessary / necessities

2.

Noun (person): shoplifter
Noun (thing): shoplifting, compulsion, emotion, guilt, shame, excitement, necessities
Verb: shoplift
Adjective: compulsive, inexpensive, expensive, emotional, guilty, ashamed, exciting, necessary
Adverb:

18 Hot Topics 1 • Chapter 6

Reading Skills
Using Headings and Subtitles (Page 68)

1. a. Each subtitle is a type of shoplifter. They help you understand that the reading is actually a list.
   b. Each title describes the type of shoplifter and helps you understand the paragraph about that type.
2. a. Each subtitle is a question. They show that the reading is organized as questions and answers.
   b. When you read the question, you can predict what the answer might be.

PART II (Page 69)

1. Because shopping is an important part of the holiday, which increases the chance that they might steal.
2. The stores become more crowded with shoppers and it is hard to catch the shoplifters.
3. Everyone pays higher prices.
4. "Cleptomaniacs" and Shoplifters Anonymous
5. To get help and support so that they can stop shoplifting

Vocabulary Work
Guess Meaning from Context (Page 70)

1.

stress / stressful
crowds / crowded
increase / decrease
pricey / price
stolen / steal

2.

detectives: They are people who watch customers.
merchandise: It is something that people steal and sell.

afford: It says when people do not have enough money, they cannot buy something. Therefore, it must mean having enough money to buy something.
at risk: The sentence uses the synonym *in danger*.
judge: World knowledge tells me that the legal system can make people do things when they break the law. This person must be part of the legal system.

3.

It means that people carry things out of the store without paying for them. Items cannot walk out of the store by themselves.

Reading Skills
Using Grammar to Increase Understanding (Page 71)

Although the holidays are stressful for many people, kleptomaniacs have an <u>even greater problem</u> than average. Imagine being afraid to go shopping because you have a compulsion to steal. Large crowds in malls and stores make holiday shopping time <u>more difficult</u> for storeowners too. As stores become more crowded, store detectives have a <u>harder time</u> watching the customers. Larry Mason of the Ohio Storeowners Union says that there is an <u>increased problem</u> with shoplifting. "During the holiday season we have more shoppers and <u>more shoplifting</u>—the problem is <u>worse</u> because there are a lot <u>more sales</u>," he says.

CNN Video Activities: Actress Nabbed in Shoplifting Scandal
Understand It (Page 174)

1. b   2. a   3. d   4. a   5. d   6. c

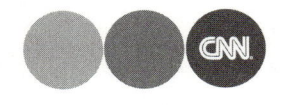

VIDEO TRANSCRIPT—Chapter 6: Actress Nabbed in Shoplifting Scandal
DVD Title 7   Running time: 01:44

Video Vocabulary

burglary   the act of breaking into a building especially with intent to steal
defendant   a person or group (business, organization, etc.) accused of wrongdoing and called into court
prosecution   the person starting a lawsuit, (the plaintiff) and his or her lawyer(s)
vandalism   willful or malicious destruction or defacement of public or private property
verdict   a decision of guilty or not guilty
witness   a person who saw something and can tell about it

Video Script

Reporter: Oscar nominee, Golden Globe winner, and now convicted felon.

Jury member: We the jury, find the defendant, Winona Ryder, guilty of the crime of vandalism.

Reporter: Winona Ryder appeared stoic as the jury returned a guilty verdict on one count of grand theft and one count of vandalism. The panel found the 31-year-old actress not guilty of commercial burglary.

Ann Rundle: I'm very comfortable with the jury's verdict. We're very happy. They followed the evidence and they followed the law.

Reporter: During the week long trial, the prosecution called Ryder's December 2001 arrest a simple case of theft. Saying the actress stole more than $5,500 worth of merchandise for the thrill of it. The jury was shown a 90 minute Saks Fifth Avenue surveillance tape detailing most of Ryder's movements. The store's security manager testified he first became suspicious after viewing Ryder on camera stuffing items into a hat. One Saks employee testified she saw Ryder through the slats of a fitting room door using scissors to cut security tags from merchandise. And three prosecution witnesses testified they heard the actress apologize and say she was doing research for a role as a shoplifter. Following the verdicts, Ryder's bond was continued and she was ordered to return December 6th for sentencing. Prosecutor Ann Rundle says she'll seek probation, community service, and restitution to Saks.

Ann Rundle: This case was never about jail time. We never asked for any jail time, and we will not be asking for any jail time in this matter. We were simply asking for Ms. Ryder to take responsibility for her conduct.

Reporter: Ryder and her attorney left the courthouse without commenting on the verdicts, but Ryder's publicist did issue a written statement reading, "Winona is grateful to her family and friends and those who have supported her, especially during this time."

Eric Horng, CNN, Beverly Hills, California.

CHAPTER 7 — GLUTTONY: YOU ARE WHAT YOU EAT!
Pages 73–83

Summary Most people know that overweight and obese Americans are numerous, but the problem is also becoming widespread outside the United States. Readings 1 and 2 of Chapter 7 present statistics about the world's overfed and underfed, and indicate that sedentary lifestyles and cheaper food are responsible for the increase in the former. Part II focuses on obesity in children, and places most of the blame squarely on advertisers who promote junk food.

Audio The readings in this chapter can be heard on the *Hot Topics 1* Audio CD 1 Tracks 19–21 or Audio Tape 1 Side B.

Background You won't find the list anywhere in the Bible. In fact, the "seven deadly sins" were conceived of by Pope Gregory the Great. Gluttony, pride, lust, greed, envy, sloth, and anger are thought to be sins one commits against oneself, at great cost to spiritual health. The interface between morality and nutrition is what makes gluttony a hot topic. Is it possible to attribute all of the obesity epidemic to changes in lifestyle, new eating practices, and the unscrupulous practices of advertisers? Or are overweight people guilty of a sin? Be aware that opinions may be strong and emotions may run high.

Teaching Note Section #3 on page 79 focuses attention on compound words and phrases, which can be a problem for second language readers who look at only one word at a time. One of these words, *labor-saving*, is a hyphenated adjective. After working with the reading in Part II, ask the students to find all of the hyphenated adjectives in that reading, and discuss the meaning of each one. (They should find *high-calorie, high-fat, toxic-food, well-advertised, soft-drink,* and *fast-food*.)

Internet Activity If your students are wondering about their own eating habits, have them calculate their daily caloric needs using an online calculator such as the one at http://www.parknicollet.com/tools/nutritionCalorie.cfm that considers age, sex, and activity level. Next, they can keep a food diary, writing down everything they eat and drink for a week. Students can use labels and an online calorie table such as the one at http://www.myfoodbuddy.com/foodCalorieTable.htm to determine their average daily caloric intake and compare it with the recommendation of the online calculator.

CNN Video Clip Summary Reporter Walter Rogers speaks with a doctor about the growing international problem of obesity, which is as prevalent in places such as the U.K. and the Middle East as it is in the U.S. The doctor is alarmed at the health and financial consequences, but only the reporter seems to have an easy answer to the problem.

Video Script Go to page 23 in this Instructor's Manual for the "Obesity: Not Simply an American Problem" video script and recommended video vocabulary for review.

Video Activity Go to page 175 in the student book for activities to accompany the CNN video clip.

ANSWER KEY—Chapter 7: GLUTTONY

PREVIEW (Page 73)
1. Answers will vary.
2. all of these countries

PART I

Predict (Page 74)
1. Readings 1 & 2
2. Reading 2
3. Reading 1
4. Reading 2

Reading Comprehension

Check Your Predictions (Page 76): Answers will vary.

Check the Facts

Reading 1 (Page 76)

A.
1. False
2. True
3. False
4. True
5. False
6. True

B.
1. We eat more. We don't move much. People lead sedentary lives.
2. leaf blowers; riding lawn mowers; dishwashers; robot vacuum cleaners; television remote controls

Reading 2 (Page 77)

A.
1. False
2. True
3. True
4. True
5. True

Analyze (Page 77)
1. heart disease; high blood pressure; diabetes
2. They don't agree. Reading 1 says that 65 percent of Americans are overweight and 31 percent are obese. Reading 2 says the numbers are 55 percent and 23 percent.
3. People have more money to buy food, so they eat too much.
4. No. Starvation is not a large problem in rich countries because people have enough money to buy food.

Vocabulary Work

Guess Meaning from Context (Page 77)

1.
a. *glutton:* a person who eats too much
b. *obese:* a person who is more than 20 percent overweight
c. *sedentary:* a person who does not move much

2. (Answers may vary.)
a. *malnutrition:* My knowledge of nutrition and health allows me to guess that this word means not having the correct type of food.
b. *starvation:* My knowledge of the problem of hunger allows me to guess that this means a condition of not having enough to eat.

Guess Meaning from Related Words

1.

Reading 1 (Page 78)

weigh / overweight
obese / obesity
glutton / gluttony

Reading 2 (Page 78)

weight / overweight / underweight
overfed / underfed
nutrition / malnutrition / nutritious
starving / starvation
hungry / hunger

2.

Noun (person): glutton
Noun (thing): weight, obesity, gluttony, nutrition, malnutrition, starvation, hunger
Verb: weigh
Adjective: overweight / underweight, obese, overfed / underfed, nutritious, starving, hungry
Adverb:

3.

Reading 1 (Page 79)

1. desk job: desk and job
2. lawn mower: lawn and mower
3. leaf blower: leaf and blower
4. robot vacuum cleaner: robot and vacuum and cleaner
5. television remote control: television and remote and control
6. labor saving: labor and saving

Reading 2 (Page 79)

overweight: over and weight
overeating: over and eating
overfed: over and fed

Reading Skills

Understanding Statistics (Page 79)

overweight people: 65 percent; 47 percent
obese people: 31 percent; 59 million; four out of ten; 15 percent, 20 percent

PART II (Page 80)

1. everywhere
2. An environment that offers a lot of bad food.
3. Because we see it advertised everywhere and it is cheap.
4. Governments should educate people about the dangers of eating the wrong food.

Vocabulary Work

Guess Meaning from Context (Page 82): (Answers may vary.)

worrying (1)
consume (4)
toxic (4)
unavoidable (1)
rates (2)
turn into (3)
junk foods (3)

Reading Skills

Main Ideas and Supporting Details (Page 82)

Paragraph 1: *Main idea*—the number of overweight children is increasing
Type of supporting details—statistics

Paragraph 2: *Main idea*—our diets and amount of activity are different
Type of supporting details—examples

Paragraph 3: *Main idea*—advertisements persuade us to eat unhealthy foods
Type of supporting details—reasons

Paragraph 4: *Main idea*—advertisements persuade children to eat unhealthy foods
Type of supporting details—statistics

Paragraph 5: *Main idea*—food companies want to sell unhealthy food to developing countries
Type of supporting details—statistics, quotations

Paragraph 6: *Main idea*—we can do something about this problem
Type of supporting details—examples

CNN Video Activities: Obesity: Not Simply an American Problem

Understand It (Page 175)

1. d   2. e   3. a   4. c   5. b

VIDEO TRANSCRIPT—Chapter 7: OBESITY: NOT SIMPLY AN AMERICAN PROBLEM

DVD Title 8   Running time: 03:13

Video Vocabulary

affluent   wealthy
ballooning   rapidly increasing
life expectancy   the average age to which people can expect to live

Video Script

Reporter: That is definitely not a goose down parka under that coat keeping this lady warm. It's fat. Fat is also what makes these blue jeans tight. This too is fat and so is this. These are not obese Americans, but Londoners. And obesity is not simply a problem of affluent Americans and British, it's a ballooning global problem. Some experts believe obesity is becoming the most serious health problem in the world.

Doctor: We now know that the problem in the Middle East is just as bad as in the United States. There's an enormous problem in Central and Eastern Europe.

Woman: We're having 300,000 deaths in the UK per year because of it. And average life expectancy is reduced in obese people compared to lean people by almost nine years.

Reporter: In Asia where successive generations have been conditioned to fear famine and starvation, obesity is becoming a huge problem. Traditionally malnourished Chinese and Indians, now consume gobs of fat and sugar.

Doctor: We're eating ourselves to death and the current calculations are that the fat and obese children who are more likely to get diabetes even in their teens, their life expectancy is going to be less than their parents or grandparents.

Reporter: Men with fat bellies are thought to be in real trouble. The bloat often signals diabetes, high blood pressure, stroke, heart disease, and some cancers. Thin and fit people pay for the obese. Taxed for higher health care costs. Government meters are staring down the barrel of national healthcare crises.

Doctor: If they're not careful, the health services of their country, currently becoming overwhelmed, are going to be in major crisis, already the calculation is that 40 percent, 2/5 of the budget of the United States, spent on health relates to obesity associated problems.

Reporter: Fatty foods and lack of exercise cause obesity. Governments are to blame too. Food production has been subsidized to the tune of billions of dollars funding food and huge servings, which bodes ill for the next generation. British solution:

Newscaster: A bill is being introduced in the Commons calling for a ban on the TV advertising for under fives of food and drink high in salt, sugar, and fat.

Reporter: The private sector here says educating young people, not legislating diets is the answer.

Man: We don't want quick, easy, short-term fixes because where it has been tried, and if you take a place like Quebec where it's been tried for something like twenty years, the level of overweight and obese children in Quebec is no lower than other Canadian provinces.

Reporter: Surprisingly, weight loss diets don't eliminate obesity problems according to health experts. Many say the diets are just gimmicks, a different technique to get you to eat less. And it would appear it all comes down to this: the fat and the soft drinks simply have to go.

Walter Rogers, CNN, London.

CHAPTER 8 — Get-Rich-Quick Scams: Have I got a deal for YOU!
Pages 84–95

Summary The people in the television infomercials certainly look happy and prosperous, but the viewers at home who call in their credit card numbers may be in for some nasty surprises. In the form of a newspaper article, Reading 1 tells the story of a company that recruits people to market their diet pills. Reading 2 is an advertisement for a pyramid scheme that promises big money for little effort. Another pyramid scheme, this one targeting women, is outlined in Part II.

Audio The readings in this chapter can be heard on the *Hot Topics 1* Audio CD 1 Tracks 22-24 or Audio Tape 1 Side B.

Background Behind every "get rich quick scam" is someone who plans to take in a large amount of money and pay out a much smaller amount, just as in lotteries. But just as in lotteries, there are people who believe they might be one of the lucky ones who ends up a winner. Besides pyramid schemes and businesses whose real purpose is to sell investors a lot of set-up materials, there are scams involving chain letters, real estate, vending machines, and promises of large salaries for easy work that can be done at home.

Teaching Note Help students understand the CNN video clip by teaching them the idioms it contains, including: *a win-win* (or *win-lose* or *lose-lose*) *proposition, to crack down on, a sting, one's life savings, no deal.*

Internet Activity Direct students to the website of the Better Business Bureau or a government website to search for ways to avoid being fooled by get-rich-quick scams. Enter the terms *get rich quick scams* in an Internet search engine to find reliable sites with accessible English. Have the students print out the tips they find in order to discuss the ideas in class and answer language questions.

CNN Video Clip Summary The CNN video clip tells the story of a man who lost money in a vending machine business despite checking references beforehand, and what the Federal Trade Commission is doing to protect consumers from scams.

Video Script Go to page 26 in this Instructor's Manual for the "Fortune or Fraud? The Truth about Business Opportunity" video script and recommended video vocabulary for review.

Video Activity Go to page 176 in the student book for activities to accompany the CNN video clip.

ANSWER KEY—Chapter 8: Get-Rich-Quick Scams: Have I got a deal for YOU!

PREVIEW (Page 84): Answers will vary.

PART I

Predict (Page 85)

A.
1. Reading 1
2. Reading 2
3. Reading 1
4. Reading 1

B. Answers will vary.

Reading Comprehension

Check Your Predictions (Page 88): Answers will vary.

Check the Facts

Reading 1 (Page 88)

A.
1. False
2. False
3. False
4. True
5. False
6. True
7. True

B.

	Amount they paid	Amount they made	Amount they lost
Kelly Eagan	$5175	0	$5175
Susan Kauffman	$2000	$839.70	$1160.30
Igor Spilsak	$5000	$918.85	$4,081.15

Greg Cheney made $6816.45 from these people.

Reading 2 (Page 89)

1. You can make a lot of money without working. Your profit is guaranteed. You don't have to sell anything. You don't have to talk to anyone, answer questions, or be rejected.
2. a group of marketing professionals
3. Audiotapes, videotapes, and textbooks.
4. So you can start making money quickly.

Analyze (Page 89): (Answers may vary.)

1. He doesn't like him. He criticizes him. He says that he lies. He says that his business is a scam.
2. It was written for people who want to get rich quick.
3. It is probably very expensive. They want to get you interested. They don't want to scare you with the price.
4. Pyramid schemes may not be legal, and they may not work.

Vocabulary Work

Guess Meaning from Context (Page 89)

1. scam / rip-off
2. fortune: probably means a lot of money
   sign up: to join
   market: a place to sell things
   professional: a person who does something to make money
   profit: the money you make
3. sponsor: the person who told you about the program

Guess Meaning from Related Words (Page 90)

1.
a. rejection / reject
b. automated / automatically
c. profitable / profit
d. market / marketing
e. wealth / wealthy
f. successful / success

2.
Noun (person):
Noun (thing): rejection, profit, marketing, market, sales, wealth, success
Verb: reject, market, sell
Adjective: automated, profitable, wealthy, successful
Adverb: automatically

3.
a. moneymaker: (money + maker) = a person who makes money
b. con artist: (con + artist) = a person who cons or cheats people

Reading Skills

Identifying the Author's Purpose (Page 91)

1. Reading 1 informs readers. The writer wants the readers to know about Greg Cheney. He also wants to tell them about these kinds of scams in general.
2. Reading 2 persuades people. The writer wants readers to buy the program.

3. a. The writer uses quotes to support his opinions.
   b. Yes, he thinks Greg Cheney's program is a scam.
4. a. He uses italics and underlining for emphasis. He also uses exclamation points.
   b. powerful / incredibly profitable / guaranteed / huge market / automatically / explode / successful / happy / wealth
   c. Obviously the writer writes as if he thinks the program is great.

PART II (Page 91)

1. For women to help women.
2. $5000
3. $40,000
4. The pyramid splits.
5. Because soon there are no people.
6. Because they think they can get money and help other people too.

Vocabulary Work

Guess Meaning from Related Words (Page 93)

1.
a. sisterhood: (sister) something to do with sisters
b. backbone: (back + bone) the bone in your back (your spine)
c. uneducated: (education) people who did not go to school
d. payment: (pay) money you give to someone
e. safety: (safe) not dangerous

2.
a. in need — people who need something
b. pyramid — a geometric figure
c. cycles — complete circle
d. pep talk — trying to make people enthusiastic by talking to them
e. blew the whistle — told the police

Reading skills

Understanding Organization (Page 94)

Paragraph 1: *Purpose*—introduction
Most important idea—The idea sounds good but it doesn't work
Paragraph 2: *Purpose*—description of the plan in general
Most important idea—It looks like a pyramid.
Paragraph 3: *Purpose*—problems with the plan in general
Most important idea—There are not enough people.

Paragraphs 4 & 5: *Purpose*—description of a specific group
Most important idea—Even rich, educated people can get fooled.
Paragraph 6: *Purpose*—conclusion
Most important idea—Although it sounds like it helps people, it really hurts them.

CNN Video Activities: Fortune or Fraud? The Truth about Business Opportunity
Understand It (Page 176): Students should check 1, 3, 6, and 7.

VIDEO TRANSCRIPT—Chapter 8: Fortune or Fraud? The Truth about Business Opportunity
DVD Title 9   Running time: 01:39

Video Vocabulary
claim   a statement that something is true
deceptive   causing someone to believe what is not true
earnings   wages, salary, or income from work or investments
proposition   an offer, especially in business
references   a recommendation, especially for employment
unsubstantiated   not supported by evidence
vending machine   a machine that gives packaged food, soft drinks, or other items after coins are placed in it

Video Script
Reporter: He doesn't want his last name known, but he does want his story told. Jeffrey came across a business opportunity; it sounded like a win-win proposition.
Jeffrey: I bought about twenty machines and thought that I'd get about two to three thousand dollars monthly from profits from the vending machines.
Reporter: The initial cost $9,000, but before investing with the company, Accent Marketing of Alabama, Jeffrey checked first with the Better Business Bureau then a family member in the vending business and lastly he called the references given by the company.
Jeffrey: One guy even said he's getting ready to retire to work this business full time, it was so profitable for him.
Reporter: Jeffrey bought the machines, but hasn't come close to the company's projected earnings. Now the Federal Trade Commission is cracking down on 77 operations and has taken 11 to Federal Court to get them to stop, including Accent Marketing in a sting called Project Busted Opportunity. The common violation: using deceptive or unsubstantiated earnings claims.
J. Howard Beales: These are frauds that in the aggregate have cost consumers tens of millions of dollars, that individually they've cost some consumers their life savings and their dream of owning a successful small business.
Reporter: The FTC says the operations involved a variety of scams from distributing CDs and tapes to envelope stuffing. Its advice to consumers: unless a company can thoroughly back up its earnings claims in its ads and with disclosure statements, tell them no deal.

Elaine Kihano, CNN, Washington.

CHAPTER 9 — SPORTS DOPING: DOES IT MATTER IF YOU WIN OR LOSE?

Pages 96–107

Summary Athletes and performance enhancing drugs are under discussion in Chapter 9. Reading 1 includes a chart showing the types of drugs that are commonly used and their purposes. Reading 2 contains examples of some of the drug violations at the 2004 Olympics in Athens. The reading in Part II is an editorial that explains why sports doping is a problem, and that the source of the problem is the importance placed on winning at all costs.

Audio The readings in this chapter can be heard on the *Hot Topics 1* Audio CD 2 Tracks 1-3 or Audio Tape 2 Side A.

Background Sports doping may be as old as sports themselves, with stimulants and pain killers known to have been used by ancient Greek and Roman athletes. In the twentieth century, however, sports organizations began to make efforts to eliminate doping. The first reliable drug tests appeared in the 1970's, but the number of doping substances and techniques has kept growing despite the health risks, and the list of athletes who have been caught doping is a long one.

Teaching Note Use the *Idea Exchange* section of Part II to do role-plays. After students have a chance to read and think about the situations, assign one of the situations to each pair or small group and give them a few minutes to plan their conversation without writing it down. After students perform the role-plays, allow some time for general discussion of the issues involved.

Internet Activity Create a while-reading worksheet to help your students tackle a current news article on sports doping while conveying the idea that it is possible to understand main ideas without understanding every word. First, enter the terms *sports doping* in the search engine at www.google.com, then click on "news results" near the top of the page and choose one of the current stories. Write main idea questions, perhaps one question for each paragraph, for the students to answer as they read the article without using dictionaries.

CNN Video Clip Summary This video clip from the 2004 Olympic Games in Athens focuses on sports doping in American track and field, and on Justin Gatlin, a runner who wants to show by example that it is possible to win without doping. His coach, Trevor Graham, was partly responsible for the investigation into U.S. track and field doping following the Sydney Olympics.

Video Script Go to page 29 in this Instructor's Manual for the "Racing Toward Stardom—or Scandal?" video script and recommended video vocabulary for review.

Video Activity Go to page 177 in the student book for activities to accompany the CNN video clip.

ANSWER KEY—Chapter 9: SPORTS DOPING: DOES IT MATTER IF YOU WIN OR LOSE?

PREVIEW (Page 96): Answers are on page 97.

PART I

Predict (Page 97)

A.

1. Reading 2
2. Readings 1 & 2
3. Readings 1 & 2
4. Readings 1 & 2

B. Answers will vary.

Reading Comprehension

Check Your Predictions (Page 100): Answers will vary.

Check the Facts

Reading 1 (Page 101)

A.

1. True   2. False   3. True   4. True   5. False

B.

1. (Answers may vary.) Increase muscles. Cover pain. Reduce weight. Make you relax.
2. In order to get an advantage. To win.
3. Because they can make a lot of money if they win.

Reading 2 (Page 101)

A. Greece / Russia / Ukraine / Hungary / Belarus / Colombia / Kenya / Puerto Rico / Morocco / Moldova / India / Turkey / Myanmar / Switzerland / Spain / Ireland / the United States

B.

weightlifting / shot-putting / rowing
running / boxing / high jumping / cycling
wrestling / baseball / canoeing

C.

1. weightlifting
2. (Answers may vary.) They did not allow some athletes to compete. They asked some athletes to leave. They took away the medals of some athletes.

Analyze (Page 102): Answers will vary.

Vocabulary Work

Guess Meaning from Context (Page 102)

1.

a. the big game: My knowledge of sports lets me guess that this refers to an important game. Perhaps it is with a team that they always play.
b. & c. bragging rights / talk big: *Bragging rights* and *talk big* are used in the same way. My knowledge of sports tells me that this means feeling proud because your team is the best.

2.

a. mask: This must mean something like stop pain or make it less.
b. banned: not allowed
c. restricted: This is contrasted with banned. It also says that drugs that are restricted are necessary, so they aren't banned. Therefore, they must be allowed at certain times.
d. consequences: The article talks about bad consequences. This must mean bad things that can happen such as not being allowed to compete or hurting yourself.

3. Athletes are banned when they are not allowed to compete. Drugs are banned when they are not allowed to be used.

Guess Meaning from Related Words (Page 103)

1.

Reading 1

1. compete / competition / competitor
2. risks / risky
3. advantage / disadvantage

Reading 2

(note: One form is used as a noun and as an adjective.)
Olympics / Olympian / Olympian

2.

Noun (person): competitor, Olympian
Noun (thing): competition, risks, advantage, disadvantage, Olympics / Olympiad
Verb: compete
Adjective: risky, Olympian
Adverb:

3.

a. weightlifting (weight + lift)
b. motorcycle (motor + cycle)
c. unclean (un + clean)
d. baseball (ball)
e. teenagers (teen + age)

Reading Skills

Using Charts (Page 104)

1. to give extra information
2. c. the use of each drug

PART II (Page 104)

1. because athletes should have control over their bodies
2. because drugs are dangerous
3. Every athlete will think that they must use them in order to be competitive.
4. They may let their children take drugs.
5. the idea that winning is the only thing that is important

Vocabulary Work

Guess Meaning from Context (Page 106)

1.

control / out of control: The reading talks about athletes controlling their bodies and drugs being out of control. Control probably means managing.
fair / unfair: The reading talks about an unfair environment and a fair chance. Fair must mean just, reasonable and unfair is the opposite.
professional / amateur: I know that a professional is a person that is paid. Amateur must mean a person who is not paid.

2.

Environment usually means nature or our surroundings; here it is more like a situation.
Costs usually refers to money; here it means no matter what the consequences are.
Win usually means not lose a game; here it means to receive.

Reading Skills

Understanding the Use of Examples

1. He pretends that he is an athlete competing against the reader.
2. Imagine that . . .
3. The idea that drug use can easily get out of control.
4. Yes, because it illustrates the problem.

Video Activities: Racing toward Stardom—or Scandal?

Understand It (Page 177)

1. coached
2. sent
3. coach
4. nice
5. banned
6. use

VIDEO TRANSCRIPT—Chapter 9: RACING TOWARD STARDOM—OR SCANDAL?

DVD Title 10   Running time: 02:19

Video Vocabulary

allegedly   not yet proven
anonymously   not being named, unknown
evidence   words or objects that support the truth of something
investigation   a search for facts and information, especially by people with power
regrets   a bad feeling about having done something
syringe   a hollow tube with a plunger, usually attached to a needle through which it draws or injects fluids out of or into the body
tainted   a trace of scandal or corruption
vow   to swear, solemnly promise

Video Script

Reporter: Trevor Graham made news at the last summer Olympics, if not headlines. In Sydney he coached Marion Jones who collected five medals. Since Graham cut ties with Jones, the headlines have become bolder and darker for U.S. track and field, reeling from a federal investigation of BALCO, a company allegedly providing illegal performance enhancing drugs to athletes. Graham has admitted to anonymously sending a syringe to U.S. anti-doping officials containing the steroid THG, starting the investigation. Now, back at the summer games, Graham's back in the news as well. He's the coach of the newly crowned men's 100-meter champion, Justin Gatlin. And Graham's latest pupil has vowed to help clean up his sport's image.

Justin: I'm not saying that anybody has tainted this sport but I think it's my turn to show there are a lot of good people out there in track and field with a lot of good character and I just wanted to show everybody that hey, nice guys can finish first.

Reporter: As the man responsible for turning in the key piece of evidence in what's become the biggest doping scandal in U.S. track and field history, Graham said quote "I was just a coach doing the right thing at that time . . . I have no regrets." By his actions, the former Olympic silver-winning relay champion for Jamaica has changed the way athletes are tested. At the Athens Olympics, six athletes have tested positive for banned substances. None for THG.

Olympics Official: The good news, coming out of the THG affair, is it shows that the cheaters are out there and they're ahead. But they're only one step ahead. As soon as you know what it is you're looking for, you can devise a test for it and, as I say, THG is now a dinosaur drug. Nobody will use it.

Justin: Every other question now is a drug question, which doesn't bother me at all either. You know? Because it's part of sports, you just have to roll with the punches. But I'd like to see more questions about "what is your next race?" "how did you feel in that race?"

Reporter: Gatlin's next race is the 200 meters. Should he win double gold, he'll find himself in the fast lane to stardom and with his coach alongside.

Mark McKay, CNN, Athens.

CHAPTER 10
Pages 108–120

WHITE-COLLAR CRIME: WHEN A LOT JUST ISN'T ENOUGH!

Summary One topic that is sure to raise some hackles is that of the rich getting richer. In Reading 1, ideas from the sociologist who first used the term "white-collar crime" are presented, including the similarities and differences between white-collar crime and street crime. Reading 2 provides three lists: definitions of white-collar crimes, the motivations of white-collar criminals, and the reasons that white-collar criminals often go unpunished. In Part II, a Harvard professor comments on the well-known cases of Martha Stewart and Dennis Kozlowski.

Audio The readings in this chapter can be heard on the *Hot Topics 1* Audio CD 2 Tracks 4-6 or Audio Tape 2 Side A.

Background The collapse of the Enron corporation in 2001 resulted in huge financial losses for ordinary workers and focused public attention on corporate corruption. Fraud and identity theft are ways that smaller white-collar criminals extract money from their victims. Whatever their methods, white-collar criminals line their pockets at the expense of the people who can least afford it.

Teaching Note The *Analyze* section on page 113 includes a list of crime-related vocabulary. Help the students move from passive recognition of the words to the ability to use them actively by having them write two paragraphs describing two crimes—one street crime and one white-collar crime. Ask them to use every word in the list. Doing this as an in-class writing would allow students to ask for help from you and from each other, and following up with read-alouds would provide further reinforcement, a speaking opportunity, and possibly good entertainment value.

Internet Activity Direct students to http://www.ckfraud.org/whitecollar.html to view a list of white-collar crime terms and schemes. Ask them to look up the terms from the *What Do White-Collar Criminals Do?* section of Reading 2 and compare the definitions, then invite them to read about some of the white-collar crime schemes described in the second half of the website. Alternatively, students can search the Internet to find out more about the white-collar criminals mentioned in Chapter 10.

Video Clip Summary The reporter explains that the rates of punishment for white-collar crime are low while the potential rewards are high, making it very tempting for some businesspeople.

Video Script Go to page 32 in this Instructor's Manual for the "White-Collar Crime: Is It Worth It?" video script and recommended video vocabulary for review.

Video Activity Go to page 178 in the student book for activities to accompany the CNN video clip.

ANSWER KEY—Chapter 10: WHITE-COLLAR CRIME: WHEN A LOT JUST ISN'T ENOUGH!

PREVIEW (Page 108): Answers are on page 109.

PART I

Predict (Page 109)

A. 1. Reading 1
   2. Reading 1
   3. Reading 2
   4. Readings 1 & 2

B. Answers will vary.

Reading Comprehension

Check Your Predictions (Page 112): Answers will vary.
Check the Facts

Reading 1 (Page 112)
A.
1. True   3. False   5. True
2. False 4. False   6. True

B.
1. Respected, usually educated people; not poor people.
2. FBI (The Federal Bureau of Investigation)

Reading 2 (Page 113)
A.
1. embezzlement   4. money laundering
2. forgery   5. fraud
3. kickbacks   6. bribery

B.

1. Greed, power, anger and bad role models.
2. People are afraid of them. Sometimes the crimes don't seem to have victims.

Analyze (Page 113)

1. White collar criminals are not poor. They are educated and respected.
2. computer/ the Internet / telephone

Vocabulary Work

Guess Meaning from Context (Page 114)

1.

Reading 1

social institutions: examples
greedy: They were people who had a lot, but wanted more.
forensic accounting: description of the job

Reading 2

property: something that can be stolen
control: different from owning
associate: with
greed: They want more money.
stretching the truth: similar to lying

2. b. There are many different kinds of punishment for "white collar crime."

Guess Meaning from Related Words (Page 115)

1.

poor / poverty   crimes / criminals
violent / nonviolent   trust / distrust

2.

Noun (person): criminals
Noun (thing): poverty, crimes
Verb: trust, distrust
Adjective: poor, violent, nonviolent
Adverb:

3.

white-collar workers = workers who wear white collars
well-respected (well + respect) = respected a lot
victimless (victim + less) = without a victim

Reading Skills

Finding Referents (Page 115)

1. white-collar workers
2. white-collar crime and street crime
3. white-collar criminals
4. people
5. sociologists
6. people
7. wealthy people
8. white-collar crime
9. white-collar crime
10. no referent
11. white-collar criminals
12. They often cover their crimes in complex financial arrangements.

PART II (Page 117)

1. for insider trading
2. She teaches business at Harvard University.
3. He stole $135 million from Tyco International.
4. They are rich, famous, drunk on success, selfish, and don't think they have to follow rules.
5. They must have values and know when they have enough.

Vocabulary Work

Understanding Words in Italics (Page 118)

1. *Inside* means secret here.
2. He didn't plan to pay it back.
3. They didn't know about the loan, or else it was a gift.
4. They were not really loans, but rather stolen money.
5. They didn't forget anything; they hid the information.
6. This isn't like being drunk from alcohol.
7. This doesn't mean play a game; it means to obey rules and laws.

Reading Skills

Finding Referents (Page 119)

1. $50,000
2. insider trading
3. go for the maximum
4. Stewart and many other business executives
5. $100 million a year
6. millions of dollars more
7. his wife's birthday party in Italy
8. the "loans"

Chapter 10 • Hot Topics 1   31

9. the company
10. business superstars (famous, rich, drunk on success)
11. happiest, most caring, wealthiest
12. what the person already has

Video Activities: White-Collar Crime: Is it worth it?
Understand It (Page 178)

1. 43 percent
2. 20 percent
3. 82 percent
4. 57 percent
5. 41 months
6. jail

VIDEO TRANSCRIPT—Chapter 10: WHITE-COLLAR CRIME: IS IT WORTH IT?
DVD Title 11   Running time: 02:43

Video Vocabulary
civil   of citizens in general, not religious or military
complex   having many parts or details that make something hard to understand or deal with
cross the line   do something unacceptable
deterrent   something that prevents (an attack, a crime, etc.)
guidelines   ideas or rules on what to do (or not to do)
lure   the power of something that attracts
reward   something pleasant for something well done

Video Script

Reporter: Legal experts say the lure of white collar crime is stronger than ever.

Jan Handzlik: People are seeing huge rewards from very little effort using a little brain power and so the temptation is there for people to cross the line and to do things that are improper because they will be rewarded so heavily.

Reporter: The Justice Department does not keep precise statistics on white collar crime, but smart crooks are betting correctly that the risk of getting caught is slim because it takes a lot more to catch white collar criminals than common street criminals.

Henry Pontell: White collar crime, because it can certainly involve very complex financial transactions and rather large amounts of investigation, require correspondingly many more enforcement resources and that's a real problem.

Reporter: Even if you do get caught, the odds are still in your favor. In 2001, of the 41,000 cases referred to the justice department for prosecution of a white-collar crime, 43% were prosecuted and 20% went to jail. Of the 22,000 drug crimes referred, 82% were prosecuted and 57% went to jail. But if you do get convicted, sentencing guidelines are strict. Shoe magnate Steve Madden was given 41 months for stock fraud and ordered to pay back millions of dollars he swindled. Jail is seen as the number one deterrent to white collar crime. That's why the SEC, which only has civil authority, is urging state and federal prosecutors to launch their own criminal investigations and offering up SEC resources in hopes of putting more crooks behind bars.

Ira Sorkin: How much does it deter? We'll never know. For some people one day in jail is a lifetime, for others it's the cost of doing business.

Reporter: A spokesman for New York Attorney General Elliot Spitzer says so far the SEC has talked about more cooperation, but not really taken action. He says while they've worked together on some high profile cases, the relationship continues to be mostly a one way street.

Kathleen Hayes, CNN Financial News, New York.

CHAPTER 11 — THE HOMELESS: IT'S NOT THEIR CHOICE
Pages 121-131

Summary Chapter 11 takes a sympathetic view of the homeless, people who are often feared and despised. In the form of a movie review, Reading 1 tells the story of a young woman who grew up homeless yet overcame many disadvantages and eventually received a scholarship to Harvard. Reading 2 give facts and statistics on the working poor, and explains that many working people are in a precarious position with regards to housing. The reading in Part II is a newspaper editorial urging city officials to provide more housing and services for the homeless.

Audio The readings in this chapter can be heard on the *Hot Topics 1* Audio CD 2 Tracks 7-9 or Audio Tape 2 Side A.

Background Although many people think of the homeless as single men with mental problems who don't have jobs, the facts are otherwise, according to Goodwill Industries. Only around 25 percent of the homeless in the U.S. have mental illnesses, and about the same number abuse alcohol or drugs. A surprising 30 percent of homeless people are employed, and at least 20 percent of all homeless people are children. They are victims of crimes much more often than they are dangerous criminals, and less than 6 percent of the homeless have chosen to live that way.

Teaching Note Since the articles in Chapter 11 focus on homelessness in the U.S., give your students a chance to discuss homelessness in their countries. In small groups, ask each student to explain what they know about who the homeless are, why they are homeless, and how and where they live. Alternatively, give small groups discussion questions about homeless issues on index cards (e.g., Is it a good idea to give money to homeless people?) Students can take turns reading the cards aloud and leading brief discussions on each topic.

Internet Activity Students may be interested in organizations like Habitat for Humanity (www.habitat.org) which work to provide housing for homeless families. Habitat for Humanity's website contains brief news articles as well as a way to search for local affiliates. If there is one in your area, contact them and ask about guest speaker or field trip possibilities. Alternatively, have students search the Internet for tips on how to help the homeless.

Video Clip Summary The reporter visits Tamikio Bailey and her seven children in their room at a homeless shelter. It is Christmas time, and the children have received donated toys and other gifts, but both women indicate that needs at other times of the year are not always met.

Video Script Go to page 35 in this Instructor's Manual for the "Homeless at Christmas: One Family's Story" video script and recommended video vocabulary for review.

Video Activity Go to page 179 in the student book for activities to accompany the CNN video clip.

ANSWER KEY—Chapter 11: THE HOMELESS: IT'S NOT THEIR CHOICE

PREVIEW (Page 121): Answers will vary.

PART I

Predict (Page 122)

A.
1. Reading 1
2. Reading 2
3. Reading 2
4. Reading 1

B. Answers will vary.

Reading Comprehension

Check Your Predictions (Page 124): Answers will vary.

Check the Facts

Reading 1 (Page 125)

A.
1. True   2. False   3. True
4. False   5. True   6. False

B.
1. from the government
2. outside on the streets of New York City
3. They asked people on the street.

Reading 2 (Pages 125-126)

A.
1. True   2. True   3. False
4. True   5. False

B.

1. $5.25
2. $500
3. 168
4. 30 percent
5. 50 percent

Analyze (Page 126)

1. It was very difficult to live on the money from the government.
2. Her parents didn't work. They were drug addicts and used the money from the government to buy drugs.

Vocabulary Work

Guess Meaning from Context (Page 126)

1. Everything in the paragraph is related to the "difficult" way in which Liz and her family lived.
2. Answers will vary. (Examples below)
   <u>Homeless shelter</u>: homeless probably means someone is without a home. A shelter may be a place where someone without a home goes for protection or a place for someone without a home to stay.
   <u>Child Welfare System</u>: a government system that looks after the welfare of a child.
   <u>Foster Family</u>: a family who takes care of someone under legal age who is not biologically related to them. A family that fosters a child's development.
   <u>Group home</u>: a place where a group of children without parents may live.
3. If the car breaks down or someone gets sick a family may have an extra expense.
4. *live from paycheck to paycheck:* spend all the money one makes in one paycheck without saving any money
   out on the street: homeless

Guess Meaning from Related Words (Page 127)

1.

paycheck (pay + check) = the check you get when you get paid
subway (sub + way) = sub means under; way means route
underground (under + ground) = under the ground

2.

public parks: a park that everyone can use
garbage cans: a can to put garbage in

3.

the working poor

Reading Skills

Understanding Transition Words (Page 127)

1. *however:* to introduce an opposite idea
2. *therefore:* to give a result
3. *so:* to give a cause

PART II (Page 128)

1. San Miguel (a city in the United States); the editor of a newspaper
2. giving homeless people tickets or arresting them
3. (Answers may vary.) The police actions are embarrassing and possibly illegal; city officials should help homeless people find homes instead of punishing them.
4. increase housing and services for homeless people

Vocabulary Work

Guess Meaning from Context (Page 129)

1. (Answers may vary slighty, examples are below.)
   illegal: legal means lawful, illegal must mean the opposite, unlawful
   criminalizing: a criminal is someone who commits a crime, criminalizing must mean treating people as if they have commited a crime.
   interestingly: to have an interest means to be absorbed or curious. Interestingly must be a form of interest or interesting.
   embarrassment: shameful
   standard of living: the type of lifestyle one has
   mayor: a position of authority in the city/a city official
   well-being: being well, happy, or content.
2. It is contrasted with a helping hand. A helping hand is nice. A slap across the face is not nice.

Reading Skills

Identifying the Author's Purpose (Page 130)

1. The writer is trying to persuade people that the government is wrong.
2. The last paragraph has examples such as: "we shouldn't punish people because they have no place to live."

Analyzing an Argument (Page 130)

1. & 2.
   a. *statistics:* There is not enough affordable housing and police are giving out more tickets, especially in one part of town.

b. *quotations:* The government is doing something illegal.
3. Answers will vary upon student's opinion.

CNN Video Activities: Homeless at Christmas: One Family's Story

Understand It (Page 179)

1. False   3. True   5. False
2. False   4. False   6. True

VIDEO TRANSCRIPT—Chapter 11: HOMELESS AT CHRISTMAS: ONE FAMILY'S STORY
DVD Title 12   Running time: 02:43

Video Vocabulary

donation   a gift
evicted   to be forced out of a property by threat, law, or physical force
exemplify   to serve as an example, illustrate
misconception   a misunderstanding

Video Script

Reporter: Tamikio Bailey has lived in this room at DC Village Shelter for the past two months with her seven kids.

Tamikio Bailey: Oh this is Tayana Bailey. She's three years old. That's Takia. She's four years old.

Reporter: And for the Bailey children, Santa came early this year.

Reporter: Show me your stuff. Do you have toys around here?

Reporter: Tamikio's family exemplifies a growing number of the homeless population and a frustrating misconception for those who work to end it.

Nan P. Roman: We think the homeless people are the men we see on the street, people with mental illness, substance abuse disorders, physical ailments, and those people are indeed homeless, but a large percentage of homeless people also are people living in families.

Reporter: Homeless children battle a unique set of challenges.

Takia: I want to be living in my own house!

Nan P. Roman: What's very difficult for children is the lack of stability and not having a place to live, so they do often not as well in school. They have more illnesses. It's stress.

Reporter: How families get to the streets—another common misconception.

Nan: That perhaps they become ill or their car breaks down, they lose their job, they can't pay the rent one month, they get evicted and it's so expensive and difficult to get back into housing once they've lost their housing.

Reporter: Donations pour in during the holidays, something the Baileys are grateful for.

Tamikio Bailey: Well this is my first Christmas in a shelter, so it's been really good.

Reporter: A happiness and generosity this mother wishes could continue year round.

Tamikio Bailey: Sometimes it's like they care and they give us things and then after that it's back to the normal routine.

Nan P. Roman: It's a year round situation and while it's wonderful that people give so generously during the holiday season, we need people also to give when it's not the holiday season.

Reporter: Nevertheless, the Bailey children are grateful this year.

Woman: We want you all to say thank you to the people that came in to give you gifts.

Tamikio Bailey: There's nothing like your own home where you can cook for them and talk to them and play with their stuff, so it gets depressing sometimes but they keep me going. They happy, I'm fine.

Reporter: The latest study by the U.S. Conference of Mayors shows that request for shelters by homeless families last year was up 15 percent and of the total population of homeless, 40 percent of them were families with children.

Jennifer Coggiola, CNN, Washington.

CHAPTER 12 — Beauty Contests: The business of beauty
Pages 132–143

Summary There is a beauty contest for nearly everyone in Chapter 12, whatever their age, gender, culture, or digital nature. Reading 1 presents both the attractive and the ugly sides of child beauty pageants, while the search for the perfect digital woman is the subject of Reading 2. In Part II, the topic is standards of male beauty, whether in western bodybuilding contests or the lifelong beauty contest of the African Wodaabe culture.

Audio The readings in this chapter can be heard on the *Hot Topics 1* Audio CD 2 Tracks 10-12 or Audio Tape 2 Side B.

Background In 1996, six-year-old Jon Benet Ramsey was murdered in her Boulder, Colorado home, and newspapers and magazines showed pictures of young Jon Benet in the heavy make-up and frilly costumes that she wore as part of her life as a child beauty queen. Much of the public was shocked by the idea of sexy toddlers on pageant runways, but child beauty pageants have continued to be popular. Outside of that specialized arena, the debate over standards of beauty also continues, with some evidence of evolutionary components, and other evidence showing shifts in the ideal over time and across cultures.

Teaching Note Recycle the vocabulary in the *Vocabulary Work* section on page 138 by having students create their own rules for a beauty pageant. They can decide on the particulars, but encourage them to use as many of the terms as possible, and be sure to share the results with the whole class.

Internet Activity Have each student locate a photograph on the Internet of a person they consider to be very beautiful, then explain to the class exactly what appeals to them. Encourage the students to visit a variety of websites with good photography, although the ubiquitous shots of celebrities will also serve the purpose. If your class is multi-cultural, the resulting discussion could be very interesting. Be sure to remind everyone that beauty is in the eye of the beholder, and nobody's ideas about beauty are wrong.

Video Clip Summary Scenes from child beauty pageants are featured, with supporters describing how the pageants boost children's self-esteem, and detractors pointing out the inappropriateness of young girls mimicking adults. Although it is not directly stated, the photography and statements imply that the beauty pageants sexualize little girls.

Video Script Go to page 38 in this Instructor's Manual for the "Child Beauty Pageants: Fulfilling dreams?" video script and recommended video vocabulary for review.

Video Activity Go to page 180 in the student book for activities to accompany the CNN video clip.

ANSWER KEY—Chapter 12: Beauty Contests: The business of beauty

PREVIEW (Page 132): Answers will vary.

PART I

Predict (Page 133)

A.

1. Reading 1
2. Reading 2
3. Reading 1
4. Reading 1

Reading Comprehension

Check Your Predictions (Page 136): Answers will vary.
Check the Facts

Reading 1 (Page 136)

A.

1. True
2. False
3. True
4. False
5. False
6. False
7. False

B.

1. **Tina Crosby:** contestant
   Megan Palmer: beauty pageant organizer
   Ted Cohen: publishes a directory of pageants
2. **Megan Palmer:** She likes them. She thinks that they help children learn things. She thinks they are like sports teams. But she thinks that parents are sometimes a problem.

Hot Topics 1 • Chapter 12

Psychologists: The children grow up too fast.
Ted Cohen: There are more and more of them every year.

Reading 2 (Page 137)

A.

1. False 2. True 3. True 4. False 5. True 6. True

B.

1. The winner must be beautiful. She must also be "good" and a role model.
2. She isn't a real person. Internet users will vote for the winner.

Analyze (Page 138): (Answers may vary.)

1. Women might think they have to compete with a virtual woman.
2. You have to give the virtual contestants date of birth and her address.
3. So that she can be used to advertise products.

Vocabulary Work

Guess Meaning from Context (Page 138)

1. Answers will vary.
2. *calm down:* to become calm
   wash off: to wash in order to remove something
3. *push their children too hard*
   clue: the example of a parent hitting her child

   makeup
   clues: something that goes on a face that makes little girls look older; you can wash it off

   big business
   clue: there are a lot of pageants, therefore this must be a successful business

   heroines
   clue: example of Lara Croft

Guess Meaning from Related Words (Page 139)

1.

Reading 1

1. advantages / disadvantages
2. psychological / psychologist

Reading 2

1. contest / contestants
2. presenter / presentation

2.

Noun (person): contestant, psychologist, presenter
Noun (thing): contest, presentation, advantage, disadvantage
Verb:
Adjective: psychological
Adverb:

3.

well-spoken: speaks well
self-confident: having confidence in yourself

Reading Skills

Understanding Organization (Page 139)

1. Reading 2 starts with a general introduction. Reading 1 starts with a story about one beauty contest contestant.
2. In Reading 1 it helps you to understand how children's beauty contests work. It is more interesting than starting with a general introduction.

PART II (Page 140)

1. Not really, but there are bodybuilding contests.
2. The men with the most well-developed muscles win the contests.
3. beauty not strength
4. Beautiful men should have long thin arms and legs and pointed noses. They should also have beautiful costumes, face paint and personal magnetism. In addition, magic helps the winner.
5. They win the most beautiful woman as their bride.

Vocabulary Work

Guess Meaning from Context (Page 142)

1. *appearance:* It contains the verb appear. The writer also talks about women's appearance as beautiful and men's as handsome. Both of these refer to physical characteristics.
2. *bodybuilding:* It contains the words body and building. I can guess this means making muscles.
3. *pose:* I can use my world knowledge of bodybuilding and also the clue about the audience.
4. *overall:* It contains the words over and all.
5. *strength:* It looks like strong. The writer compares strength and beauty.
6. *magnetism:* It contains the word magnet. Magnets attract things.

Reading Skills
Summarizing (Page 142)
a. In the Wodaabe culture men compete in beauty contests.
b. The most beautiful man wins the contest.
c. He wins the most beautiful woman as his bride.

Video Activities: Child Beauty Pageants: Fulfilling dreams?
Understand It (Page 180)
1. 100,000
2. 3,000
3. life
4. inappropriate
5. self-esteem
6. overdo
7. makeup
8. dream

VIDEO TRANSCRIPT—Chapter 12: Child Beauty Pageants: Fulfilling dreams?
DVD Title 13   Running time: 03:04

Video Vocabulary
ambition a goal, objective
grown up not childish or immature
overwhelmed overcome with emotion

Video Script

Announcer: Katerina's ambition is to make it to pre-school.

Reporter: Katerina Johnson is one of more than 100,000 children under the age of twelve who compete in child beauty pageants.

Sylviane Kitchen: And I do ask my audience, "please applaud for each one of them." Because that gives them the courage of "Oh, look at me. They do like me."

Announcer: Her favorite song is The Wheels on the Bus.

Reporter: There are about 3,000 pageants for children each year. Entry fees range from $20-500. The prizes vary from toys to thousands of dollars in scholarships. Child pageants are viewed by some as cute slices of American life. By others as curious or odd. And now with the focus on Jon Benet Ramsey, critics are calling the pageants inappropriate. They point to the young girls' grown up makeup, hairstyles, clothes, as well as grown up actions and appearance.

Bunny Bennet: I think they're taking and they're making it look like we're creating little Barbie dolls and that is not the image that we're creating here.

Reporter: Bunny Bennet's two nieces came to live with her six years ago.

Bunny Bennet: And when they came they had very low self-esteem. They could not be in public easily and since they've started in the pageants they have just blossomed.

Heather Brinegar: I feel comfortable in front of the people who are applauding me because I feel proud of myself.

Reporter: Organizers say the public doesn't understand that pageants can involve the whole family, that most contestants don't wear expensive clothes, and that some makeup is necessary.

Peggy York: It's like any spotlight when it shines on you, you need something to enhance that.

Reporter: Psychiatrist Duane Hopson says whether a pageant is good or bad for a young girl depends on the child.

Dr. Duane Hopson: I think for some children it may provide them the opportunity to work on their development of the social skills they need to interact with their peers, whereas another child the same age perhaps might be totally overwhelmed.

Reporter: Pageant organizers admit sometimes parents overdo it.

Man: A lot of times these parents go way too far with their children and sometimes the dresses are too low, there's too much padding.

Woman: It seems to me that in pageants, the children are primarily taught to mimic adults.

Reporter: Organizers fear the current controversy could hurt child pageants.

Sylviane Kitchen: I feel so sorry for the girl who want to enjoy come to pageant and now people will say, "Oh you're in the pageant, that's no good."

Reporter: Because for some young girls, pageants help fulfill a dream, a dream of someday being Miss America.

Tony Clark, CNN, LeMark, Texas.

CHAPTER 13
Pages 144–155

Drug Trends: Legal but lethal

Summary The topic of Chapter 13 is drugs, particularly drugs that are available at the local pharmacy or grocery store. Reading 1 tells the story of cocaine, a popular and legal drug in the nineteenth century. Reading 2 exposes the dangers of tobacco, alcohol, and inhalants, the legal drugs that are most popular with teenagers. Part II focuses on caffeine and the various products in which it can be found.

Audio The readings in this chapter can be heard on the *Hot Topics 1* Audio CD 2 Tracks 13-15 or Audio Tape 2 Side B.

Background The dangers of illegal drugs are often discussed, but legal drugs can also be abused and can be much easier to obtain. Alcohol, for example, can often be found in the liquor cabinet at home, while cold tablets, cough syrup, and a few prescription drugs are in the bathroom medicine cabinet. Aerosol cans might be under the kitchen sink or in the garage, perhaps near a parent's forgotten pack of cigarettes. For adults, of course, any of these can easily be purchased at the store, with no need for a dark alley.

Teaching Note Reading 1 uses chronological organization. Having students create a timeline of the events can help them focus on the time signals in the passage and can help visual learners understand the order of events. Depending on your resources and the size of the class, timelines can be drawn on the board, drawn on poster-size paper, or drawn on regular paper. Afterwards, work with the class to check for accuracy, drawing attention to the language used to convey chronological order.

Internet Activity Search the Internet for anti-drug public service announcements (PSAs) that the students can watch and listen to. Try to find a site with several PSAs so that students can later explain which one they liked best, or why the PSAs would be effective or ineffective in curbing drug abuse. Be aware that different sites require the use of different media players. Try visiting http://www.drugabuse.gov/drugpages/PSAs.html or http://www.unodc.org/unodc/en/multimedia_video.html

Video Clip Summary The CNN video clip draws attention to the abuse of prescription drugs by young people. One young man tells of snorting $250 worth of OxyContin® every day, and a government education campaign compares the dangers of legal prescription drugs to those of more notorious illegal drugs.

Video Script Go to page 41 in this Instructor's Manual for the "Just This Once? Teen Drug Abuse" video script and recommended video vocabulary for review.

Video Activity Go to page 181 in the student book for activities to accompany the CNN video clip.

ANSWER KEY—Chapter 13: Drug Trends: Legal but lethal

PREVIEW (Page 144)
1. all of them
2. Answers will vary.

PART I

Predict (Page 145)
1. Reading 2
2. Reading 1
3. Reading 2
4. Reading 2

Reading Comprehension

Check Your Predictions (Page 147): Answers will vary.
Check the Facts
Reading 1 (Page 148)

A.
1. False
2. False
3. True
4. False
5. True
6. False
7. True

B.
1. It made people feel better and more awake.
2. People became dependent on cocaine; People went a little crazy; People died from cocaine poisoning.

Reading 2 (Page 148)
A.
1. False
2. False
3. True
4. True
5. False
6. False
7. True
8. True
9. True

B.

Type of drug	Legal use	Illegal use	Effects
Tobacco	smoked by people 18 or older	smoked by teenagers	diseases and addiction
Alcohol	legal for adults to drink	illegal for teenagers to drink	relaxation for some; dangerous loss of inhibitions for others; addiction (alcoholism)
Inhalants	used as ingredients in common household products	inhaled or sniffed to get *high*	a *high* feeling; brain damage; death

Analyze (Page 149)

(Answers may vary.)

1. Tobacco is legal today just as cocaine was in 1880, and both are addictive; Tobacco is not thought to be a wonder drug and people don't die of tobacco poisoning.
2. Alcohol is legal today just as cocaine was in 1880, and both are addictive; Alcohol is not thought to be a wonder drug, and it makes people more relaxed, not more awake.
3. Inhalants are legal today just as cocaine was in 1880, and can be found in many products; Inhalants and cocaine are both dangerous and can lead to death.

Vocabulary Work

Guess Meaning from Context (Page 149)

(Answers may vary.)

1.
a. depression and alcoholism / I guess *depression* is a kind of illness like alcoholism.
b. heroin, ecstasy, cannabis, cocaine, and LSD / This is a list of illegal drugs, so *cannabis* must be a kind of illegal drug.
c. emphysema, heart disease, and lung cancer / The text says "serious diseases such as . . .", so *emphysema* is a serious disease

2. (Answers may vary.)
a. The Incas *chewed* coca leaves for energy, so chewing was a way to get the drug into the body. Maybe the leaves went into their mouths somehow, like eating or smoking.
b. The *Spanish conquistadors* took coca plants to Europe, so they must have been explorers from Spain who met the Incas.
c. *Cocaine* is a drug, and it comes from coca leaves, so it must give you energy.
d. A *wonder drug* must be a good thing, because cocaine immediately became very popular.
e. *Awake* must be like having energy, since the Incas chewed coca leaves for energy, and Coca-Cola also contained caffeine, like coffee.
f. *Dependent* is followed by, "they couldn't live without it," so dependent must be like addicted.
g. *Poisoning* is followed by the phrase, "they took to much of it," so poisoning must be taking too much of something.

3.
a. "cigarettes, cigars, and chewing tobacco" are examples of *tobacco products*
b. *Regularly* looks like regular. Maybe it means smoking is a normal part of their day.
c. Alcohol is a *depressant*, and alcohol can make people relaxed or make them do stupid things, so depressants must make people relaxed or stupid.
d. *Inhibitions* must keep people from doing stupid, sometimes dangerous things.
e. The text contains a definition. It says that *alcoholics* are people who are addicted to alcohol.

Guess Meaning from Related Words (Page 150)

1.

Reading 1

medicine / medicinal
benefits / beneficial

Reading 2

addiction / addicted
illegal / legal

40 Hot Topics 1 • Chapter 13

2.
Noun (person):
Noun (thing): medicine, benefits, addiction
Verb:
Adjective: medicinal, beneficial, addicted, illegal / legal
Adverb:

3. long + term (a period of time) = a long period of time

Reading Skills

Understanding Organization (Page 151)

Reading 1 uses chronological organization; Reading 2 is a list. In Reading 1, we can find the words and phrases *long ago, immediately, until, in the 1880s, one hundred years ago, at that time, soon, by the beginning of the twentieth century,* and *today.*

PART II (Page 152)

1. caffeine
2. coffee, tea, cola, and chocolate
3. It stimulates the brain.
4. Some people feel fine; others feel nervous and jumpy.
5. 250 mg a day

Vocabulary Work

Guess Meaning from Context (Page 153)

(Answers may vary. Examples are below.)

milligrams: must be a type of measurement because the article says people consume more than 300 milligrams of caffeine a day.

consume: caffeine comes in forms of liquids and foods in a person's diet, so *consume* must mean to eat or drink
take in: similar to the meaning of *consume* based on it's context in the article.
illegal: Legal means lawful so illegal must be against the law.
jumpy: article says some people feel nervous and jumpy after one drink. Must have a negative meaning, perhaps to feel anxious as a reaction to the caffeine.
stimulate: caffeine acts an "energizer" so it must excite, invigorate, or add energy.
stimulant: caffeine stimulates energy so it must be a stimulant.

Reading Skills

Identifying Referents (Page 154)

1. caffeine
2. most people
3. cocaine and heroin
4. anyone
5. 250 mg a day
6. people
7. the body
8. no referent

CNN Video Activities: Just This Once? Teen Drug Abuse

Understand It (Page 181)

1. True
2. False
3. False
4. True
5. True
6. False

VIDEO TRANSCRIPT—Chapter 13: *Just This Once? Teen Drug Abuse*
DVD Title 14   Running time: 02:22

Video Vocabulary

awareness   having or showing realization, perception, or knowledge
hooked   addicted; obsessed
launch   to start; put into operation, etc.
mode   a manner, way, condition of doing something
reformed   a goal; objective
resort   one who is looked to for help
zombie   a person who acts like a walking dead person, especially from being very tired

Video Script

Reporter: To make its case about the dangers of prescription drugs, the government presented a 19-year-old reformed addict who struggled with a $250-a-day habit.
Kyle Moores: I regret doing it because it put me in basically a zombie mode for a year and a half and screwed up my family financially and emotionally.
Reporter: It was the prescription drug OxyContin®, Oxy for short, that threatened Moores' life. He told CNN he would take the coating off a single tablet, crush it up, and then inhale for an instant high.

Kyle Moores: It's really, really addictive, like you could do it once or twice and you'll be hooked.

Reporter: Moores apparently has lots of company. According to the Department of Health and Human Services, almost 3 million children between the ages of 12 and 17, 12% have used prescription drugs to get high. And almost 7 million young adults between the ages of 18 and 25, nearly 1 in 4. For many of the nation's youth, illegal drugs are no longer the problem.

Westley Clark: Illegal drugs are sort of going in a little roller coaster. But this is not. This has taken off, prescription drugs, particularly narcotic pain relievers, have taken off over the past five years.

Reporter: The new awareness program will feature ads like these and television spots.

Commercial: It starts with just this once. But misuse of prescription pain relievers can kill you. Just like illegal drugs.

Reporter: In an accident of timing, the government is launching its education program within days of a general accounting office report showing that another drug education effort, the so-called DARE program, had no effect in deterring the use of illegal drugs among young people. And even Kyle Moores said he fully understood the Oxys he snorted were harmful and had the potential to kill him. How much good can an education program do? The sponsors of this one acknowledge it's only a small part of a larger solution. The awareness effort here is aimed not just at young people who abuse prescription drugs, but also at their families and friends. Families and friends who may be the remedy of first resort.

Tim O'Brien, CNN Financial News, Washington.

CHAPTER 14 — NATURE: PARADISE LOST—CAN WE GET IT BACK?
Pages 156–168

Summary This chapter looks at three cases of ecological disaster caused by humans. The testing of nuclear bombs on Bikini island is the topic of Reading 1, while Reading 2 outlines the disastrous effects of a Soviet irrigation project on the Aral Sea. Part II features another island, Polynesia's Nauru, where strip-mining provided great wealth, but also spelled the end of a tropical paradise.

Audio The readings in this chapter can be heard on the *Hot Topics 1* Audio CD 2 Tracks 16-18 or Audio Tape 2 Side B.

Background In 1872, the U.S. Congress declared Yellowstone the first National Park, arguably the beginning of the environmental movement in the United States. The interest in preserving wildlife was fueled in the twentieth century by writers like Aldo Leopold, who once worked for the U.S. Forest Service, and *Silent Spring* author Rachel Carson of the U.S. Fish and Wildlife Service. When Wisconsin Senator Gaylord Nelson founded Earth Day, first observed in 1970, many Americans had serious ecological concerns and were ready to fight to protect the environment.

Teaching Note Take a field trip to a place in your community that reflects environmental awareness such as a botanical garden, an arboretum, or a university agricultural research station. Prepare the students with important vocabulary, and if possible, give them an opportunity to ask an expert questions. Follow up with a writing assignment in which students describe the place and explain how it benefits the environment.

Internet Activity Have the students find out about and report on environmental protection efforts in their countries. Try Yahoo's directory which includes a regional listing at http://dir.yahoo.com/Society_and_Culture/Environment_and_Nature/organizations/

Video Clip Summary Reporter Gary Strieker talks to people who depend on fishing in the Bering Sea, where fish populations are decreasing. The fishermen blame the drop on huge factory trawlers, but the U.S. authorities who manage fishing in the region state that fluctuations in wildlife populations are normal and caused by climate conditions.

Video Script Go to pages 45-46 in this Instructor's Manual for the "Endangered Arctic Ecosystem" video script and recommended video vocabulary for review.

Video Activity Go to page 182 in the student book for activities to accompany the CNN video clip.

ANSWER KEY—Chapter 14: NATURE: PARADISE LOST—CAN WE GET IT BACK?

PREVIEW (Page 156)
a. The Great Flood?
b. Visit the Rainforest Now or You May Be Too Late
c. A Way of Life Dies as the Sahara Desert Moves South

PART I

Predict (Page 157)
1. Reading 1
2. Readings 1 & 2
3. Readings 1 & 2
4. Readings 1 & 2

Reading Comprehension
Check Your Predictions (Page 160): Answers will vary.
Check the Facts
Reading 1 (Page 160)

A.
1. False
2. False
3. True
4. True
5. True

B.
1. They are very powerful and the radiation can kill people for years after the explosion.
2. They told the Bikinians that the tests were good for all people and could end wars, and that the islanders could return after the tests.

Reading 2 (Page 161)

A.
1. True (but less than today)
2. True
3. False
4. False
5. True
6. False

B.
1. It is smaller and saltier, and there are fewer kinds of fish.
2. Farmers must use pesticides and fertilizers, and the growing season is shorter because of climate changes. Some fishermen live far from the sea. Poor drinking water causes health problems.

Analyze (Page 161)
(Answers may vary.)
1. Both problems happened because the governments did not understand the effects their actions would have.
2. No. The U.S. government underestimated the power of the nuclear bomb, and the Soviet government didn't know that the irrigation project would cause so many problems.
3. Both situations are important, but it's possible that the Aral Sea situation is affecting more people than the Bikini Island testing.

Vocabulary Work

Guess Meaning from Context (Page 162)
1. Answers will vary.
2. (Answers may vary.)

In exile contrasts with *could return* in the previous paragraph.
Starved is a negative thing; perhaps it happens when people don't take care of each other.
Harmonious might be like cooperative since people did things together.
Shrinking is similar to *getting smaller* in the next sentence.
Survive is like live; it contrasts with *cannot live* in the previous sentence.
Sand is where the lake used to be, so it's dry land, but not *soil*, since it destroys the soil.
Climate must be like weather because they talk about heat, rain, cold, and snow.
Diarrhea is a kind of *serious health problem*.

Guess Meaning from Related Words (Page 162)

1.

Reading 1
Bikini / Bikinians
protection / protectorate
stronger / strength

Reading 2
irrigate / irrigation / irrigated
salt / salty

2.

Noun (person): Bikinians
Noun (thing): Bikini, protection / protectorate, strength, irrigation, salt
Verb: irrigate
Adjective: stronger, irrigated, salty
Adverb:

Reading Skills

Identifying Transition Words and Phrases (Page 163)

1.
a. however
b. therefore / in the end
c. (none)
d. now / after / then / meanwhile
e. sadly / unfortunately
f. in the same way

2.
(Answers may vary.) Examples below:
in the 1960s / at that time / from 1960 to 1990 / soon / within decades / in 1989 / now

Analyzing the Organization of a Reading (Page 164)

CAUSE: Water from rivers used to irrigate crops
    RESULT: Region becomes world's fourth largest cotton producer
    RESULT: Aral Sea becomes smaller
        RESULT: Some fishing communities now far from sea
        RESULT: Very few fish
        RESULT: Sea is very salty
            RESULT: Most of the native plants and animals cannot live there
    RESULT: Land is sandy
        RESULT: Farmers us a lot of insecticides and fertilizers
        RESULT: Climate is changing because of the sand
            RESULT: short, hot, dry summers and long, cold, dry winters
    RESULT: Water is a problem
        RESULT: Water has insecticides and fertilizers
            RESULT: Water is unsafe for humans and animals
        RESULT: Drinking water is salty
            RESULT: increases in serious diseases

PART II (Page 165)

1. Nauru is an island in the Pacific.
2. People were part of twelve clans and lived in small houses. They had little communication with Europeans.
3. phosphate
4. removing the top layer of soil and taking away the desired material
5. The government was getting a lot of money, but using it unwisely. The surface of the island was nearly destroyed and the phosphate was running out.
6. Nauru is almost bankrupt; the Naurans have nothing.

Vocabulary Work

Guess Meaning from Context (Page 167)

ecological nightmare—There are many negative words in the paragraph.
heartbreaking—*Heart* sometimes refers to emotions, and *saddest* is used earlier.
remote—similar to *far from*
whaling ship—whale + ship, so it's probably a ship used to hunt whales
clans—It says *clans or family groups*, so it's a family group.
alcohol—It's in a list with guns, and destroyed the social balance, so it's bad.
reduced—900 is less than 1,400, so *reduced* means made smaller
strip-mining—This paragraph describes the process of *strip-mining*.
running out—With 90 percent of the island destroyed, there wasn't much left.
bankrupt—Now the Naurans have nothing.
unwisely—not + wise, so in a way that was not wise

Reading Skills

Identifying Transition Words and Phrases (Page 167)

(Answers may vary.)

<u>Mark Time</u>: then / now / for thousands of years / in 1798 / at first / in 1888 / in 1899 / in that year / gradually / in 1968 / every year / soon / by 2000
<u>Add Ideas</u>: also / in addition
<u>Emphasize an Idea</u>: in fact

Video Activities: Endangered Arctic Ecosystem

Understand It (Page 182)

1. no
2. trawlers (huge nets)
3. more than half
4. St. George is one of the Pribilof Islands in the eastern part of the Bering Sea near the edge of the continental shelf.
5. It agrees with the big fishing and processing companies that the ecosystem is very healthy; fisheries are not causing declines in marine mammals and birds.
6. Climate change and pollution

VIDEO TRANSCRIPT—Chapter 14: ENDANGERED ARCTIC ECOSYSTEM
DVD Title 15   Running time: 03:47

Video Vocabulary

consolation   comfort from a loss
decline   a lowering
rake   to gather material using a rake
trawl   a large, sack-shaped fishing net that is pulled on the bottom of the ocean

Video Script

Reporter: On the island of St. George, it's the start of fishing season.
David Fox: This is our jig line. This is what we use to catch the halibut when we're not long lining.
Reporter: But finding halibut off this island is not as easy as it used to be. What's causing this, do you think?
Rodney: Trawlers.
Reporter: Trawlers, are causing it?
Rodney: Yeah, a lot of them.
Reporter: Factory trawlers, owned by big fishing companies dragging miles of huge nets across the Bering Sea.
Man: And us poor little fisherman are, you know, we're trying to make a living in the summer and they're just killing us out there. They're just raking the sea.
Reporter: And it's not only some fish populations that are dropping, marine mammals are also in trouble with Stellar sea lions listed as an endangered species and locals reporting reductions in northern fur seals, as well as declining populations of many kinds of sea birds nesting and breeding here. The people on these islands have seen it and researchers are now producing evidence that many wildlife species here are quickly declining in numbers. Scientists tell us something is upsetting the natural balance in the Bering Sea and what might result from that could be serious.
   More than half of the annual fish catch in the United States and in Russia comes from the Bering Sea. St. George is one of the Pribilof Islands in the eastern part of the sea near the edge of the Continental Shelf. Biologically, it's a highly productive area, important for science and conservation.
Evie Witten: By looking at the Pribilof Islands and monitoring what's going on there, it's like taking the temperature of the rest of the sea. It gives us an indication of the biological health of other parts of the Bering Sea.
Reporter: And because fur seals and sea birds survive on a diet of fish, declining numbers of these animals could be a warning signal that giant trawlers are over fishing the Bering Sea.
Dorothy Childers: If fisheries are having a serious impact on this food web question and we don't do anything because we can't prove it, then someday we may be in a heap of trouble, and we may already be there.

Reporter: That's not so, say the big fishing and processing companies and they're supported by U.S. authorities responsible for managing fisheries in the region.

David Witherell: The ecosystem itself is considered very healthy.

Reporter: They sight a recent scientific study concluding it's highly unlikely fisheries are causing declines in marine mammals and birds. And they say stability in wildlife populations should not be expected.

David Witherell: That's not the case with nature, especially in these near arctic ecosystems. Things fluctuate due to environmental conditions.

Reporter: Maybe there's more to this problem than over fishing. Maybe it's climate change or pollution or maybe it's all natural. But that's small consolation to these fisherman looking for halibut that are no longer there.

Gary Strieker, CNN, on St. George Island in the Bering Sea.

HOT TOPICS 2: Instructor's Manual

CHAPTER 1 — REALITY TV: WOULD YOU BE A SURVIVOR?
Pages 1–9

Summary This chapter explores the topic of reality television. Supporters of reality television find it entertaining, while critics claim the content is too simplistic and is often offensive. Part I describes four popular reality shows; Part II gives the results of a psychological study about who watches reality shows.

Audio The readings in this chapter can be heard on the *Hot Topics 2* Audio CD 1 Tracks 1-2 or Audio Tape 1 Side A.

Background Reality television is a genre that does not rely on scripts or defined characters. Instead, viewers apply to be on the show and, if chosen, are videotaped performing the tasks required by the particular program. There are many types of reality television shows. Some focus on personal relationships or business; others challenge participants in unusual or extreme environments. There has even been a historically-set reality show where participants were required to survive in a house equipped with the technology of the year 1900.

While reality television has seen a recent wave of popularity, the genre is not new. The earliest "reality" show was *Candid Camera*, which began in 1948. The show recorded how people reacted to unusual situations when they did not know they were being filmed. Since then, there have been many programs with unscripted content, for example, *America's Funniest Home Videos*, *Real World*, *America's Most Wanted*, and *Cops*.

Teaching Note The reading skills section of this chapter focuses on synonyms as a cohesion device. Encourage students to generate synonyms themselves by conducting a competitive game. Divide the class into small groups, and have each group select a "secretary." Write a familiar word such as *friend*, *store*, or *nice* on the board, and give the students one minute to brainstorm as many synonyms as possible. The group with the highest number writes their synonyms on the board. Give feedback, and add additional words from other groups. Repeat the process.

Internet Activity Instruct students to conduct an Internet search about reality television. They can visit sites like www.infoplease.com and follow the menus to articles about television and reality shows. Have them choose an article about one of the following topics: the history of reality television, a popular reality show, or a celebrity from a reality show. Have them take notes on the article they read, and then share the information they gather in small groups. Alternatively, have students share information from a realty show's homepage such as www.idolonfox.com (*American Idol*) or www.cbs.com (select *Survivor* or *The Amazing Race*). These sites contain video clips, message boards, trivia quizzes, and interactive games, along with information about the show and the contestants.

Video Clip Summary In this CNN video clip, the reporter, Wolf Blitzer, discusses the popularity of reality television shows and covers the issues that surround them. For example, he alludes to criticisms that reality television shows have questionable values and oversimplify their portrayal of personal lives. He also focuses on the criticism that reality shows promote the "peeping Tom" attitude of viewers.

Video Script Go to page 49 in this Instructor's Manual for the The Reality of Would You be a Survivor? "Reality TV" video script and recommended video vocabulary for review.

Video Activity Go to page 168 in the student book for activities to accompany the CNN video clip.

ANSWER KEY—Chapter 1: REALITY TV

PREVIEW (Page 1)
1. Answers will vary.
2. Answers will vary.

PART 1

Predict (Page 2)
A. 1. c 2. c 3. a

Chapter 1 • Hot Topics 2 47

B. 4. b   5. a
C. Answers will vary.

Reading Comprehension

Check Your Predictions (Page 5)

1. Answers will vary.
2. Answers will vary.

Check the Facts (Page 5)

1. ten people
2. The people on *Big Brother* cannot contact the outside world.
3. In the U.S., the contestants vote the people out of the house.
4. They often have to eat live worms and other small animals such as insects. In addition, their bodies may be covered with bees or they may be asked to get inside a box full of snakes.
5. Female competitors, siblings, parent and child teams
6. They must live outside and cook their own food.
7. Successful players must be able to make agreements with other players.
8. The previously eliminated contestants vote to give one of the finalists $1,000,000.
9. four couples
10. If a single person can convince a man or woman to leave his or her mate, he or she wins.
11. Many religious organizations say the show is immoral because it is about sex, not relationships.
12. He said the show helps couples learn about themselves.

Analyze (Page 6)

1. Similarities: competitive, voting system, people live together, cut off from society
   Differences: *Big Brother* takes place within a house; *Survivor* takes place in the wilderness. *Big Brother* activities consist of housework and special jobs; *Survivor* competitions are based on physical tests and survival in the wilderness.
2. (Answers may vary.) Suggested responses: *Fear Factor* because the contestants aren't living together; *Temptation Island* because it has a romantic theme
3. Answers will vary.

Vocabulary Work

Guess Meaning from Context (Page 6)

1. Answers will vary.
2. *media:* television, radio, and newspapers
   worms: small, soft crawling animals with no legs
   relationships: connections between two people, especially regarding behavior and feelings
   separated: not together
   convince: persuade
3. Answers will vary.

Guess Meaning from Related Words (Page 6)

1. Answers will vary.
2. *compete:* competitors; competition
   survivor: survival
   tempt: temptation

Reading Skills

Understanding Cohesion (Page 7)

players: competitors; contestants
audience: public
task: job
program: show

Discussion (Page 7)

1. Answers will vary.
2. Answers will vary.

PART II

Read It (Page 7)

1. a. People watch the programs to be part of the "in" crowd.
   b. Some people think that only people who are unintelligent watch reality television.
2. People who watch reality television were more competitive than people who don't watch it; People who enjoy reality television generally agreed with statements such as, "Prestige is important to me." and "I am impressed with designer clothes."

Vocabulary Work

Guess Meaning from Related Words (Page 9)

compete
New word: *competitive*
Meaning: someone who likes to compete
celebrate
New word: *celebrities*
Meaning: famous people
intelligent
New word: *unintelligent*
Meaning: not bright, not clever

Video Activities: The Reality of Reality TV

Understand It (Page 168)

1. True
2. False
3. False
4. False
5. False
6. True
7. True

VIDEO TRANSCRIPT—Chapter 1: THE REALITY OF REALITY TV
DVD Title 2   Running time: 02:47

Video Vocabulary

aghast   shocked; horrified

network   a large television or radio company with stations across the country: ABC, CBS, and NBC are the three major television networks.

voyeur or peeping Tom   a person who gets pleasure, especially sexual thrills, from secretly watching others

Video Script

Bachelor: Nice to meet you.

Woman 1: Nice to meet you!

Bachelor: She seems so down to earth and not . . . and not at all like a gold digger.

Reporter: You may shudder with indignation.

Man 1: There's a little card inside.

Bachelorette: Thank you very much.

Man 1: I'll see you later.

Bachelorette: OK. I'll see you, tonight.

Reporter: You may defiantly say, I never watch those shows.

Female Voice: Oh, my God!

Reporter: But you also may, ever so secretly, be watching. Others certainly are . . . many others. The reality is that reality TV, what some <u>network</u> executives call "unscripted programming," is a raging success. This week Joe Millionaire on Fox attracted 18.6 million viewers. And ABC's the *Bachelorette* wasn't far behind, burying NBC's popular West Wing by three and a half million viewers.

Woman 2: . . . and so I expect my husband to make a certain amount of money, yeah.

Reporter: They're bringing viewers back to the networks. They're also bringing out the critics who are aghast at the perceived voyeurism, lack of intellect, and questionable values.

Sandy Rios: We've got a fifty percent divorce rate, at least. And you know so when you present programs like these where the end game is marriage based on marrying this fake millionaire, or a marriage based on picking out of twenty five girls the one who, you know, rings your chimes the best, that's a terrible reason to choose a mate.

Reporter: Trista Rehn who's dating twenty-five guys on the Bachelorette to find her mate says, don't be so quick to judge.

Trista Rehn: It's really hard, I think, to meet good people. And I had a whole casting department out there looking for me. ABC was basically playing match maker and these guys are all blood tested and psychologically screened.

Reporter: But do we need to be psychologically screened? Why is it that we can't wait to watch someone squirm in a tank full of snakes on NBC's *Celebrity Fear Factor?*

Michael Medved: These shows exist for one reason only, and that's to humiliate really good looking people.

Reporter: But don't judge this format as just a disrespectful Johnny-come-lately. Reality TV has been around for decades, even before MTV's the *Real World*, now in its twelfth season. And the networks will keep those shows coming. From their standpoint, what's not to like about a popular show that's much cheaper to produce than a sitcom or a drama. And one of those critics . . .

Critic: The negative part of all these shows, the negative part of all these shows, is that they make us all into <u>peeping Toms</u>. But the point is, compare it to the rest of the stuff on TV.

Wolf Blitzer, CNN, Washington.

CHAPTER 2 — Violence in Sports: When is a game not a game?

Pages 10–20

Summary Whether they are celebrating their team's victory or expressing anger and frustration over a defeat, sports fans can become violent after a game. This chapter uses newspaper articles to outline three cases of such violence, and to explore some of the causes of and ways to prevent post-game fan violence.

Audio The readings in this chapter can be heard on the *Hot Topics 2* Audio CD 1 Tracks 3-6 or Audio Tape 1 Side A.

Background Although competitive sports by their nature involve aggressive play tactics and glorify the physical domination of one athlete over another, the rules of any game and the idea of good sportsmanship prohibit actual violence. During the game, of course, fights do sometimes break out between the athletes, and fans might hurl verbal abuse along with bottles and cans. It's during the aftermath of the game, however, when large crowds and alcohol contribute to dangerous "celebrations."

Teaching Note The reading skills section of this chapter points out that newspaper articles usually begin with a general statement which summarizes the article. To reinforce this idea, cut out newspaper headlines and leading sentences (or write simplified versions of the leading sentences) for the students to match. As a follow-up activity, cut out photos from newspapers and have students write their own headlines and leading sentences. Point out that headlines use simple verb tenses and contain no function words.

Internet Activity Direct students to websites such as www.cnn.com or www.yahoo.com to find a short news article on a topic that interests them. Have the students print the article, circle unknown words as they read, then use context clues to guess meanings. After they are familiar with the article, students create a simple poster with the article's headline and first sentence, which they read aloud to the class before giving an oral summary of the article. If students want to read more about fan violence, a search engine can be used to find additional articles on the topic.

CNN Video Clip Summary This CNN video clip looks at cases of fan violence in the United States and Europe, describing a riot after a Los Angeles Lakers game and police efforts to control the violence there. The reporter explains potential sanctions against fans and players in England following violent incidents, and Tony Blair expresses support for the sanctions.

Video Script Go to page 52 in this Instructor's Manual for the video script "Sports fans or foes?" and recommended video vocabulary for review.

Video Activity Go to page 169 in the student book for activities to accompany the CNN video clip.

ANSWER KEY—Chapter 2: Violence in Sports: When is a game not a game?

PREVIEW (Page 10) 2. Answers will vary.

PART I

Predict (Page 11)

1. a. Answers will vary.
   b. Answers will vary.
2. a. (Answers may vary.) Reading 2
   b. (Answers may vary.) Reading 1
   c. (Answers may vary.) Reading 3
3. Answers will vary.
4. Answers will vary.

Reading Comprehension

Check Your Predictions (Page 15)

1. Answers will vary.
2. Answers will vary.

Check the Facts

Reading 1 (Page 15)

1. False   2. True
3. True   4. True
5. False

Reading 2 (Page 15)
1. False
2. True
3. False
4. False
5. False

Reading 3 (Page 16)
1. True
2. False
3. False
4. True
5. True

Analyze (Page 16)
1. Similar: Violent riots; cars were burned; destructive; both following sporting events
   Different: People injured in Russia; people not injured in Columbus. People died in Russia; no one died in Columbus. Russian riot due to loss; Ohio students celebrating a win.
2. Russians think showing the match on an outdoor screen caused the riot.
3. Similar: Both are international competitions.
   Different: Olympic fans are different from soccer fans: Riots and fights never happen at the Olympics, while they are common at soccer matches.
4. Yes; in their song they mention throwing bottles and their song is threatening.

Vocabulary Work

Guess Meaning from Context (Page 16)
1. a. False
   b. True
   c. True
   d. False
2. *fan:* a person who likes a person or thing very much
   arrest: to seize or hold by legal authority
   riot: violence by a crowd of people
   injured: hurt
   mob: a very large group of angry people
   smash: break
   shout: call out in a loud voice
   ban: not allow

Guess Meaning from Related Words (Page 17)
1. **Verb:** rioted;—; celebrate; destruct
   Noun (thing): riot; violence; celebration; destruction
   Noun (person): rioter;—; celebrity
   Adjective:—; violent; celebratory
2. trouble maker
   over turn
3. *a war zone:* area of destruction or violence
   turn ugly: go bad

Reading Skills

Understanding Organization (Page 17)
1. <u>Reading 1:</u> Students should underline, "Officials said about 50 people were injured and two died in a riot after Japan beat Russia 1-0."
   <u>Reading 2:</u> "Police arrested 46 people in a celebratory riot after Ohio State University's football team defeated the University of Michigan 14-9."
   <u>Reading 3:</u> "The World Cup finals begin in Japan next Friday. People here are both excited and worried. They're excited about the games and worried about the fans."
2. a. Reading 1
   b. Reading 2
   c. Reading 3

Discussion (Page 17)
1. Answers will vary.
2. Answers will vary.

PART II

Read It (Page 18)
1. Two main causes of mob violence are alcohol and the crowd itself.
2. Officials can make sure that an area is not overcrowded. They should think of games as "big parties." They can put cameras in all the stadiums.

Vocabulary Work

Guess Meaning from Related Words (Page 19)
1. *destroy*
   Other form(s): destructive
   Meaning: causing great damage
2. *celebrate*
   Other form(s): celebratory
   Meaning: having to do with celebration, festive
3. *normal*
   Other form(s): abnormal, normally
   Meaning: abnormal: not normal, unusual; normally: usually
4. *violent*
   Other form(s): violence
   Meaning: injury or damage, brutality
5. *crowd*
   Other forms(s): overcrowded
   Meaning: too many people in one area

CNN Video Activities: Sports fans or foes?

Understand It (Page 169)

A.

1. happy
2. outside
3. English
4. EUFA

B.

1. 2; 70; a (one); a (one)
2. 23; 11; thousand; 2; thousand

VIDEO TRANSCRIPT—Chapter 2: Sports fans or foes?
DVD Title 3   Running time: 01:43

Video Vocabulary

*EUFA**   European Football Association
expel   to send away for a reason
hooligan   a thug, troublemaker
loot   to rob, steal from
mayhem   serious destruction of property or harm to someone
rucku   a lot of noise and confusion
torch   to set afire

Video Script

Reporter: Monday night, <u>mayhem</u> in Los Angeles. Outside the Staples Center downtown, hundreds of Laker fans who watched the game on giant screens outdoors celebrated the NBA championship violently—vandalizing a limousine, <u>torching</u> two police cars and a city bus, destroying two television satellite trucks, damaging more than 70 cars lined up at auto dealerships, and <u>looting</u> a furniture store and a computer store.

The fire department responded to 23 calls; 11 people were arrested. Police used riot gear and rubber bullets against the crowd, which they estimated at three thousand, and which two news organizations put at ten thousand.

Mayor Richard Riordan: These are not fans; they're losers who only know how to trash our city.

Reporter: It's a frequent occurrence—fans causing a ruckus at sporting events, casting a shadow on the sports world. In Belgium this week thousands of riot police are on hand to keep soccer fans at the Euro 2000 tournament in check.

Over the weekend more than 800 English fans were arrested in Brussels and Charles-le-Roi for violence.

<u>EUFA</u>, European football's controlling body, threatened to <u>expel</u> England from the tournament if its fans caused any more trouble. England's professional soccer league said it would ban for life fans found guilty of <u>hooliganism</u>.

Tony Blair: I most certainly deeply regret what has happen, because I think that's important. But now we have to make sure that we're doing everything possible for the future matches. . .

Hot Topics 2 • Chapter 2

CHAPTER 3
Pages 21–33

ADVERTISING: WE KNOW WHAT YOU WANT *BEFORE* YOU DO!

Summary Advertising seems to be everywhere, and Part I of this chapter takes a look at some of the questionable forms it can take, describing Candie's shoe ads that feature celebrities in the bathroom, and "Schmio awards" given to the advertising world's worst examples. Part II outlines the common ways advertisers try to convince consumers to buy products.

Audio The readings in this chapter can be heard on the *Hot Topics 2* Audio CD 1 Tracks 7-10 or Audio Tape 1 Side A.

Background The image of fifteen-year-old Brooke Shields posing topless in her Calvin Klein jeans made a splash in 1980, and advertisers have been pushing the boundaries of acceptability and good taste ever since. Today, advertising is rapidly evolving, taking advantage of our web-surfing habits with banner and pop-up ads, and reaching out to the teen market with websites that promise prizes for members who can recruit a large number of friends. Consumers who know about advertising techniques can be more sophisticated judges of the ads they see and hear every day.

Teaching Note The reading in Part II describes fourteen techniques used by advertisers. Collect English language magazines of different types (fashion, news, business) and ask small groups of students to locate ads that exemplify as many of the techniques as possible. (You could offer a prize for the group that finds the most.) Have the students cut out the ads, hold them up or tape them to the wall, and explain to the rest of the class how each ad tries to appeal to consumers.

Internet Activity Follow up on the CNN clip's discussion of marketing to children and teenagers by assigning an Internet research topic such as "advertising and childhood obesity" or "age compression"—the advertising industry's term for marketing sexy adult products like make-up or lingerie to young people. Students should find an article they can read and understand, then write a report (or fill out a chart) with key information to share with the class. Alternatively, send students to www.aef.com, the Advertising Educational Foundation, to read articles from the advertising industry that may contrast with the textbook articles, and look for links to Clio Award-winning ads. Other interesting websites include www.adcouncil.org, which highlights public service advertising, and www.aeforum.org, with international advertising news.

Video Clip Summary The CNN clip focuses on marketing to American children and teenagers, who spend $170 billion each year themselves, and also influence the purchases their parents make. Critics say that kids can't objectively weigh the power of celebrities and the subtle messages that ads send, but one advertising agency points to their campaign that encourages kids to eat healthier foods.

Video Script Go to page 55 in this Instructor's Manual for the "Selling to Kids" video script and recommended video vocabulary for review.

Video Activity Go to page 170 in the student book for activities to accompany the CNN video clip.

ANSWER KEY—Chapter 3: ADVERTISING: WE KNOW WHAT YOU WANT *BEFORE* YOU DO!

PREVIEW (Page 21)
1. Answers will vary.
2. Answers will vary.

PART I

Predict (Page 22)
1. Answers will vary.
2. Answers will vary.
3. Answers will vary.
4. Answers will vary.
5. Answers will vary.

Reading Comprehension

Check Your Predictions (Page 25)
1. Answers will vary.
2. Answers will vary.

Check the Facts

Reading 1 (Page 25)
1. True
2. False
3. True
4. False

Reading 2 (Page 26)
1. False
2. False
3. False (Jenny McCarthy who starred in the ad won the award.)
4. True
5. False

Reading 3 (Page 26)
1. True
2. False
3. True
4. False
5. False

Analyze (Page 26)
1. (Answers may vary.) Both techniques are out of the ordinary, and both target young women.
2. (Answers may vary.) The Media and Democracy Congress most likely disapproves of undercover advertising because it is deceptive and sneaky.

Vocabulary Work
Guess Meaning from Context (Pages 26–27)
1. Answers will vary.
2. *controversial:* something people don't agree about
   in bad taste: not polite
   awards: prizes; things given for achievement
   false: not true
   cool: fashionable
   deceptive: not telling the truth
   enthusiastic: excited
3. Answers will vary.
4. Answers will vary.
5. Answers will vary.

Guess Meaning from Related Words
Reading 2 (Page 27)
1. *harmless* (harm + without): not causing hurt or damage
   influential (influence + adjective): having an impact
   critics (criticize + noun): people who review and give opinions about things
   empowerment (power + noun): giving power to someone or something
   empower: to give power to

Reading 3 (Page 28)
undercover (under + cover): disguised
stylish (style + adjective): fashionable, attractive
traditional (tradition + adjective): passed from one generation to the next
underground (under + ground): below the ground, secret
overhear (over + hear): to hear something by accident
performance (perform + noun): presentation before an audience

2. (Answers may vary.) Usually: noun; Phrase: verb
3. (Answers may vary.) Usually: of a yellow or gold color; Here: valuable or excellent

Reading Skills
Identifying Cultural References (Page 28)
1. (Answers may vary.) They are all influential American organizations. They all play a part in present day advertising.
2. Answers will vary.

Understanding Cohesion (Page 29)
1. Candie's
2. the ads
3. the ads
4. Candie's Inc.
5. the customers
6. the customers

Discussion (Page 29)
1. Answers will vary.
2. Answers will vary.

PART II
Read It (Page 30)
1. Heart Strings
2. Put Downs
3. Star Power

Vocabulary Work
Guess Meaning from Context (Page 32):
(Answers may vary.)
1. *strategies:* plans in order to achieve a goal
2. *lifestyle:* the manner in which one lives
3. *hottest:* most popular
4. *in-crowd:* popular people
5. *left out:* not included, on the outside
6. *competitor:* a person involved in competition
7. *statistics:* collection of numerical information
8. *misleading:* leading to the wrong idea
9. *deceptive:* causing someone to believe what is not true
10. *sugary:* too sweet
11. *uncool:* unacceptable, socially awkward
12. *hip:* aware, fashionable

Reading Skills

Understanding the Author's Viewpoint (Page 32)

1. Answers will vary.
2. Answers will vary.

Video Activities: Selling to Kids

Understand It (Page 170)

1. b. kids
2. c. tweens
3. a. clothes
4. d. cool
5. c. strategies
6. b. shop
7. d. hip

VIDEO TRANSCRIPT—Chapter 3: SELLING TO KIDS

DVD Title 4   Running time: 03:05

Video Vocabulary

allowance   money for everyday expenses
demographics   demographic information about groups of people used especially in politics and marketing
fit in   to be accepted by other people in a group
full-fledged   complete
manipulative   to be controlling
tween*   a child between the ages of 8 and 12

Video Script

Reporter: Britney is just the beginning. Before parents were finished complaining about how their young daughters were copying everything the star wore and ate, marketers decided it was the next big wave. Now the Olson twins make every young pre-teen or tween aspire to their coolness, selling clothing and a fragrance line at Wal-Mart.

Seventy-five percent of kids watch what stars on TV wear. Top of the list is Hilary Duff—the star of *Lizzy Maguire*.

Tween boys are into skateboarding and other sports; tween girls are into sports and clothes.

Cameron Diaz: Let's get dirty.

Reporter: . . . with plenty of impact from stars like *Charlie's Angels* and other bubble gum girls.

Girl 1: Cameron Diaz is really pretty. I have a lot of different friends. Some like being dressed up, like, one of my friends—Lauren—she likes being dressed up.

Reporter: Kid-buying power is the obsession of Tim Coffey, head of the Wonder Group, a youth marketing and advertising consulting firm.

They point out this market of 20 million preteen customers is barely tapped. Spending power, mostly from allowances is about $300 a year. But building customers is key. Last year, full-fledged teens spent $170 billion on stuff.

Tweens influence other purchases, for example 65 percent of tweens help with the grocery shopping.

TV announcer: Introducing Air Heads Xtremes.

Reporter: Air Heads is an example of the kind of sell that makes a success, and goes to core of the demographic.

Tim Coffey: Air Heads is one of those candies that most adults don't know about, but every kid does. They're uniquely formulated for kids' tastes, and we portray that brand in a way that, you know, speaks to their, again, this notion of power and freedom that, you know, eating an Air Heads allows you to do things that you might not be able to do all the time.

Reporter: Some see the messages as manipulative—too subtle for kids to see through and too powerful to resist.

Expert: It's exploiting their vulnerabilities. I mean . . . and, and why should we eat because it's cool, you know? We should eat because we're hungry, or because it tastes good. But the notion of eating to be cool or to fit in is actually really problematic

Reporter: Nonsense, say marketers like Wonder Group. The firm was hired by Chiquita to make bananas cool. They point out healthy products like yogurt and cereal fall into basic food groups.

But boring is not necessary. A trip through the grocery aisle finds Incredible Hulk Jell-O, highly animated yogurts, and cereal bars for kids to grab on their way to the car pool instead of skipping breakfast altogether.

Marketers say it's a question of "getting with the program." Kids do drive purchases. The typical customer in a grocery store or anywhere else is a parent and a child and the most frequently asked question is: what do you want to eat? The kids decide.

Kitty Pilgrim, CNN, New York.

Chapter 3 • Hot Topics 2

CHAPTER 4 — Fashion: You mean you're wearing THAT?
Pages 34–43

Summary Clothing *can* be controversial. Just ask a teenager who has to follow a dress code, a man who wants to wear a skirt, an Edinburgh taxi driver who doesn't want to wear flannel trousers, or a religious person going to school in France. This chapter provides a lot of fuel for the fashion fire!

Audio The readings in this chapter can be heard on the *Hot Topics 2* Audio CD 1 Tracks 11-14 or Audio Tape 1 Side A.

Background When the Beatles first traveled to the U.S. in 1964, most Americans had not heard their music, yet they soon formed strong opinions about their "long" hair and their "Beatle boots". As an outward symbol of who we are, clothes can indicate cultural background, religious or political beliefs, socioeconomic status, and even gang affiliations. They can also serve to erase such distinctions, for instance as ethnically distinct traditional clothing gives way to more uniform Western clothing in many parts of the world, or else becomes an inspiration for high-priced designer couture.

Teaching Note Write thought-provoking questions on index cards for small groups of students to draw and discuss. Include questions such as the following:
What are some practical reasons for wearing certain clothes?
What do you wear when you're feeling happy?
What kinds of clothing make a man/woman look attractive?
How do you decide which clothes to put on each morning?
Which celebrity is well-dressed, in your opinion?
Give the students an opportunity to write their own questions, too.

Internet Activity Challenge your students to find interesting fashions from another era. The Louvre Museum in Paris (http://www.louvre.fr/llv/commun/home_flash.jsp?bmLocale-en), The Metropolitan Museum in New York (http://www.metmuseum.org/home.asp), and the Museum of Fine Arts in Boston (http://www.mfa.org/) all offer online galleries arranged by historical period. Tell the students to find a painting or sculpture that depicts a person wearing interesting clothing. They can write a report describing the outfit, or play a game of "Describe and Draw" in class. To play, they will need to right-click on the image, save it to a document, and print it—preferably in full-page size. Then without showing the picture, students describe it to a small group or the whole class in as much detail as possible while their classmates draw. After the classmates have a chance to ask some questions, they reveal their drawings to see which is closest to the original.

Video Clip Summary The reporter interviews Marcus Ross, owner of the construction company Carpenters in Kilts. Ross explains that he wears a kilt at work to honor his Scottish ancestry, and while he doesn't require his employees to wear kilts, all of them do, either for the freedom of movement the kilts afford, or, as Ross suggests, because young women find the men in kilts attractive.

Video Script Go to page 58 in this Instructor's Manual for the "Men in Kilts" video script and recommended video vocabulary for review.

Video Activity Go to page 171 in the student book for activities to accompany the CNN video clip.

ANSWER KEY—Chapter 4: Fashion: You mean you're wearing THAT?

PREVIEW (Page 34)

1. Answers will vary.
2. Answers will vary.

PART 1

Predict (Page 35)

1. Answers will vary.
2. Answers will vary.
3. Answers will vary.
4. Answers will vary

Reading Comprehension

Check Your Predictions (Page 38)

1. Answers will vary.
2. Answers will vary.

Check the Facts

Reading 1 (Page 38)

1. False 2. True 3. True
4. False 5. False

Reading 2 (Page 38)

1. False 2. True 3. True
4. True   5. True

Reading 3 (Page 39)

1. False 2. False 3. True
4. True   5. True

Analyze (Page 39)

1. (Answers may vary.) Similar: Both dress codes require people to wear specific types of clothing and both are strictly enforced. Different: The dress code in the first reading is for students; the dress code in Reading 3 is for cab drivers. The dress code in the first reading is used to stop the "fashion race"; the dress code in the third reading has been created so that cab drivers will make a good impression on the public.
2. Reading 3 and the CNN video both mention kilts, a kind of skirt for men. This is related to the clothing situation in Reading 2, an exhibit about men's skirts in history.

Vocabulary Work

Guess Meaning from Context (Pages 39–40)

1. (Answers may vary.)
   Edinburgh Street Taxi Association: a group for Edinburgh taxi drivers
   The Modern Social Research Institute: a place where modern society is studied
   The Metropolitan Museum of Art: a place where art is exhibited
2. Answers will vary.
3. *fit in:* be one of a group
   alike: similar
   peer group: people of the same age and social group
   taboo: forbidden
   feminine: female
   gladiator: a Roman fighter
   masculine: male
   kilt: men wear this skirt in Scotland
   fine: financial punishment
4. Answers will vary.
5. b

Guess Meaning from Related Words (Page 40)

1. (Answers may vary.)
   identical: the same
   identity: a sense of oneself
   dress code: rules about dress
   unisex: suitable to both men and women
   strict: requiring obedience, rigid
   restrictive: limiting
   disagreed: to differ, to hold a different opinion
2. (Answers may vary.) Both uses of "judge" involve making as assessment. In Reading 1, judge is used as a verb, meaning that teenagers decide if their peers are acceptable or not. In Reading 3, judge is used as a noun, referring to the judge in a court of law who makes legal decisions.
3. (Answers may vary.) "appropriate", "inappropriate" and "appropriately" all relate to what people consider to be proper and acceptable.

Reading Skills

Understanding Cohesion (Page 41)

1. 1—fashion; 2—the pressure of dressing in a certain way; 3—some schools; 4—students; 5—being laughed at; 6—people at the school; 7—the dress code; 8—the dress code
2. (Answers may vary.) "Another side" of fashion is the problems that come with the pressure to dress a certain way as opposed to the "fun" side mentioned in the first sentence.

Discussion (Page 41)

1. Answers will vary.
2. Answers will vary.

PART II

Read It (Page 41)

1. The French government banned all obvious religious symbols from public school. The hijab is a religious symbol. The commission felt that conspicuous religious symbols set people apart and stopped them from feeling truly French.
2. The Sikhs wear turbans to cover their hair, which is a symbol of their religion.

Vocabulary Work
Guess Meaning from Related Words (Page 43)

1. (Answers may vary.)
   a. undressed: without clothes
   b. newcomers: new people, people new to an area
   c. hearings: a legal proceeding in which a judge listens to concerns
   d. headed: going toward
2. a. Related word: recommendation
      Meaning: a suggestion
   b. Related word: immigrant
      Meaning: a person who moves to a new country
   c. Related word: humiliating
      Meaning: embarrassing

CNN Video Activities: Men in Kilts
Understand It (Page 171)

1. False
2. False
3. True
4. False
5. True
6. True
7. False
8. False
9. True

CNN VIDEO TRANSCRIPT—Chapter 4: Men in Kilts
DVD Title 5   Running time: 01:37

Video Vocabulary

attire/garb   clothing, dress
don   to put on, dress
double take   a surprising, delayed act of recognizing someone or something
opt out   decide against
snicker   to laugh unkindly or to show disbelief
to get down to the nitty-gritty   to begin discussing the most important issues

Video Script

Reporter: This is no ordinary construction site.
Debbie McKinnon: We're not quite sure what . . . Halloween or what it is.
Reporter: It's not the usual music . . . or your typical construction <u>attire</u>.
Carpenter 1: You're a lot freer; you can move everywhere a lot quicker.
Reporter: Meet Carpenters in Kilts.
Marcus Ross: The heritage that my parents gave me, what my parents taught me—we just took it and turned it into a company . . .
Marcus Ross: (. . . hit it into the grid in four places.)
Reporter: . . . as a way to honor his late Scottish father. In fact, Marcus Ross says he doesn't even own a single pair of pants.
Marcus Ross: We've had a lot of real interesting reactions.
David Longwith: They laugh, they <u>snicker</u>, they have their little comments: nice dress!
Marcus Ross: There's a lot of <u>double takes</u>.
David Longwith: It's all the way you look at it.
Reporter: All right, let's <u>get down to the nitty-gritty</u>: What everybody really wants to know—just how authentic are these guys?
Marcus Ross: Nothing but my boots, darling.
David Longwith: When you climb up a ladder and maybe a little old lady walks out on the deck and she looks up . . . we can't do that, we'd get in trouble, so we actually have to have the shorts underneath.
Reporter: Ross makes their kilts. Real or not, nothing with these tartans comes cheap. Average cost? Some $600, depending on the season and the material used. Although <u>donning</u> the <u>garb</u> is strictly optional, so far none of them has opted out.
Marcus Ross: The true story is: the young guys like the kilts because the young girls like the young guys in the kilts.
Reporter: And the carpenters in kilts like it, too.

Kimberly O'Sykes, Denver.

Hot Topics 2 • Chapter 4

CHAPTER 5 — WORK: Is it interfering with your life?
Pages 44–56

Summary Part I of Chapter 5 focuses on finding a good match between personal characteristics and careers. The readings describe three unusual jobs: policing web access at workplaces, studying hurricanes, and working as a disc jockey. Part II gives helpful advice for people who have not been lucky enough to find their dream jobs, but instead do work that can be stressful and unrewarding.

Audio The readings in this chapter can be heard on the *Hot Topics 2* Audio CD 1 Tracks 15-18 or Audio Tape 1 Side B.

Background Children are often asked what they want to be when they grow up. Some people have a strong opinion on the topic at a very young age, others find a career path in high school or college, and many seem to stumble into jobs by accident. For those who actually decide on a career, careful consideration of personal preferences, such as a dislike of formal clothing or a desire to work with their hands, can lead people to jobs that are very satisfying. Unfortunately, increased workloads, a lack of control and autonomy, and fewer resources at work are also a reality of the working world. People who can achieve a positive outlook despite such negative circumstances are better able to cope with stress at work.

Teaching Note The chapter preview lists fifteen occupations, and the readings in Part I present three more. To expand on the idea of matching people and jobs, ask your students to write a list of their own traits, skills, and preferences that relate to employment. Next, let partners or small groups choose one of the occupations from the book and create a job announcement—something similar to those that appear in the classified section of a newspaper. Groups can then exchange job announcements, and discuss which person in their group would be best suited for the job, based on the lists they wrote. Finish the activity by asking the groups to report out, telling the class about the job announcement they received, and how they decided who was best qualified.

Internet Activity Create an Internet scavenger hunt for your students. Visit a website such as http://hotjobs.yahoo.com, www.monster.com, or www.careerbuilder.com, and generate a list of questions for students to answer as they read job listings. Use the job categories, for example *healthcare*, to lead students to actual job listings in various fields. Ask questions about salary, education requirements, and job duties for specific positions in several of the categories. (In a computer lab setting, you could impose a time limit to encourage students to quickly scan for the information.) Afterwards, discuss the results, along with the pros and cons of the various jobs.

Video Clip Summary Kathy Slobogin reports that about half of Americans, who work more hours than people in any other industrialized nation, feel overworked. This is partly due to long work weeks, and partly due to stress and a feeling that one's work isn't valued. She points out that businesses need to be concerned about this since it affects employee retention, the number of mistakes made on the job, and ultimately a company's profit margin.

Video Script Go to page 62 in this Instructor's Manual for the "Time Crunch" video script and recommended video vocabulary for review.

Video Activity Go to page 172 in the student book for activities to accompany the CNN video clip.

ANSWER KEY—Chapter 5: WORK: Is it interfering with your life?

PREVIEW (Pages 44–45)

Jobs for people who Answers may vary. Suggested responses below.
- . . . don't like to wear formal suits or clothing. Artists, astronaut, baker, chef, coach, farmer, mechanic
- . . . are very organized. Architect, banker, hotel manager, lawyer, stockbroker, zoologist
- . . . like unpredictable days. Actor, artist, astronaut, coach, stockbroker
- . . . love people. Banker, coach, dentist, hotel manager, lawyer
- . . . want to work with their hands. Artist, baker, chef, dentist, farmer, mechanic

PART I

Predict (Page 45)

(Answers may vary.) Suggested responses:

1. Internet police are people who determine which websites people have access to.
2. A hurricane hunter follows hurricanes and flies into them to do research.
3. To be a disc jockey you should have training in broadcasting, English, public speaking, drama, and computer science.
4. The first two articles have quotations from people in the field.
5. Answers will vary.

Reading Comprehension

Check Your Predictions (Pages 48-49): Answers will vary.

Check the Facts (Page 49)

Reading 1

1. A big red hand appears on the screen and a warning about unauthorized Web surfing appears on the bottom of the screen.
2. a Web-filtering company
3. She looks for sites that employers do not want their employees visiting.
4. gambling, travel, and shopping sites
5. Companies want to block Internet sites where employees may waste time at work.
6. Yes; she says she likes spending time on the Internet and that she feels like she is in touch with what people are thinking and doing.

Reading 2

1. Karla Williams, a hurricane hunter
2. She likes working with other scientists and traveling around the world.
3. She responded to an ad for a hurricane researcher.
4. One part is collecting information during hurricane season; the other is working with the information later.
5. meteorology

Reading 3

1. DJ
2. radio, clubs, dances, restaurants and weddings
3. a pleasant, well-controlled voice, good timing, excellent pronunciation, a strong grasp of correct grammar, and the ability to speak off the cuff and work under tight deadlines
4. Probably. Disc Jockeys should have formal training in broadcasting as well as coursework in several other areas.
5. Salaries vary widely.

Analyze (Page 50): Answers will vary. Suggested responses below.

Hurricane hunter is the most dangerous.
Hurricane hunter requires the most education.
Answers will vary.
Content specialist requires the least education.
DJ is probably for young people.

Vocabulary Work

Guess Meaning from Context (Page 50)

1. *take a break:* to stop working and rest in the middle of work or school
   waste time: to spend time doing unproductive things
   in touch with: knowing about
   in advance: beforehand
   pretty much: mostly
   on the air: on the radio or television
   off the cuff: without preparation
   public speaking: speaking in front of a group of people
2. Bad. Answers will vary.

Guess Meaning from Related Words (Page 51)

1. (Answers may vary.)
   blacklisted (black + list): censured, excluded
   white-listed (white + list): approved of
   background (back + ground): previous experience
   timing (time): pace
   well-controlled (well + control): managed well
   personality (person + noun): a person's qualities
   announcer (announce + one who): a person who makes announcements
   likable (like + adjective): capable of being liked
   pleasing (please): causing pleasure or happiness
   technical (tech + adjective): having to do with technology
2. *blacklisted:* put on a forbidden list
   white-listed: put on an approved list
   background: past education or work experience
   timing: doing something at the correct time
   well-controlled: nicely used or managed
   personality: a person's qualities or behavior
   announcer: presenter

likable: nice
pleasing: enjoyable
technical: vocational or mechanical

3. The people listed in column 2 do the things listed in column 1.

Reading Skills

Understanding the Purpose of a Reading (Page 51)

1. Reading 3 provides a list of facts.
2. Reading 1 uses humor in the title and describes a scenario at work.
3. Reading 2 focuses on interesting and exciting parts of job.

Discussion (Page 52): Answers will vary.

PART II

Read It (Page 52)

1. Workers have less job security, heavier workloads and less autonomy.
2. With layoffs, strikes and shutdowns, workers do not feel like valued employees.
3. People take jobs for a paycheck when they are unable to find jobs in their field.
4. Find different ways of doing everyday tasks.
5. Get involved in activities outside of work.
6. Colleagues can provide mutual support.

Vocabulary Work

Guess Meaning from Context (Page 54)

(Answers may vary.)

1. *downsizing:* reducing the number of people that work for a company
2. *layoffs:* getting rid of employees to save money
3. *strikes:* when employees refuse to work to try to get better pay or benefits
4. *shutdowns:* when a company is closed

Guess Meaning from Related Words (Page 54)

1. *autonomy:* positive / independence and self-direction
2. *long-term:* positive / for a long time
3. *powerless:* negative / having no power
4. *rewarding:* positive / when you feel good about doing something
5. *significant:* positive / important
6. *temporary:* negative / for a short time
7. *uncertain:* negative / not definite
8. *valued:* positive / regarded as important
9. *worthwhile:* positive / worth the time or effort spent

Reading Skills

Understanding Main Ideas (Page 55)

Answers will vary. Suggested responses:

1. Although work is difficult, there are ways to reduce the stress.
2. working professionals
3. Yes; the author is explaining ways to reduce the stress of a bad job.

CNN Video Activities: Time Crunch

Understand It (Page 172)

1. the United States
2. 46 percent or nearly half
3. 29 percent
4. women
5. baby boomers
6. 35 hours
7. 22 percent
8. Answers will vary. Possible responses: feeling pressured and pushed; not feeling respected; having tension at work; feeling one's work isn't of real value
9. neglect themselves; not feel successful in their personal and family relationships
10. Answers will vary. Possible responses: employees are more likely to look for a new job; employees feel angry at their employers; employees make mistakes

VIDEO TRANSCRIPT—Chapter 5: Time Crunch

DVD Title 6   Running time: 02:52

Video Vocabulary

baby boomer*   a person born during a baby boom in the U.S. between 1947 and 1961
bottom line   profit or loss
clarion call*   loud and clear
Gen Xer   a person born in the U.S. in the second half of the 60s or the early part of the 70s.
get burned out   to become extremely fatigued
overwhelmed*   to feel powerless because there is too much to do
wake-up call*   a shocking event that changes the way people think
workaholic   a person who works all the time

Video Script

Man 1: I have no, absolutely no, personal life at all. I just work. That's all I do.

Man 2: I probably work maybe fifty hours a week.

Woman: It can be maybe 40, which is nice. Or it can be more like 80.

Reporter: We've become a workaholic nation. American workers put in the longest hours of any industrialized nation—surpassing the next closest country, Japan, by nearly two full work weeks a year. Now a new study finds we're paying a price.

Ellen Galinsky: Nearly half of the U.S. workforce, 46 percent, feel overworked in one way or another. This study is a clarion call for all of us—companies and individuals—to look at how we're working.

Reporter: The Families and Work Institute survey of a thousand U.S. workers, found that 28 percent often felt overworked, 28 percent felt overwhelmed by how much work they had, and 29 percent felt they had no time to step back and reflect on their work.

Women felt more overworked than men, baby boomers more than Gen Xers or older workers. Although the survey found that employees on average would like to work about a 35-hour work week, for many that's a distant fantasy. Twenty-four percent of American workers work 50 or more hours a week. Twenty-two percent work 6 to 7 days a week. A quarter don't take the vacation time they're entitled to.

But Ellen Galinsky says it's not just the hours.

Ellen Galinsky: When you feel pressured and pushed, when you feel not respected, when you have tension at work, when you feel that the work that you're doing isn't of any real value—that it's low value work, all of those lead us to feeling more overworked. And sizeable proportions of the U.S. workforce are having these feelings.

Reporter: The survey found those who felt overworked were more likely to neglect themselves, less likely to feel successful in their personal and family relationships.

Man 2: I feel tired and I feel like I'm juggling five or six different balls in the air at one time between work and family.

Woman: You feel stressed, frazzled. You feel like you're missing out on a lot of your life.

Reporter: What's more, the survey found overwork can lead to serious on the job consequences. Overworked employees are more likely to look for a new job, feel angry at their employers, and make mistakes. Seventeen percent of those who feel overworked report often making mistakes on the job compared to only 1 percent of those who don't feel overworked.

All that means that overwork is costing business, from higher healthcare costs for stressed employees to training new workers to replace those who get burned out and leave. Survey researchers say it's that impact on the bottom-line that will be the wake-up call for American business.

Kathy Slobogin, CNN, Washington.

Hot Topics 2 • Chapter 5

CHAPTER 6
Pages 56-66

Internet Dating: Is this really YOUR photo?

Summary Chapter 6 takes a look at positive and negative aspects of Internet dating services. In Reading 1, a reporter posts the same description of herself with different photos at several dating websites, and discovers that when it comes to Internet dating, image does matter. Reading 2 provides rules for managing the risks of online dating. Part II explores some of the reasons so many people are turning to the Internet to find a mate.

Audio The readings in this chapter can be heard on the *Hot Topics 2* Audio CD 1 Tracks 19-21 or Audio Tape 1 Side B.

Background Internet dating is the latest in a long line of matchmaking methods, ranging from arranged marriages to "getting set up" by friends, video dating services with libraries of tapes, and even "speed dating" events—all offering the hope of meeting the right person.

Online dating services utilize large databases of personal information and charge a monthly subscription or membership fee in exchange for the opportunity to post a photo and description of oneself and view the profiles of other members. Although these databases provide access to large numbers of potential dates, the truthfulness of the profiles and the accuracy of the photos may be questionable.

Teaching Note One of the exercises in the Vocabulary Work section introduces two and three-word verbs. These phrasal verbs are frequent, and also difficult for language learners to identify, which means they can have a significant impact on reading comprehension. After the students understand the phrasal verbs in the exercise, tell them that the reading in Part II also contains two and three-word verbs, and ask the students to locate them as they read. This may be difficult at first, so offer hints such as how many phrasal verbs are in the article, or that sentence X contains a two-word verb. They should find: *give up, look for (2), set up, go out with, get together,* and *look through*. Discuss the meanings of the verbs in the context of the article.

Internet Activity Although websites such as www.Match.com allow visitors to browse through photos of local singles free of charge, one is asked for an email address and other personal information fairly quickly. Instead, have your students learn about another type of dating service that interests them. Use a search engine such as www.google.com to find articles on professional matchmaking, arranged marriages, video dating, or speed dating. Each student should choose an article that interests them and discuss it with a small group of classmates.

Video Clip Summary The reporter talks to people who use online dating services, and points out that more men than women look for dates online, and that the services make it possible to search very specifically, for example stipulating an age group or religion. One service, Matchmaker.com, saw a 70 percent jump in clients after September 11th, and states that singles didn't feel right watching such a significant news story alone. For the people in the clip, the results of the online search for a mate are mixed, but they remain optimistic about this method of meeting people.

Video Script Go to page 65 in this Instructor's Manual for the "Internet Dating" video script and recommended video vocabulary for review.

Video Activity Go to page 173 in the student book for activities to accompany the CNN video clip.

ANSWER KEY—Chapter 6: Internet Dating: Is this really YOUR photo?

PREVIEW (Page 56): Answers will vary.

PART I

Predict (Page 57)

Answers will vary. Suggested responses below.
1. Reading 1 is written from a woman's perspective, while reading 2 is geared toward both men and women
2. The sexy photograph got the most replies.
3. Answers will vary.
4. Answers will vary.

Reading Comprehension

Check Your Predictions (Page 60): Answers will vary.

Check the Facts

Reading 1 (Page 60)
1. whether men responded more to picture or profile
2. a profile and a picture of herself
3. Each picture was different.
4. the "Sexy Lady" picture
5. No; men were more responsive to the pictures than to the description in the profile.

Reading 2 (Page 61)

1. in a public place
2. to avoid anger and disappointment later
3. Save them. If you think someone is lying to you, you can check previous messages.
4. Ask for his/her home phone number, work number, and references.

Analyze (Page 61)

Answers will vary. Suggested Responses:
1. The writer does not like online dating services.
2. Answers will vary.

Vocabulary Work

Guess Meaning from Context (Page 61)

1. Answers will vary.
2. *profile:* basic facts about someone's life
   tracksuit: comfortable clothes for exercising
   risk: danger
   anger: strong feeling of dislike or hate towards someone
   up-to-date: current, new
   face-to-face: in person
   persuade: convince
   previous: before
   fake identity: not a real name
3. Answers will vary.
4. Bad. The article gives advice on protecting yourself from liars and cheaters.

Guess Meaning from Related Words (Page 62)

(Answers may vary.)

1. *runaway:* won by a long lead
   impolite: rude
   sports-minded: interested in sports
   predictable: easy to guess
2. They have the same root: *disappoint*

Understanding Two- and Three-Word Verbs (Page 62)

Answers will vary. Sample sentences below.

1. I would never go out with someone that I met at a bar.
2. Many people worry that credit card companies will give out their personal information.
3. I made plans to get together with an old friend to have dinner.
4. When you go on vacation, it's a good idea to bring along an umbrella in case it rains.
5. Make sure that you have written your name on your homework before you hand it in.
6. Talking about hobbies is a good way to get to know someone.
7. Beware of people who try to convince you to do things that make you uncomfortable.
8. Sometimes looking back at old assignments can help you understand your new assignment.
9. Look in a phone book to find out someone's phone number.
10. You shouldn't jump into a relationship if you don't know the person well.

Reading Skills

Using Subtitles (Page 62): Answers will vary.

Summarizing Main Ideas (Page 63)

Answers will vary. Suggested responses below.
Paragraph 2: Be Honest
Paragraph 3: Take your Time
Paragraph 4: Save Everything
Paragraph 5: Get Personal Information
Paragraph 6: Have fun

Discussion (Page 63)

Answers will vary.

PART II

Read It (Page 63)

1. Advantage: Online dating allows you to choose from thousands of people.
   Disadvantage: It is difficult to judge physical chemistry through computer communication.
2. Most couples met in high school or college.
3. People marry at an older age, and there have not been new social organizations to replace traditional ones.

Vocabulary Work

Guess Meaning from Related Words (Page 65)

Answers will vary. Suggested responses below.

life partner: someone you marry or spend your life with
physical chemistry: physical attraction
singles bars: places where you can go to drink and meet other single people
in person: face-to-face

Reading Skills

Understanding Cohesion (Page 65)

1. *of them*: the 120 men she e-mailed
   Of these: the 11 men she met in person
   the one: the person she wants to spend her life with
2. the person she wants to spend her life with

CNN Video Activities: Internet Dating

Understand It (Page 173)

1. False
2. False
3. True
4. False
5. True
6. False
7. False
8. True

VIDEO TRANSCRIPT—Chapter 6: Internet Dating

DVD Title 7   Running time: 02:19

Video Vocabulary

booming   growing rapidly
heart's desire*   whatever someone wants
scroll   (in computers) to move quickly through a file
stigma   a mark of shame or disgrace
to cater to   to satisfy someone's special needs or desires
uncertainty   doubt

Video Script

Reporter: A bit nervous, Faith Sedline waited for her date to show up—a man she'd only met online.

Faith Sedline: Hi, nice to meet you.

Matt: Nice to meet you, Faith.

Reporter: Internet dating services are booming. Match.com reports that in the two months following the September 11th attacks, membership went up 70 percent.

Announcer: Match.com provides "the who."

Reporter: Love experts say that's not surprising in times of uncertainty.

Pepper Schwartz: Even if it doesn't happen to you, it reminds you that you don't even want to watch that news without your special someone, you know, beside you. So I believe that the services are being used more.

Reporter: Services that cater to just about every heart's desire. Want someone over fifty? There's Senior Friend Finder. How about a churchgoing friend? For Jewish singles there's JDate.com. And for the rest Matchmaker, Match.com and Kiss.com, and the list goes on.

Doug Wyllie: Is there any equipment that's been damaged?

Reporter: Doug Wyllie began scrolling for "the one" in September. It was soon obvious to him that more men than women were hitting their keyboards for a date. Nothing like a little competition.

Doug Wyllie: I don't make a lot of money, and I don't have any power per se, so that makes it very tricky. But it's fun, you know, it's fun to, to meet new people.

Reporter: Men still outnumber women, because for many women, looking for "Mr. Right" on the Internet is just a little scary. But Sedline says after her experiences, the greatest danger in online dating is getting carpal tunnel syndrome.

Faith Sedline: You don't know who's going to walk up and you're going, oh, what did I just do? Why am I doing this? But that fades pretty quickly.

Reporter: And how about the stigma of using the classifieds?

Faith Sedline: When people hear that I cough up to online dating, they go . . . their first thought is, oh, you can't get a date. And, you know, I just, I just thought it would be fun. And you get to meet a lot of people.

Matt: When I, when I first got out of college . . .

Reporter: So Faith met Matt and had lunch, and well, that was that. But she ended up meeting someone else online. For Doug Wyllie, the hunt continues in hopes that the woman on the screen will match the woman of his dreams.

Rusty Dornin, CNN, San Francisco.

Chapter 6 • Hot Topics 2

CHAPTER 7 — ANGER: I'M NOT ANGRY! YOU'RE ANGRY!
Pages 67–78

Summary This chapter focuses on anger. Part I opens with a quiz that lets readers determine their own anger level. It also contains advice for managing anger, and a fable with an interesting take on expressing anger. The reading in Part II is an intercultural comparison of attitudes toward the expression of anger.

Audio The readings in this chapter can be heard on the *Hot Topics 2* Audio CD 1 Tracks 22-25 or Audio Tape 1 Side B.

Background Many psychologists see anger as normal and healthy, and only a problem when it interferes with one's life. They argue that suppressing anger can result in depression or physical illness. On the other hand, anger has been linked to diseases such as ulcers and atherosclerosis, and as this chapter points out, its expression is simply not acceptable in many places or situations. Whether anger is healthy or unhealthy, anger management is widely taught and written about. Techniques include relaxation, behavior modification, and learning problem-solving skills.

Teaching Note Teach your students idioms involving anger and heat. For example:

> to be hot under the collar
> to have a heated discussion
> to be a "hothead"
> to burn someone (i.e. insult them)
> to keep (or lose) one's cool
> to blow off steam
> to be hot-tempered
> to make one's blood boil

Provide example sentences, and discuss the type of situations in which the idioms are used. (Just for fun, and to assist in memorization, students could draw illustrations for the idioms and compile an "idiom picture dictionary.")

Internet Activity Direct students to a good search engine such as www.google.com to search for articles on anger management. Ask each student to find at least one technique that sounds practical and useful to them personally, and report back to the class. Follow up by creating a class list of bullet points similar to the list in Reading 2.

Video Clip Summary Holly Firfer reports on the link between feeling angry and developing hardening of the arteries, which can occur even in young people. She explains that anger raises blood pressure, and this in turn contributes to arterial calcification. She recommends several anger management techniques, and suggests focusing on the positive and getting enough exercise.

Video Script Go to page 68 in this Instructor's Manual for the "Young Angry Hearts" video script and recommended video vocabulary for review.

Video Activity Go to page 174 in the student book for activities to accompany the CNN video clip.

ANSWER KEY—Chapter 7: ANGER: I'M NOT ANGRY! YOU'RE ANGRY!

PREVIEW (Pages 67-68): Answers will vary.

PART I

Predict (Page 68)

1. all
2. Answers will vary.
3. Reading 3
4. Answers will vary.

Reading Comprehension

Check Your Predictions (Page 71): Answers will vary.

Check the Facts (Page 72)

Reading 1

1. other people's mistakes, unfair treatment, criticism, driving
2. say hurtful things, hit people
3. headaches, depression
4. low scores

Reading 2

1. True
2. True
3. True
4. False. When you are angry, you should avoid drinking alcohol.
5. True
6. True

Reading 3

1. a priest
2. The man kept asking the same questions repeatedly.
3. The snake bit the villagers on their way to church.
4. stop biting people
5. The children dragged the snake behind them when they ran.
6. not to bite, but to hiss

Analyze (Page 73)

Answers will vary. Suggested responses below.

1. low
2. Yes, because both encourage acknowledging anger, and both agree that anger must be controlled or managed. (On the other hand, the Swami advises *acting* angry at times in order to affect the behavior of others, which the writer of Reading 2 would probably disagree with.)
3. Hissing and biting are reactions to things that are threatening or unpleasant, and so is anger. In Reading 3, hissing is similar to angry shouting, while biting would be physically harming someone in anger.

Vocabulary Work

Guess Meaning from Context (Page 73)

1. Answers will vary.
2. *moderate:* not extreme
   manage: run or operate
   criticize: to say someone is bad
   tension: stress
   temple: a Hindu place of worship
   cobra: a kind of snake
   hiss: the noise a snake makes
3. Answers will vary.

Guess Meaning from Related Words (Pages 73-74)

1. *hurtful* (hurt): causes pain
   enjoyment (enjoy): pleasure
   machinery (machine): mechanical equipment
   relaxation (relax): rest

2. Anger is the name of the emotion; angry is how you feel.
   To meditate is what you do; meditation is the name of the practice.
   Depressed is how you feel; depression is the name of the emotion.
   To manage is something that you do; management is the name of the skill.

Reading Skills

Finding Referents (Page 74)

1. the people in the village
2. Swami Ramala
3. Swami Ramala; the snake; the snake; bite people
4. X

Discussion (Page 74): Answers will vary.

PART II

Read It (Page 75)

1. United States, Middle East, Mediterranean
2. England, Finland, China, Japan, Utku Eskimo

Vocabulary Work

Guess Meaning from Related Words (Page 77)

1. a. *accept:* accepted, unacceptable
   b. *avoid:* avoidance
   c. *effect:* effective
   d. *express:* expression
   e. *communicate:* miscommunication
   f. *destroy:* destructive
   g. *understand:* misunderstanding
   h. *friend:* friendliness
   i. *polite:* impolite
   j. *violent:* violence
2. a. negative
   b. negative
   c. negative
3. (Answers may vary.) Anger when driving

CNN Video Activities: Young Angry Hearts

Understand It (Page 174)

1. c   3. e   5. b
2. d   4. a   6. f

Chapter 7 • Hot Topics 2   67

VIDEO TRANSCRIPT—Chapter 7: YOUNG ANGRY HEARTS
DVD Title 8   Running time: 01:50

Video Vocabulary

clench   to force together, grip tightly
coronary artery   one of several large blood vessels going from the heart
*cynical**   having a negative attitude
prone   inclined toward, likely to do something

Video Script

Reporter: You feel your heart race, your blood pressure rise, and jaw <u>clench</u>. You're not just getting angry—a new study in the Journal of the American Medical Association says you might also be shortening your life.

Researcher: Those who had hostility levels above average had a two and a half higher risk of developing <u>coronary artery</u> calcification.

Reporter: Most alarming to the researchers, this coronary calcification, or hardening of the arteries, was found in young adults ages eighteen to thirty.

Excluding other risk factors such as smoking, diet, and exercise, researchers speculate anger or hostility can result in the release of stress hormones which cause blood pressure to rise. The high blood pressure, in turn, increases the tendency of platelets—the blood cells responsible for clotting—to stick together and begin to clog the artery walls, which eventually collects calcium, even at a young age.

Although it's normal to feel bursts of anger, those at highest risk exhibit day-to-day hostile personalities.

Researcher: . . . mistrusting other people, the second component is having a <u>cynical</u> view of the world and the third characteristic is being <u>prone</u> to aggression.

Reporter: Anger management can help prevent these biological reactions.

Expert: . . . and then the very first thing is to stop and do three diaphragmatic breaths, because the breathing is going to short circuit the stress reaction.

Reporter: Experts also recommend talking about your feelings, but express yourself calmly, listen to responses from others, and negotiate alternative solutions to problems. Another suggestion: keep track of pleasant events in your life and exercise before it's too late.

Holly Firfer, CNN, Atlanta.

CHAPTER 8
Pages 79–90

Psychics: What do they know that we don't?

Summary Chapter 8 invites readers into the realm of parapsychology to consider the topic of psychics. The first reading in Part I is an advertisement for an online service that offers psychic readings at a reasonable price. Reading 2 is a newspaper article about an organization that offered $1,000 to anyone who could prove their psychic abilities, and Reading 3 offers advice on distinguishing the real psychics from the phonies. In Part II, techniques for making a psychic reading believable are presented.

Audio The readings in this chapter can be heard on the *Hot Topics 2* Audio CD 1 Tracks 26–29 or Audio Tape 1 Side B.

Background In Hollywood's version of *The Wizard of Oz*, Dorothy meets a fake but observant fortune teller who is able to figure out that Dorothy is running away from home. He later appears in Dorothy's dream as the Great and Powerful Oz, who turns out to have no more supernatural powers than the fortune teller in Kansas. But are there people with true psychic powers? Since the sixteenth century the visions of Nostradamus have been interpreted as foretelling world events such as the rise of Adolf Hitler and the assassination of John F. Kennedy. More recently, Uri Geller amazed live television audiences with his ability to affect objects like spoons and clocks with the power of his mind. For skeptics, believers, and the undecided, the debate goes on!

Teaching Note The reading in Part II is a guide to doing "cold" psychic readings. Give your students the chance to apply the information in the reading to a role-play situation. First, approach the reading as you usually would, asking students to aim for overall understanding. After doing the language exercises, tell the students they will be doing cold readings themselves, and have them read the article again and ask questions about it. In small groups, students should discuss how to do a believable cold reading, for example by acting confident and using props. Depending on your students and the class size, organize the role plays to involve everyone and create a light, enjoyable atmosphere, keeping in mind that some students may be sensitive about participating in something they see as superstitious or sacrilegious.

Internet Activity Encourage your students to have fun reading their online horoscopes and evaluating the accuracy of the statements. At www.dailyhoroscopes.com, they can click on their astrological sign, and http://astrology.yahoo.com/astrology/ offers personalized horoscopes based on one's birth date. Students can also read their Chinese zodiac horoscopes. (Naturally, there are psychic readings for sale alongside the free horoscopes, so remind students to use their Internet savvy.)

Video Clip Summary The video clip looks at psychics who do readings over the telephone, including the Psychic Friends Network, which was very profitable before being sued and going bankrupt. The reporter refers to a Gallup poll that indicates that the percentage of Americans who believe in psychic powers is increasing.

Video Script Go to page 71 in this Instructor's Manual for the "Calling All Psychics" video script and recommended video vocabulary for review.

Video Activity Go to page 175 in the student book for activities to accompany the CNN video clip.

ANSWER KEY—Chapter 8: Psychics: What do they know that we don't?

PREVIEW (Page 79): Answers will vary.

PART I
Predict (Page 80)

Answers will vary. Suggested responses below.

1. Readings 1 and 3
2. Reading 1
3. Reading 3
4. Reading 2
5. Answers will vary.

Reading Comprehension

Check Your Predictions (Page 83): Answers will vary

Check the Facts

Reading 1 (Page 83)

1. via the Internet
2. any subject you want
3. Your situation is more complicated than you thought.
4. It's cheaper, faster, and you will be able to sit and analyze your reading for as long as you want

Chapter 8 • Hot Topics 2   69

Reading 2 (Page 83)
1. no
2. $1,000
3. none
4. no
5. hold another challenge for a $10,000 award

Reading 3 (Page 84)
1. by running experiments and offering money for proof of psychic ability
2. No. The person may try to keep you talking as long as possible so that you pay more.
3. No.
4. No.
5. No, but some have.

Analyze (Page 84)
Answers will vary. Suggested responses below.
1. You should be suspicious of Cyberpsychic because they make the unrealistic claim of letting you see your future and require payment in advance.
2. Answers will vary.
3. Answers will vary.
4. Probably. Reading 3 encourages using caution when dealing with psychics, and checking the psychics abilities by asking questions and recording the reading.

Vocabulary Work

Guess Meaning from Context (Pages 84-85)
1. a. Answers will vary.
   b. expensive; fortunately / luckily; old
   c. In Reading 3: without preparation. Usually "cold" refers to temperature, but we do talk about "warming up"—preparing—so "cold" can be the antonym of "warmed up."
2. *accurate:* correct
   confusing: puzzling
   skeptic: someone who doesn't believe things without proof
3. Answers will vary.

Guess Meaning from Related Words (Page 85)
Answers will vary. Suggested responses:
1. a. *confident:* sure
   b. *confidential:* private
   c. *reading:* interpretation
   d. *unconscious:* thoughts that you are not aware of
   e. *unsatisfactory:* not good enough
   f. *strengthen:* make stronger
   g. *expectation:* what you think will happen
2. Answers will vary. Suggested responses:
   a. Psychic abilities allow people to know things without being told. Psychics are people who have these abilities.
   b. Skeptics are people who do not believe things without proof. Skeptical is how they feel.
   c. You prove something is true. You disprove something that is false.

Reading Skills

Detecting Bias (Page 86): Answers will vary. Suggested responses below.

Reading 1 is biased toward a particular organization. Words like fast, accurate, clear, and efficiently praise the organization. Phrases like "at last" imply that no other organization has ever offered equal services. The author of Reading 2 uses the terms "crazies" and "supposed psychics" to show a bias against people who say they are psychics. Reading 3 shows a bias in favor of people who claim to have psychic abilities by using the term "real psychics".

Discussion (Page 86): Answers will vary.

PART II

Read It (Page 86)
1. No. The writer is teaching "tricks" people use in order to pass as psychics, showing that anyone can be a "psychic" despite having no special abilities.
2. Make use of the latest polls and surveys; Get the subject's cooperation in advance; Make statements that are true for almost everyone; Use your observations to begin guessing; Use the technique of *fishing;* Learn to be a good listener
3. You can use observations about the subject's age, clothes, jewelry, behavior, and speech.
4. *Fishing* is a way to get the subject to tell you about himself or herself. You rephrase what he or she has told you and feed it back to the subject.
5. Yes, the subject will provide answers.

Vocabulary Work

Guess Meaning from Context (Page 89)
1. key: important
2. subject: a person that is looked at or examined
3. probability: the likelihood or chance that something will happen

4. **cooperation:** the act of working with someone toward a common goal
5. **mysterious:** having no known cause
6. **delay:** a time that something is slowed or stopped

Reading Skills

Understanding Idioms (Page 89): (Answers may vary.)

1. *to sell:* to make a sale
2. *enter the picture:* become part of a situation
3. *fit:* to be suitable for a specific purpose
4. *click:* go smoothly, to be successful
5. *atmosphere:* special tone or mood of a particular place
6. *feed it back:* to repeat, to reword

CNN Video Activities: Calling All Psychics

Understand It (Page 175)

1. True	4. True	7. False
2. True	5. True	8. True
3. True	6. True	9. False

CNN VIDEO TRANSCRIPT—Chapter 8: *Calling All Psychics*
DVD Title 9   Running time: 02:02

Video Vocabulary

bankruptcy — the legal state of being without money or credit
fraud — deceit with the purpose of gaining another's money or property
harness — to capture the power of something
sixth sense — the ability to feel things beyond the five senses of sight, smell, hearing, taste, and touch

Video Script

Psychic 1: Uhmm . . . there's a beautiful smell of flowers around you. I don't know why. Are you around flowers right now?
    Voice on phone: There's a plant with some flowers . . .
Patricia Masters: It's not as if you are actually hearing words. What it is, is a knowing. It feels as if I go out of myself for a moment and I know something that comes into me—very quickly.
Reporter: Patricia Masters calls herself a "clairaudient psychic." Working over the phone, she claims to harness voices she hears around her . . .
Patricia Masters: Very good. Do you know it's a mineral level?
Reporter 1: . . . offering life advice to dozens of callers each week.
Patricia Masters: They are not coming to find out if they're going to get married next year. They are coming to find out why they haven't gotten married yet. As a psychic, I can look at the pattern and I can say: Ah, this is where it is.

Reporter: Masters is just one of many psychics who claim to utilize the phone to tap into their sixth sense. Remember Miss Cleo and the TV Psychic Friends Network?
Miss Cleo: You know I'm telling you the truth, don't you?
Reporter: At one time it was estimated they were making as much as $100 million a year, that's before they were sued for fraud and declared bankruptcy.
Miss Cleo: I am who I say I am. I am not a fake, and I am not a fraud.
Reporter: Despite cases like Miss Cleo, the number of Americans who believe in psychics is actually on the rise. According to a recent Gallop poll, 54 percent of us believe in psychics or spiritual healing. That's up 8 percent since 1990.
Psychic 1: Hey, it's a good opportunity. Go for it!
Reporter: This comes as no surprise to Patricia Masters, who says that in particular after September 11th, many more people are seeking her help and for different reasons.
Patricia Masters: Now, the need for it is greater. And people are understanding it. They're not . . . they're not looking for the fortune-teller anymore, they're looking for the bigger questions.

Anderson Cooper, CNN, New York.

Chapter 8 • Hot Topics 2   71

CHAPTER 9 — BEAUTY: MIRROR, MIRROR, ON THE WALL...
Pages 91–102

Summary It may be only skin deep, but people are going to great lengths to achieve beauty. Reading 1 explains why: research shows that physically attractive people have significant advantages in life. Reading 2 describes the reality TV show *Extreme Makeover*, and Reading 3 indicates that the pressure to look good is having an effect on men, too. And where is the pressure coming from? The reading in Part II outlines social research in a Kenyan village where everyone is happy with their appearance. The village has no access to the media.

Audio The readings in this chapter can be heard on the *Hot Topics 2* Audio CD 2 Tracks 1–4 or Audio Tape 2 Side A.

Background Watching television, flipping through magazines, or driving past billboards, we're confronted with images of youth and beauty. This focus on appearance is good for the cosmetics industry and has contributed to a boom in plastic surgery in many countries, and people may have an easier time finding a job or a mate if they can improve on nature a little. But as the readings in this chapter point out, there is also the widespread feeling of not measuring up to the ideal. This chapter challenges readers to consider both the advantages of having more control over one's appearance and the potential price—whether financial, physical or emotional.

Teaching Note Have a discussion about what things besides physical beauty make people attractive. Use the adjectives for behavior and character in Part II as a starting point, and give the students time to brainstorm and use dictionaries to generate their own descriptive words. List the adjectives on the board, discuss meanings as needed, and ask the students to explain why the characteristics make a person attractive.

Internet Activity Dove's www.campaignforrealbeauty.com, which it says is in response to women's desire for a broader definition of beauty, offers an interesting angle on physical appearance. At the website, students can click on photos sent in by women, and read each woman's ideas on attractiveness. There is an opportunity to vote on whether a physical feature—for example wrinkles or freckles—is beautiful or ugly, and also short articles about the campaign. Alternatively, have students research plastic surgery in their countries and report on recent trends.

CNN Video Clip Summary The reporter visits plastic surgeons and talks about the kinds of procedures people have and how much they typically cost. The surgeons explain that there are risks involved with plastic surgery, but that most people are confident that they'll get good results without a long recovery period. In the end, the reporter decides he'll keep his own nose just the way it is.

Video Script Go to page 74 in this Instructor's Manual for the "Quick Fix Surgery" video script and recommended video vocabulary for review.

Video Activity Go to page 176 in the student book for activities to accompany the CNN video clip.

ANSWER KEY — Chapter 9: BEAUTY: MIRROR, MIRROR, ON THE WALL...

PREVIEW (Page 91)
(Answers may vary.)
1. The wicked queen in Snow White. She wanted the mirror to tell her that she was the most beautiful woman.
2. Answers will vary.

PART I
Predict (Page 92)
(Answers may vary.) Suggested responses below.
1. Readings 1 and 3
2. Reading 2
3. Reading 1
4. Reading 2
5. Answers will vary.
6. Reading 3
7. Answers will vary

Reading Comprehension
Check Your Predictions (Page 95): Answers will vary.
Check the Facts
Reading 1 (Page 95)
1. No, because attractive people have many advantages in society.

2. Attractive children are more popular. Teachers give attractive children better grades. Attractive job applicants have a better chance of getting hired and higher salaries. People generally believe attractive people have other desirable characteristics such as intelligence, competence, confidences, and morality.
3. No; people often think that attractive people are more intelligent.
4. No; every period of history has had standards of beauty.
5. Even though appearance has been important in every age and every culture, it has not always been as important as it is today. Western societies today are obsessed with physical appearance.

Reading 2 (Page 96)

1. The purpose of *Extreme Makeover* is to help people change their appearance by undergoing makeover procedures.
2. The people on the show undergo various makeover procedures.
3. Thousands of people apply.
4. An *Extreme* makeover is different because it involves plastic surgery; a regular makeover involves changes in clothing, make-up, and hairstyle.
5. You can apply for an Extreme Makeover by writing to the TV show and describing your physical flaws.

Reading 3 (Page 96)

1. They are pretty. Traditionally, women have worried about their appearance.
2. 25 percent
3. Men are dying gray hair. They are paying money to grow back hair. They are using plastic surgery to fix their noses and remove fat. Men are even getting bicep implants.
4. They want to be more attractive to get better jobs, to be more athletic, and to attract women.
5. No; he says that men are unhappy with their appearance because they see ideal men in movies, in advertisements, and on television and music videos.

Analyze (Page 96)

(Answers may vary.) Suggested responses below.

1. Reading 1 explains that people want to be attractive in order to achieve certain goals and have certain advantages. Reading 3 explains the measures men take in order to become "attractive." Reading 1 gives reasons that the people in Reading 3 do the things that they do.

2. Readings 1 and 3 emphasize the importance people place on being attractive, while Reading 2 describes a TV program that changes people's appearance through plastic surgery. Reading 2 supports the ideas in the other readings since surgery is arguably the most drastic way to try to achieve beauty, yet many people are willing to do it.

Vocabulary Work

Guess Meaning from Related Words (Page 97)

(Answers may vary.)

1. To apply is to request or seek admission or assistance. An applicant is the person who is seeking admission or assistance. Apply is the verb form; applicant is the noun form.

    Obsessed is the state of having something control one's mind or behavior. An obsession is the idea or habit that controls the mind. Obsessed is the adjective form; obsession is the noun form.

    Attractive is appealing or charming. Attraction is the ability and quality in a person to attract. Attractive is the adjective form; attraction is the noun form.
2. (Answers may vary.)

Guess Meaning from Context (Page 98)

1. Answers will vary.
2. *vanity:* pride
   extreme: radical
   motto: saying
   dying: coloring
   implants: something put inside the body, for example to increase its size
3. Answers will vary.
4. a. *plastic surgeon:* operates on people to alter their appearances
   b. *eye surgeon:* operates on people's eyes
   c. *cosmetic dentist:* improves the appearance of people's teeth
   d. *hair stylist:* cuts and styles people's hair
   e. *fashion consultant:* helps people with their wardrobes
   f. *makeup expert:* helps people with their make up
   g. *personal trainer:* helps people exercise

Reading Skills

Understanding Cohesion (Page 99)

1. candidates; participants
2. the two people who participate in *Extreme Makeover*

Discussion (Page 99): Answers will vary.

PART II

Read It (Page 99)

1. The researcher wanted to find out if people in other cultures are unhappy with their appearance.
2. Everyone in the village is completely satisfied with their appearance.
3. The Maasai look at jewelry, cleanliness, white teeth, short hair, height, and elongated ear lobes. The Maasai also think about attractiveness in terms of both physical traits and moral character.

Vocabulary Work

Guess Meaning from Related Words (Page 101)

(Answers may vary.)

attractive: unattractive (not good-looking); attractiveness (noun form)
satisfy: satisfied (happy with); dissatisfied (not happy with)
clean: cleanliness (state of being clean)

CNN Video Activities: Quick Fix Surgery

Understand It (Page 176)

1. True	3. False	5. True	7. False
2. True	4. False	6. False	8. True

VIDEO TRANSCRIPT—Chapter 9: Quick Fix Surgery

DVD Title 10   Running time: 02:26

Video Vocabulary

bulbousness* roundness
lipoplasty* cosmetic surgery in which fat is removed
rhinoplasty* plastic surgery performed on the nose
tuck a type of cosmetic surgery

Video Script

Surgeon 1: I'm going to have you hold this up underneath here just for additional lighting.

Reporter: There are few things that make us quite as self-conscious as visiting a plastic surgeon.
   So you're going to narrow the nose and bring it up a little bit? Is that what you're . . . ?

Surgeon 1: I'm going to narrow it and bring it in at the tip.
   There's a little bit of bulbousness on the tip.

Reporter: See what I mean?
   Bulbousness . . .

Reporter: A plastic surgeon sometimes does his or her job by cutting things out—whether it's rhinoplasty to fix a bulbous nose, tucks to remove extra skin, or even lipoplasty to suck out fat.

Surgeon 2: The guys are realizing they can come in with sort of a fullness in their chest area, fullness in their tummy, and just have liposuction. They'll be off of work for four days maybe seven days.

Reporter: Other times they move stuff around . . .

Surgeon 1: We are going to raise one of your brows, just slightly.

Reporter: . . . or even add new parts like a chin implant.

Surgeon 1: . . . and we are going to bring your chin out, just a little bit.

Reporter: . . . or breast implants, which are regaining public confidence.

Surgeon 2: They feel like if they want a breast augmentation, they can come and get it. They can get it safely. They can get the result that they expect to get, that their friend got, and they'll be happy.

Reporter: Although the wallet may not be quite as happy.

Surgeon 2: Total cost on a brow and a nose and a chin might be eight to ten thousand dollars, counting the doctor's fee and also the operating room.

Reporter: How about something like this gentleman here . . .

Surgeon 2: Liposuction of the chest and of the tummy—that's probably around six thousand.

Reporter: No operation is completely free of risk, and although it's extremely rare, a few patients have died during plastic surgery. Patients are warned ahead of time of the dangers. And computer

74   Hot Topics 2 • Chapter 9

simulations that predict the outcome of surgery help patients decide if the reward is worth the risk and the expense.

Surgeon 1: Now, I'm going to print these out for you, so you can take a copy home with you.

Reporter: Show everyone my bulbous nose? Personally, I think I'll choose to keep my nose like it is.

I never knew that I had a bulbous nose before I came here today.
But I'm OK with that.

Surgeon 1: Just a little bulbous.

Dr. Sangay Gupta, CNN, Atlanta.

CHAPTER 10 — Lying: What's THAT on your resume?
Pages 103–114

Summary The readings in chapter 10 expose the truth about lying. Reading 1 discusses the widespread practice of lying on resumes, while Reading 2 gives the results of a survey revealing how often and under what circumstances people lie. Reading 3 contains information about the physical signs that someone is telling a lie. Part II explores the social and psychological reasons that people lie, and asks the reader to reconsider whether honesty is always the best policy.

Audio The readings in this chapter can be heard on the *Hot Topics 2* Audio CD 2 Tracks 5–8 or Audio Tape 2 Side A.

Background Children learn from parents and teachers that they should not tell lies. At the same time, they are taught not to hurt other people's feelings. Their challenge is to find a compromise between truthfulness and tact. In the world of work, many people find that their opportunities are limited if they don't "stretch the truth", so the challenge is to lie without being caught. In either case, the delicate issue of lying is a reality of life.

Teaching Note Reading 3 suggests several ways to detect when a speaker is lying, and the students may want to try this themselves. First, the students prepare notes about their lives, including information about their families, their education, and experiences they have had. They should include a sprinkling of untrue information. Then, they tell a small group or the whole class about themselves, using their notes as little as possible and speaking as naturally as possible. The listeners try to detect the lies, and should be ready to discuss why they thought certain information was not true.

Internet Activity Have students write a simple résumé, including some true information and some lies or exaggerations. First, have students go to an online writing lab such as Purdue University's http://purdue.placementmanual.com/resume/, or the University of Minnesota's (http://www1.umn.edu/ohr/ecep/resume/). These websites contain tips for résumé writing and examples of good résumés. (Students should follow these examples and not worry too much about format in order to save time.) Have partners exchange résumés and try to guess which information is true and which is not.

Video Clip Summary The clip exposes "the cheating culture"—the practice of lying and cheating to get ahead in the business world. One-time entrepreneur and convicted felon Barry Minkow's Fraud Discovery Institute works to uncover illegal practices in business, something he knows about first-hand.

Video Script Go to page 77 in this Instructor's Manual for the "The Business of Lying" video script and recommended video vocabulary for review.

Video Activity Go to page 177 in the student book for activities to accompany the CNN video clip.

ANSWER KEY—Chapter 10: *Lying: What's THAT on your resume?*

PREVIEW (Pages 103-104): Answers will vary.

PART I

Predict (Page 104)

(Answers may vary.) Suggested responses:

1. Readings 1 and 3
2. on the telephone
3. Approximately 10 percent of job seekers "seriously misrepresent" their work histories.
4. Yes. Liars consciously try to look at you because they want to appear sincere.
5. Answers will vary.

Reading Comprehension

Check Your Predictions (Page 108): Answers will vary.

Check the Facts

Reading 1 (Page 108)

1. True
2. False
3. False
4. False
5. True

Reading 2 (Page 108)

1. False
2. True
3. True
4. True
5. False

Reading 3 (Page 109)

(Answers may vary.) Suggested response: The woman in picture #1 may be telling a lie because she is looking right at the listener. She may be trying to look sincere in pictures 2 and 3.

Analyze (Page 109)

(Answers may vary.) Suggested responses:

1. Yes; the information from Reading 3 provides further advice on spotting liars. In Reading 2, the expert provides tips for catching a liar.
2. Hancock (Reading 2) believes people are not likely to tell lies in writing, yet lies on résumés (Reading 1) are definitely written down.
3. During a job interview, the employer could ask the applicant questions about his or her résumé and study the person's behavior as he or she responds.

Vocabulary Work

Guess Meaning from Context (Page 109)

1. Checked words: cheating; fake; false; fictional; misrepresent; untruthful; untruths
   Circled words: accomplishments; untruths
   Underlined words: cheating; fake; get away with it; misrepresent
   Adjectives: automatic; fake; false; fictional; sincere; untruthful

Guess Meaning from Related Words (Page 110)

(Answers may vary.)

1. *misrepresent:* to mislead someone; to say something incorrect or untrue on purpose
   untruths: lies
   background: a person's family, education, and experience
   foolproof: safe; easily understood
   convincingly: to say or do something in a way that makes someone believe something
2. exaggeration (noun); exaggerating (verb); exaggerated (adjective or past tense verb); exaggerate (present tense verb)
   consciously (adverb); unconsciously (adverb / antonym); unconscious (adjective)
   employment (noun); unemployment (noun / antonym)
   fiction (noun); fictional (adjective)

Reading Skills

Identifying Euphemisms (Page 110)

Euphemisms: "face-to-face" and "stretch the truth"
face-to-face: in person
stretch the truth: to exaggerate

Discussion (Page 111): Answers will vary.

PART II

Read It (Page 111)

1. Although parents and teachers tell us that it's always better to tell the truth, society often rewards deception.
2. In recent years, a number of well-known people—from coaches and business executives to college professors and journalists—have admitted that they

have lied about their pasts. "'Each of us creates our own personal myth—our own story about ourselves.'"

3. Married couples are more honest than people who are dating. Dating couples lie to each other about 33 percent of the time, whereas spouses lie to each other in about ten percent of their major conversations.
4. The student tried to avoid telling lies for several weeks. The task was so difficult that the student was unable to complete his research and had to apologize to a lot of people afterward.
5. "White lies" are lies about very unimportant matters or lies that are meant to avoid hurting the listener's feelings.

Vocabulary Work
Guess Meaning from Related Words (Page 113)

(Answers may vary.)

1. *overslept:* slept for too long or slept too late
2. *untrustworthy:* not capable of being trusted
3. *incredible:* amazing, unbelievable
4. *dishonesty:* the failure or refusal to be honest or truthful
5. *well-known:* famous, renowned
6. *continual:* occurring again and again

Guess Meaning from Context (Page 113)

(Answers may vary.)

1. *confess:* to admit
2. *point out:* to note; to indicate
3. *myth:* an untrue or unproved story
4. *leave out:* to exclude

Reading Skills
Recognizing Transition Words and Phrases (Page 113)

a contrasting idea: however; in contrast; on the other hand
when two ideas are contrasted: however; in contrast; on the other hand
an additional idea: furthermore
when an additional idea is coming: furthermore

CNN Video Activities: The Business of Lying
Understand It (Page 177)

1. e	4. h	7. d
2. g	5. a	8. f
3. b	6. i	9. c

VIDEO TRANSCRIPT—Chapter 10: *The Business of Lying*
DVD Title 11   Running time: 02:28

Video Vocabulary

crook   criminal, especially a thief, cheat, or swindler
defraud   to steal money by trickery or deceit
get swindled*   to be cheated out of money or property
tax evasion   illegal avoidance of taxes by refusing to pay taxes or buying smuggled goods
theft   the act of stealing
whiz kid   a young, very smart person
witch hunt   a search for people whose political beliefs and activities are claimed to be dangerous

Video Script

Reporter: You could say Barry Minkow was a pioneer in the business world.
Barry Minkow: We were the first company really to lie to the auditors, get clean opinions from three different auditing firms, to inflate earnings, and not disclose all the debt.
Reporter: At sixteen Minkow started a carpet cleaning company, by age 20 he had a 240 million dollar company and was referred to as a whiz kid of Wall Street, and at 23 was sentenced to 25 years in prison for defrauding investors of 26 million dollars.
Barry Minkow: I was a crook, and, you know, although I started it with the best of intentions, the company ran into financial difficulty and I lied and cheated to keep it running.
Reporter: What Barry Minkow did resembles the recent accusations against many high profile corporations: lying about what you earn and owe to make more money. According to Minkow, right and wrong means something different in the business world.
Barry Minkow: Right equals forward motion wrong is anybody who gets in my way.

Reporter: That, says author David Callahan, is because the cheating culture sometimes makes it necessary to lie to get ahead.

David Callahan: Lawyers will say, hey everybody in my firm is over billing. If I don't also pad my hours I'm not going to be considered for partner; I'm not going to get a bonus; I'm not going to get ahead in the firm.

Reporter: In many cases, Callahan says, we are cheating and lying more. Tax evasion has more than doubled since 1990 to more than 250 billion dollars a year. And workplace theft totals 600 billion dollars a year.

David Callahan: If you're not cheating, then you're not playing by the real rules. You're playing by an abstract moral code that has no relevance in today's society.

Barry Minkow: We have to sleep at night, too. We don't want to look at ourselves at parties as big con men. It's a means to an end.

Reporter: And in the end, Barry Minkow paid for his crime. Today he works to prevent others from getting swindled. His Fraud Discovery Institute has helped law enforcement agencies uncover more than a billion dollars worth of fraud.

Barry Minkow: You'd have to have "been there and done that" to know what to test for. I think most CEOs are honest, so I'm not on a witch hunt. But every one of them is going to be tempted, at one time in their business life.

Heidi Collins, CNN.

CHAPTER 11 — Intelligence: How important is it?
Pages 115–126

Summary This chapter concentrates on intelligence. Reading 1 explains the origin of the word *dunce*, and offers cases in which people did poorly in school but very well in life, along with the case of the genius who became known as "The Unabomber." Reading 2 contains a table that shows the distribution of IQ scores in the population, and Reading 3 explains the loneliness that child prodigies experience. Part II talks about an Australian scientist's "creativity machine."

Audio The readings in this chapter can be heard on the *Hot Topics 2* Audio CD 2 Tracks 9-12 or Audio Tape 2 Side A.

Background A team of psychologists developed the test we know as "The IQ Test" in 1917 for the U.S. Army, which hoped that such a test would help to determine the best jobs for recruits based on their intellectual capabilities. But the idea of describing intelligence as a ratio of mental age to chronological age began in Europe with scientists such as Wilhelm Stern and Alfred Binet.

More recently, of course, intelligence testing has been criticized for racial bias, and Howard Gardner's ideas about multiple intelligences have been widely embraced by educators. Nevertheless, the idea of an "Intelligence Quotient" persists, and the definition of a genius is still based on IQ.

Teaching Note The Reading Skills section in Part I is on finding main ideas—a critically important reading skill. In order to practice this skill, revisit previous articles in the book that the class enjoyed and ask students to locate the main ideas. This could be done as a jigsaw activity, with individuals or groups assigned the task of finding the main idea of an article and reporting back to the rest of the class. Students could also create multiple choice quizzes for their classmates by pulling three or four sentences from the article, one of which states the main idea.

Internet Activity Using a search engine, enter the terms "brain teasers" or "lateral thinking" and find thinking exercises and puzzles at a good level for your students. Many of these are word problems, and will provide reading exercise and an enjoyable mental challenge as well. If the class wants to find out who among them might be a genius, send them to www.mensa.org, then "MENSA workout", a 30-minute IQ-type test.

Video Clip Summary The reporter profiles fourteen-year-old Alia Sabur, the country's youngest Ph.D. candidate. Alia explains that she picks things up more quickly than other people, but she's not a geek. She likes doing things besides studying. One of her professors explains that Alia thinks in a special way. In the future, Alia hopes to combine an academic career with playing the clarinet professionally.

Video Script Go to page 80 in this Instructor's Manual for the "Alia's Bright Future" video script and recommended video vocabulary for review.

Video Activity Go to page 178 in the student book for activities to accompany the CNN video clip.

ANSWER KEY—Chapter 11: Intelligence: How important is it?

PREVIEW (Page 115): Answers will vary.

PART 1

Predict (Page 116)

(Answers may vary.)

1. a stupid person
2. 0.1 percent
3. Their intellectual, social, emotional, physical, and chronological ages are very different. Many highly gifted children can find no one who is like them, so they end up lonely and isolated.
4. Answers will vary.

Reading Comprehension

Check Your Predictions (Page 120): Answers will vary.

Check the Facts

Reading 1 (Page 120)

1. He was a philosopher.
2. While he was alive, he was respected.
3. After he died, other philosophers began to criticize him.
4. He believed that conical hats increased learning.
5. Albert Einstein / Isaac Newton / Thomas Edison / Leo Tolstoy / Wernher von Braun / Louis Pasteur
6. Theodore Kaczynski is famous for being the "Unabomber." He sent letter bombs to people he didn't know.

Reading 2 (Page 120)

1. 68 percent of the population is average
2. around 14 percent of the population is above average

Reading 3 (Page 121)

1. Many child prodigies are lonely and friendless during childhood.
2. Child prodigies have problems making friends because their intellectual, social, emotional, physical, and chronological ages are very different. Many highly gifted children can find no one who is like them, so they end up lonely and isolated.
3. Child prodigies are too intelligent for other children their age and have trouble relating.
4. Child prodigies are not as mature socially or emotionally as older children or adults.
5. Ian is passionate about dinosaurs.
6. No, because other six-year-olds know too little about dinosaurs—even older children don't know enough.
7. Ian doesn't have anyone to talk to.
8. Ian has trouble talking to both children and adults.

Analyze (Page 121)

1. less than 0.1 percent
2. "unmeasurable" genius
3. Answers will vary, but the men in Reading 1 did poorly in school, so may not have been recognized as geniuses when they were children.

Vocabulary Work

Guess Meaning from Related Words (Page 121)

1. (Answers may vary.)
   lawmaker: person who creates laws
   friendless: without friends
   knowledgeable: to have knowledge
   gifted: having a special talent or special ability
2. a. lonely is an adverb; loneliness is a noun
   b. passion is a noun; passionate is an adjective
   c. problem is a noun; problematic is an adjective
   d. cone is a noun; conical is an adjective
   e. idiot is a noun; idiotic is an adjective
   f. stupid is an adjective; stupidity is a noun

Guess Meaning from Context (Page 122)

1. Answers will vary.
2. *absolute:* total
   eponymous: a word that comes from a person's name
   child prodigy: an unusually talented or intelligent girl or boy
   chronological: according to time
   genius: an extremely smart person
   fanatical: radical, extreme
   flunked out of: had to leave school because of bad grades
   jealous: wanting something someone else has, envious
3. Answers will vary.
4. (Answers may vary.) Genius may be considered too intelligent. These people have a hard time making friends and are often lonely.

Reading Skills
Finding Main Ideas (Page 122)
1. c
2. "However, being a dunce isn't all bad. There are a lot of famous people that seemed like dunces to their teachers."
3. a

Discussion (Page 123): Answers will vary.

PART II
Read It (Page 123)
1. Autistic savants are people who are mentally disabled but have one remarkable ability.
2. They are good at seeing details.
3. Creativity is the ability to make connections between ideas that seem unrelated.
4. His machine sends out magnetic signals which stop part of the mind from working so that we can see things in greater detail.

Vocabulary Work
Guess Meaning from Context (Page 125)
1. *remarkable:* noticeable; worthy of attention; outstanding
2. *accomplished:* skilled; experienced
3. *mentally disabled:* having a mental handicap
4. *temporarily:* not permanently
5. *unrelated:* not associated; having no connection
6. *nonautomatic:* not self-operating; requiring assistance

Reading Skills
Finding Main Ideas (Page 125)
1. The main point of this article is to describe one scientist's ideas about creativity and the machine he invented to help people become more creative.
2. The author supports his point by discussing the talents of autistic savants and explaining how his machine makes other people's brains work in a similar way to theirs.

CNN Video Activities: Alia's Bright Future
Understand It (Page 178)
1. 14 years old
2. the study and creation of very tiny electronic devices using optics
3. She does everything faster.
4. (Answers may vary.) Possible responses: going to school; playing the clarinet; making "origami"; Tae Kwon Do
5. 8 months old
6. applied math
7. no
8. clean her room; go to sleep on time
9. organized a surprise party for her
10. be a professional clarinetist

VIDEO TRANSCRIPT—Chapter 11: Alia's Bright Future
DVD Title 12   Running time: 02:24

Video Vocabulary
geek* somebody who is considered unattractive and socially awkward
refreshingly* pleasingly different

Video Script
Reporter: Most fourteen-year-old girls are worried about their social calendar, the latest fashions, and middle school. Alia Sabur's fourteen and working on her doctorate in electrical engineering, more specifically, nanophotonics.

Alia: Nanophotonics is the study and the creation of electronic devices using optics at the nano scale, or if you prefer, at the atomic scale.

Reporter: Not that Alia is above living in the meta atomic scale; it's just that she has a gift.

Professor Mun Young Choi: She's a person that really thinks in concepts. So when she tries to learn a mathematical formula, to her it's not just numbers and formulas, but she visualizes a solution and that's what makes her unique and special.

Reporter: Alia puts it another way.

Alia: OK, this is the thing. I just do everything faster. It's not that I know things or . . . I could just pick up the clarinet and start playing it. But . . . everything happens faster.

Reporter: She started reading at eight months, went from forth grade to college at State University of New York Stony Brook, and graduated *summa cum laude* with a degree in applied math. She's a concert level clarinetist, makes origami, and has a black belt in Tae Kwon Do. But she's not a geek.

Alia: I've never been one to study all day. You know? I have a life. I mean . . . I like having a life. You know, I would not want to spend the entire day doing one thing.

Reporter: Despite being the youngest female Ph.D. candidate in the country, and looking forward to lecturing undergraduate classes at Drexel University, she's also refreshingly fourteen.

Alia: I don't clean my room, and I don't go to sleep on time, and I'm always listening to music on my headset.

Reporter: And when it came time to move from her hometown of North Port, Long Island to Philadelphia, her friends surprised her with a party.

Alia: It was all my favorite friends. All of them—all, like, twelve of them. They all got together and organized it and had a surprise party for me. I couldn't believe they did that. I have nice friends.

Reporter: Alia's goal?—To be a professor and researcher by day and a professional clarinetist at night.

Bill Tucker, CNN, Philadelphia.

CHAPTER 12 — Graffiti: You call this ART?
Pages 127–138

Summary Some call it art, and some call it vandalism. The readings in Part I of this chapter outline both points of view on graffiti. The reading in Part II gives graffiti a historical perspective, starting in World War II and continuing through the writer's own experiences doing graffiti in New York.

Audio The readings in this chapter can be heard on the *Hot Topics 2* Audio CD 2 Tracks 13–17 or Audio Tape 2 Side B.

Background From the Greek and Latin words for "writing", graffiti originally referred to political sentiments written in public places. Starting around the 1970's, the practice of writing "tags"—names or initials identifying people—became more widespread. Over time, the tags have gotten larger, more stylized, and more colorful with the use of spray paint, covering outdoor walls, public structures, and train or subway cars. Property owners and municipalities spend large sums of money to remove graffiti, while the art world has begun to embrace it.

Teaching Note The Reading Skills section in Part II asks readers to identify transition words and phrases. To help students acquire these words and phrases, give a writing assignment in which students must use at least five of them. (Since the writing in Part II is chronological, a topic requiring students to relate events over a period of time would be appropriate.) Alternatively, use the transitions for a whole-class exercise by writing them on the board, providing an interesting sentence to serve as the beginning of a story, then getting suggestions from students for sentences that use the transitions and continue the story. Make changes and suggestions as needed, and focus attention on the meanings and functions of the transitions.

Internet Activity Ask your students to view online photographs of graffiti and write a reaction paragraph about what they see. Direct them to www.yahoo.com then use the words "graffiti exhibits" to search the directory. Also try www.graffiti.org, or use the search terms "graffiti artist" or "graffiti photographs" in a search engine.

CNN Video Clip Summary The CNN clip reports on a retrospective graffiti exhibit in Italy which aims to explain graffiti's place in art. The exhibit includes work by American Keith Haring and other graffiti artists, as well as a piece called *Olympic Rings* that will be used in 2006 when Turin hosts the winter games. Despite the recognition given by the exhibit, some graffiti artists claim that the show represents the work of only a small percentage of them.

Video Script Go to page 83 in this Instructor's Manual for the "Graffiti Gallery" video script and recommended video vocabulary for review.

Video Activity Go to page 179 in the student book for activities to accompany the CNN video clip.

ANSWER KEY—Chapter 12: Graffiti: You call this ART?

PREVIEW (Page 127): Answers will vary.

PART I

Predict (Page 128)
1. Reading 1A, and Reading 3 gives Yaeger's opinion
2. Reading 1B
3. Readings 2 and 3
4. Readings 1B and 3
5. Answers will vary.

Reading Comprehension

Check Your Predictions (Page 131): Answers will vary.

Check the Facts (Page 132)

Readings 1A and 1B
1. The newspaper printed a picture of graffiti.
2. Graffiti is illegal. The writer does not think graffiti is art, but vandalism.
3. The writer thinks the people who create graffiti are self-centered and don't care about anybody else's rights.
4. The tour will take place on Saturday, September 12 at 11:00 A.M. in Los Angeles.
5. There will be a bus tour, the participants will watch videos and clips, and the graffiti artists will discuss their work.

Reading 2
1. Brando thinks graffiti is an art form. He has a passion for graffiti.
2. Linda Keller is against graffiti. She believes graffiti "destroys the community."
3. Yes, creating graffiti without permission in Harrison is illegal.
4. Graffiti writers can paint on a legal concrete wall—a wall that has been designated by the city for use by graffiti artists.
5. Most graffiti paintings do not stay up for more than two or three days.
6. Brando photographs his paintings in order to keep them.

Reading 3
1. Don Yaeger is one of the nine graffiti artists who contributed to the murals at a new Teen Center.
2. The medium is more important to Yaeger.
3. He has done tattoos, drawn with pen and ink, and painted with cans and brushes.
4. Yaeger paints legally.
5. No, he does not think that graffiti painting should be against the law.

Analyze (Page 133)
1. Linda Keller from Reading 2
2. Both artists paint graffiti in areas where it is allowed in their cities. Neither artist is breaking the law.
3. Grandview has made graffiti art illegal. There has been a tour set up to display graffiti art in Los Angeles. Harrison has cleaned up some graffiti art and created spaces where graffiti art is allowed.

Vocabulary Work

Guess Meaning from Related Words (Page 133)
1. (Answers may vary.)
   homeowners: people who own a home
   taxpayers: people who pay taxes
   self-centered: full of oneself; only thinking of oneself
   criminal: someone who breaks the law
   expression: way of conveying a message; making a statement
   three-dimensional: having height, width, and depth
   typical: usual; common
2. *public / publicity / publicly:* All have the word "public" and have to do with the community and people
   vandals / vandalism: have to do with destruction of property
   annoy / annoyance: have to do with irritation
   erases / erasure: having to do with getting rid of or cleaning off
   moral / immoral: antonyms having to do with right and wrong

Guess Meaning from Context (Page 134)
1. Answers will vary.
2. *visible:* can be seen
   jail: prison
   fine: financial punishment
   mural: a large painting on a wall
   city hall: a building for city government offices
3. Answers will vary.
4. *Buffing out* is erasing graffiti pictures from a wall by covering the wall with paint.
   A *tag* is a label a graffiti artist has for him or herself. It is a sort of signature.

Reading Skills

Understanding Tone (Page 134)

1. (Answers may vary.) The writer from Reading 1A is angry. Phrases such as "big mistake" and "self-centered people who don't care about anybody else's rights" reveal his anger.
2. (Answers may vary.) No, the two graffiti artists are not angry. They understand that their art is controversial and is not widely accepted.

Discussion (Page 134): Answers will vary.

PART II

Read It (Page 135)

1. in the late 1960s
2. on public spaces
3. Street gangs began writing graffiti on bathroom walls.
4. *Real* graffiti is the graffiti that was painted on the New York City subway cars that the artists risked arrest, electrocution, dismemberment, and death in order to paint.
5. Graffiti ended on the subway in the 1980s when New York learned how to clean the subway cars permanently.
6. People write graffiti to send a message. Writers use graffiti to express thoughts on family, religion, and politics.

Vocabulary Work

Guess Meaning from Related Words (Page 137)

1. *dangerous:* danger
   mysterious: mystery
   synonymous: synonym
   (*-ous* turns a noun into an adjective.)

2. *risks:* risked
   create: created
   exist: existence

Guess Meaning from Context (Page 137)

1. (Answers may vary.) These words mean harmful or bad things. There is danger involved.
2. (Answers may vary.) Saw means viewed, believed, or considered.
3. (Answers may vary.)
   a. *canvases:* areas to paint; format for painting
   b. *logos:* design symbol of a business
   c. *Big Apple:* nickname for New York City

Reading Skills

Identifying Transition Words and Phrases (Page 138)

(Answers may vary.)
began; started; In the 1950s; in the late 1960s; Slowly; in the 1970s; First; Later; Then; Soon; became; in the 1980s; eventually; forever

CNN Video Activities: Graffiti Gallery
Understand It (Page 179)

1. checked
2. unchecked
3. checked
4. unchecked
5. unchecked
6. checked
7. checked
8. unchecked
9. checked

VIDEO TRANSCRIPT—Chapter 12: *Graffiti Gallery*
DVD Title 13   Running time: 01:41

Video Vocabulary

anarchy   a condition without governmental control, laws, military, etc.
scrawl   handwriting done quickly or messily
unsightly   unpleasant to look at, ugly

Video Script

Reporter: Some see it as an <u>unsightly</u> mess, others as a form of rebellious expression, and still others see it as art. No matter how you look at it, graffiti has been given a prime position at an exhibit in northern Italy.

The showing attempts to explain the thirty-year history of street art, beginning with the act of <u>scrawling</u> personal logos or statements on walls and buildings in New York City in the 1970s. The exhibit tells the history of graffiti in an effort to show its place in the art world.

Diego: There are no rules in our art. Our only rule is pure <u>anarchy</u>. Everyone does what one pleases and no one criticizes.

Reporter: The exhibit includes works from the big names in the graffiti world, including American Keith Haring whose work sprang from the American music culture of Hip Hop, rap and break dance. But most street artists say this exhibit doesn't truly represent them.

Riccardo: Just a few of the artists whose works are here now have done things similar to ours. All the rest is something else. Art galleries, the official art world, should give some recognition to our work.

Reporter: At least one piece will get recognition on walls and much more around the world. This was created in 1985. It's called Olympic Rings. It will be used by Turin as its Olympic insignia when it hosts the winter games in 2006.

Denise Dillon, CNN.

CHAPTER 13 — CHILD LABOR: WHO MADE YOUR SNEAKERS?
Pages 139–150

Summary Chapter 13 takes a look at child labor. Reading 1 tells the story of a child who was sold by his parents and later fought for children's rights in Pakistan. Reading 2 describes some of the horrific conditions faced by child laborers, and Reading 3 is about the Rugmark organization, which promotes carpet producers that don't use child labor. The reading in Part II discusses the reasons children work and the roles of children in developed versus developing countries.

Audio The readings in this chapter can be heard on the *Hot Topics 2* Audio CD 2 Tracks 18-21 or Audio Tape 2 Side B.

Background Child labor has never been uncommon. Children make it possible for rural families to get the farm work done, and children in cities find jobs to supplement the family income or to buy the latest fashions. The disagreement over child labor arises from the different perspectives of people in richer countries and those in poorer countries, where children who work can be denied education, health, and safety. The families of such children see their work as an economic necessity, while outside observers see it as an outrage.

Teaching Note The Reading Skills section in Part I involves the identification of referents while reading, something that is crucial for comprehension. Expand this activity to Reading 3 by having students locate all the instances of the pronouns *they, their,* and *it* in the passage, along with the phrase *these schools*, then identify what each one refers to.

Internet Activity Direct students to www.rugmark.org, where they can read about the organization described in Reading 3. The "About Rugmark" section is particularly interesting since it describes the organization and how it works, and contains profiles of children whom Rugmark has helped.

Video Clip Summary The CNN clip reports on child labor in India, where some sixty million children are employed at very low wages despite the fact that child labor is illegal. The reporter notes that pressure and sanctions from western countries will not change anything, but rather the solution will involve ending poverty.

Video Script Go to page 86 in this Instructor's Manual for the "Child Labor in India" video script and recommended video vocabulary for review.

Video Activity Go to page 180 in the student book for activities to accompany the CNN video clip.

ANSWER KEY—Chapter 13: CHILD LABOR: WHO MADE YOUR SNEAKERS?

PREVIEW (Page 139)

1. (Answers may vary.) Children cannot defend themselves. They do not have anyone to help them negotiate for better wages.
2. Answer will vary.
3. Answers will vary.

PART I

Predict (Page 140)

1. A Child Hero: Reading 1
   Uniting Help for Children: Reading 3
   Children Pay High Prices for Cheap Labor: Reading 2
2. Readings 1, 2, and 3
3. Reading 1
4. Reading 2
5. Answers will vary.

Reading Comprehension

Check Your Predictions (Page 143): Answers will vary.

Check the Facts (Page 144)

Reading 1

1. False
2. True
3. False
4. True
5. False
6. False

Reading 2

1. False
2. True
3. True
4. False
5. True

Reading 3

1. False
2. False
3. True
4. False
5. False

Analyze (Page 144)

(Answers may vary.)

1. Both BLLF and Rugmark act as advocates for child workers and raise awareness of the problems associated with child labor. Both organizations are against child labor. Both groups run schools for former child workers.
2. Rugmark works with carpet makers and provides a label that proves that the carpet maker doesn't use child laborers, while the BLLF doesn't work with the carpet makers. Rugmark does not actually free child laborers, while the BLLF does.
3. Yes, since these are other areas where child laborers are used and a tag might encourage people to buy from companies that do not use child laborers. On the other hand, rugs are luxury items that people only buy occasionally, whereas with daily necessities like food and clothing, a cheaper price might be more important than who produced the product.

Vocabulary Work

Guess Meaning from Related Words (Page 145)

1. (Answers may vary.)
   spokesman: person who speaks for a company or group
   sickly: ill; weak
   reunite: see again; meet with again
   development: growth
   eyesight: ability to see
2. *import:* export
   repetition: repetitive
   horrible: horrific
   intelligence: intellectual

Guess Meaning from Context (Pages 145-146)

1. Answers will vary.
2. *loom:* a machine for making rugs
   founder: the person who began an organization
   slave: a worker who receives no pay and is not free to leave
   decades: tens of years
   revenge: to do something bad to someone because that person did something bad to you
   inspect: to look at carefully
   label: a tag that says where a product came from
   rug: carpet
3. Answers will vary.
4. (Answers may vary.) These are bad places to work. The following sentence says, "These jobs are not only dull, repetitive, and dangerous, they often make normal physical and mental development impossible."

Chapter 13 • Hot Topics 2   85

Reading Skills
Identifying Referents (Page 146)
1. children
2. children
3. children who work as little more than slaves
4. children who work as little more than slaves
5. jobs in sweatshops, mines, garbage dumps, or on the street
6. jobs in sweatshops, mines, garbage dumps, or on the street

Discussion (Page 146): Answers will vary.

PART II
Read It (Page 147)
1. poverty; rural-to-urban migration; tradition
2. In some countries, women will not fit into traditional roles if they become educated. It is a common belief that educated females will not get married or have children.
3. Child specialization is the assignment of different roles to children by their parents.
4. Evidence suggests that the use of child labor may only be one stage in the development of a country, and the historical examples of the United States and England support this.

Vocabulary Work
Guess Meaning from Related Words (Page 149)
1. (Answers may vary.)
   well paid: makes a good living; makes a lot of money
   household: person or people living together in one home
   social class: group of people of similar economic or financial status
   specialization: a topic or subject about which someone knows a lot
2. (Answers may vary.)
   develop: (verb) to make progress
   developing: (adjective) in process; moving towards completion or maturity
   developed: (adjective) completed or matured
   development: (noun) growth; progress

Reading Skills
Understanding Organization (Page 149)
Roles of Children in Developing and Developed Countries: Section 3
Cultural Causes: Section 2
Causes of Child Labor: Sections 1, 2, 3
Economic Causes: Section 1

CNN Video Activities: Child Labor in India
Understand It (Page 180)

1. False
2. True
3. False
4. True
5. False
6. False
7. True
8. True
9. False

VIDEO TRANSCRIPT—Chapter 13: *CHILD LABOR IN INDIA*
DVD Title 14   Running time: 02:49

Video Vocabulary
hard labor* difficult physical work; a sentence of compulsory work imposed in addition to a term of imprisonment
sanction law or rule that punishes or deprives someone
veteran anyone with a lot of experience in a job, profession, or art

Video Script

Reporter: <u>Hard labor</u>—but it's the way much of India works. In industrialized countries, turning rocks into gravel is done by machines. But in the developing world, people are cheaper than machines. Cheapest of all are children.

In rural India the earnings are much less, says activist Ravi Chohan.

People work for thirty, forty, maybe twenty rupees a day. It's very difficult to feed all the children so they send them to work.

Twenty rupees a day is less than fifty cents, and that's for adults. The low wages are part of what make products from the developing world so cheap. Child labor is officially illegal in India, but at least sixty million children, some as young as six, work for a living. It's an important part of many of the country's traditional export industries like carpet weaving. Moham Kumar is eleven, but already he's a <u>veteran</u> weaver. His parents sold him for about five dollars to a man who said he'd get him a good job.

They used to make us work sixteen, seventeen hours a day, he says.

When Moham tried to leave, his employer used the same tool used for weaving carpets to leave these marks on his face.

So what's the solution? India says western pressure won't help end these abuses. Although it's a slow process, it says it's solving the problem on its own by working harder to enforce labor laws and by improving its economy.

The government says, the only way to end labor abuses is to lift families out of poverty, so children won't have to work and employers will have to offer better conditions. Banning child labor hasn't ended the practice. India says it requires a wider approach that will take billions of dollars and years to address.

Expert: Most of the problem is really that education is not accessible to people in the rural areas, and therefore the parents find it cheaper, better, more profitable to send their children to these organized factories.

Reporter: Child labor is the most visible abuse, but it is not the only one drawing fire in the West. In a country like India, where there is no shortage of cheap labor, adults often work up to eighteen hours a day with no minimum wage and no safety standards. Easy to criticize, India says. But the solution isn't <u>sanctions</u>, it's help in improving its economy

Jane Arraf, CNN, New Delhi.

CHAPTER 14 — Infidelity: Our cheating hearts
Pages 151-162

Summary This chapter presents the very hot topic of infidelity. Reading 1 outlines the two main reasons people cheat, the differences between unfaithful men and unfaithful women, the question of infidelity in unmarried couples, and the prospects for a couple after an affair. Reading 2 is an advice column, and Reading 3 describes two very unusual companies in the U.K. that help people get away with cheating. In Part II, a psychotherapist warns that infidelity can grow from the friendships we form.

Audio The readings in this chapter can be heard on the *Hot Topics 2* Audio CD 2 Tracks 22-25 or Audio Tape 2 Side B.

Background Infidelity is an extremely multi-faceted topic. First comes the question of monogamy. Is it natural? Why is it so important? Next we need to define cheating. Is it cheating when young people date more than one person? Is it cheating if it's just emotional or just over the Internet? Is it the same thing for a man to cheat as for a woman? Then the issue of why people cheat comes up. Do they miss the excitement of new romance? Is there something missing in their marriage? After that is the inevitable emotional devastation, and the question of whether or not to break up. And if that's not enough to make it interesting, infidelity is something with which nearly everyone has some personal experience.

Teaching Note Reading 2 is an example of an advice column similar to those commonly found in newspapers. For additional reading practice, locate an advice column involving infidelity online or in the local newspaper. For writing practice, have each student write a letter to Dear ____, then exchange letters with a partner and write a response containing helpful suggestions. The students will likely have a great time reading the solutions their classmates propose to their imaginary problems!

Internet Activity Invite the students to read more about the agencies mentioned in Reading 3. Articles about both agencies can be found by entering their names in a search engine. Since the nature of the agencies can elicit strong opinions, advise the students to try to detect the tone or bias of the articles they find.

CNN Video Clip Summary Reporter Anderson Cooper argues that monogamy is rare in the animal kingdom, and monogamy among humans is a choice we make for the sake of survival. Whether natural or not, statistics indicate that people think monogamy is a worthy goal—one that approximately 80 percent are able to attain.

Video Script Go to page 90 in this Instructor's Manual for the "Is Monogamy Natural?" video script and recommended video vocabulary for review.

Video Activity Go to page 181 in the student book for activities to accompany the CNN video clip.

ANSWER KEY—Chapter 14: Infidelity: Our cheating hearts

PREVIEW (Page 151)
Answers will vary. (78 percent, 44 percent, 26 percent)

PART I

Predict (Page 152)
1. a. Reading 2
   b. Reading 1
   c. Reading 3
2. d. All of them
3. Answers will vary.
4. Penelope is an advice columnist.
5. Answers will vary.

Reading Comprehension

Check Your Predictions (Page 156): Answers will vary.

Check the Facts

Reading 1 (Page 156)
1. Women are usually unfaithful because they are unhappy in their marriages.
2. Men usually cheat for sexual excitement.
3. Most men are having affairs with emotional ties. Meanwhile, women are having more affairs for the sexual excitement. With more men and women working side-by-side, there's more opportunity for strong emotional connections that didn't exist before.
4. Many unmarried couples don't discuss fidelity. Couples start having sex much sooner and they don't talk about whether the relationship is exclusive or not.
5. "'It depends.'" Most marriages survive an affair and many end up stronger afterwards.

Reading 2 (Page 156)
1. Yes, Confused in California is married.
2. No, her best friend is engaged but not married.
3. Confused in California wants to know whether she should tell her friend that she saw Brad holding hands with and kissing his old girlfriend in the park.
4. Penelope suggests Confused speak with Brad and urge him to call off the wedding if he is unsure about his feelings for Janet.

Reading 3 (Page 157)
1. The companies help the cheaters get away with their lies.
2. The companies will send a phony emergency beeper message, they'll answer the telephone if your partner gets suspicious, and they'll provide alibis.
3. Almost one-fourth of the customers are not married and 40 percent are women.
4. $1.50 from each Ace Alibi annual membership goes to help children of divorce.

Analyze (Page 157)
1. Both Blackwell and Glass would argue that the people who are involved in these affairs have built relationships outside of their marriages and want a way to end their marriages.
2. On the one hand, Reading 1 says that most marriages survive affairs, and can be stronger afterwards, so Brock's quote in Reading 3 could be justified, although it's hard to believe that the experts in Reading 1 would recommend having an affair. On the other hand, affairs usually lead to break-ups for unmarried couples, and ¼ of the agencies' clients are unmarried.
3. Blackwell and Glass would think that Brad is trying to get out of his relationship with Janet.

Vocabulary Work

Guess Meaning from Related Words (Pages 157-158)

1. (Answers may vary.)
   differ: to be different from; to vary
   primarily: mainly; first of all
   sexual: related to sexuality
   problematic: presenting difficulties
   fictional: invented; not factual
   unfaithful: not loyal to one's wife, husband, or lover
   deception: trickery; betrayal
2. (Answers may vary.)
   hows and whys: reasons
   side-by-side: next to each other; together
   the beginning of the end: something is about to end
3. (Answers may vary.)
   deep: The common meaning is far below the surface of something. In the reading it means serious or intense.
   face: The common meaning is the front of the head. In the reading it means to confront or accept a bad situation and be willing to suffer the consequences.

Guess Meaning from Context (Page 158)

1. Answers will vary.
2. *couples:* groups of two people who are married, living together, or dating
   fidelity: faithfulness; loyalty
   exclusive: not including others; restricted
   affair: sexual relationship between two people not married to each other
   engaged: having a formal agreement to get married
   innocent: pure; without sin
   deceive: fool or trick someone
   alibi: proof or excuse that a person didn't commit a crime
   phony: fake; not real
   suspicious: wary; distrusting
   charges: costs; fees
3. Answers will vary.

Understanding Two- and Three-Word Verbs (Page 159)

Answers will vary.
1. *ran off with:* left with someone; ended a relationship to be with someone
2. *deal with:* to manage
3. *end up:* to come to a particular place or position
4. *break up with:* to end a relationship
5. *get out of:* to leave; to remove oneself from responsibility
6. *call off:* to cancel
7. *sign up:* to join; to agree to do something
8. *show up:* to arrive
9. *stand by:* to see something happening and not take action

Reading Skills

Understanding Tone (Page 159)

(Answers may vary.)
Personal: Reading 2
Funny: Reading 3
Academic: Reading 1

Discussion (Pages 159): Answers will vary.

PART II

Read It (Page 160)

1. A long-term relationship both between husbands and wives as well as boyfriends and girlfriends.
2. Emotional as well as sexual relationships.
3. "'When people start trying to hide things, the friendship is becoming something else.'"

Vocabulary Work

Guess Meaning from Related Words (Page 161-162)

1. a. *commit:* committed
   b. *conscious:* unconsciously
   c. *fidelity:* infidelity
   d. *secret:* secrecy
   e. *available:* availability
   f. *unite:* reunions
2. *desirable:* positive characteristic or situation
   bright: positive characteristic or situation
   crisis: negative situation

CNN Video Activities: Is monogamy natural?
Understand It (Page 181)

1. no
2. gorillas; baboons; chimps
3. 3.5 million years ago
4. survival through co-dependence
5. one

VIDEO TRANSCRIPT—Chapter 14: Is monogamy natural?

DVD Title 15   Running time: 2:03

Video Vocabulary

copulate to perform sexual intercourse
harem a group of women associated with one man
monogamy the custom or practice of having only one husband or wife at one time
settle to come to agreement
strive for to work to achieve
urge a desire

Video Script

Minister: With this ring . . .
Bride: With this ring . . .
Minister: . . . I do thee be wed.
Bride: . . . I do thee be wed.
Reporter: It's what we're taught from childhood to believe in: choosing one partner for life. But is monogamy natural? Sure, penguins are known to be monogamous, but most mammals aren't. Of four thousand known species, the vast majority don't couple up for ever. Male gorillas have harems of females, so do baboons. And female chimps, our closest genetic relatives, copulate hundreds of times with different partners for each pregnancy.

Some anthropologists believe our human ancestors settled for monogamy about 3.5 million years ago. The reason: survival through co-dependence. Females needed the men to hunt and protect while they raised the kids. The men needed someone to raise the children while they hunted. This survival coupling slowly evolved into the exclusive relationship: marriage.

Despite estimates that as many as one in five people will have an affair at least once in their life time, most modern couples still say monogamy is something they strive for. For example a University of Chicago survey found 83 percent of adults said they only had one partner or none in the past year.

Woman 1: I don't think it's natural. I think it's a choice that we make.
Woman 2: I think once you've made the decision to partner with a spouse, then I think it is natural to be with them forever.
Man 1: It would be natural. Despite urges. Then again, you're always going to have urges.

Anderson Cooper, CNN, New York.

HOT TOPICS 3: Instructor's Manual

CHAPTER 1
Pages 1–13

The Cruelty of Strangers: Who can you trust?

Summary Chapter One addresses the way we treat our fellow human beings, particularly the ones we don't know. Reading 1 tells the story of a woman who trusted her instincts and did not help a stranger who asked for money, but then worried about her decision. The story in Reading 2 is about a man who did not help a stranger who was being attacked. He feels ashamed and questions his inaction. The reading in Part II describes a psychology experiment conducted at Stanford University in which subjects placed in the role of prison guards quickly became aggressive toward the dehumanized "prisoners" in the experiment.

Audio The readings in this chapter can be heard on the *Hot Topics 3* Audio CD 1 Tracks 1-3 or Audio Tape 1 Side A.

Background From the Greek "xenos," meaning guest or foreigner, we get the word xenophobia—a fear of the unknown or of outsiders. The chapter title, *The Cruelty of Strangers*, shows exactly what we fear: that in fact, we cannot depend on the kindness of strangers. It's not that the people we know always treat us kindly, but what is unknown about strangers allows us to imagine frightening possibilities.

Teaching Note The *Reading Skills* section on page 9 introduces the historical present. Using the present tense in a narrative draws the reader in and gives a sense of immediacy. Demonstrate this idea by asking the students to use the historical present to tell one of their own stories involving contact with a stranger. This can be either a writing assignment or an oral presentation.

Internet Activity Send the students to the Internet to read the introduction to Don George's book *The Kindness of Strangers*, which is a collection of travel stories: http://shop.lonelyplanet.com/samples/kindness_don_george.pdf Ask the students to compare George's ideas to those of the authors of Reading 1 and Reading 2. Alternatively, invite students to read more about the Stanford Prison Experiment at www.prisonexp.org, where they can find photos and video clips of the actual experiment.

Video Clip Summary The CNN clip looks at Project Opp Flop, the Federal Trade Commission's crackdown on businesses that defraud consumers with promises of good incomes for working at home.

Video Script Go to page 93 in this Instructor's Manual for the "Work from Home Scam" video script and recommended video vocabulary for review.

Video Activity Go to page 191 in the student book for activities to accompany the CNN video clip.

ANSWER KEY—Chapter 1: The Cruelty of Strangers: Who can you trust?

PREVIEW (Page 1): Answers will vary.

PART I

Predict (Page 2)
1. personal narratives
2. a. Reading 2
   b. Reading 1
   c. Reading 1 & 2
   d. neither
3. a. Reading 1 & 2
   b. Reading 1
4. Answers will vary.

Reading Comprehension

Check Your Predictions (Page 5): Answers will vary.

Check the Facts (Page 6)

Reading 1
1. a young man at the subway station
2. eight dollars

3. for bus fare to get to his parents
4. She did not believe him. She had many questions and she was suspicious.
5. Yes. She wondered if she had done the right thing, and she called her husband to ask his opinion.
6. In the end, she was jubilant. She was happy she had done the right thing.
7. The belief that she is a good person.

Reading 2

1. at a sandwich shop outside Boston
2. three male friends
3. four drunk men in their twenties
4. a man who had entered the restaurant alone
5. No, he thinks the drunk men are experienced fighters and have weapons.
6. The drunk men leave when the manager says the police are coming.
7. He is shocked by his cowardice; he is ashamed.
8. He isn't sure. He likes to think he would, but now he has a child to consider, too.

Analyze (Page 6): (Answers may vary.)

1. They both made the decision not to help a person who asked for help.
2. Both of them followed their instincts. The woman turned out to be right, but what if the man had really needed the money? The man is ashamed now, but what if he had tried to interfere and been seriously hurt?

Vocabulary Work

Guess Meaning from Context (Page 7)

1. (Answers may vary.)
   pleaded: It's something the young man is doing, and he is asking for money, so it may be similar to ask.
   escalator: It's something the woman stepped off at the subway station, and it looks similar to elevator.
   blinking: It's something the lights were doing to indicate that a train was coming.
   tendency: It could be related to always.
   instincts: She said she didn't feel comfortable giving him money, and her instincts told her something, so they're probably like feelings.
   ignored: She didn't give him the money, so ignore might be to not do something.
   staff: It's different from customers, so maybe it's the people who work at the restaurant.
   reckless: It's some effect of drinking, so maybe it's similar to drunk.
   savagely: It's an adverb to describe beaten, so something like violently.
   companions: There were four of them who escaped, and they were with him, so probably his friends.

2. **Reading 1**
   distressed: something bad
   jubilant: something good
   redeemed: something good

   Reading 2
   insult: something bad
   shame: something bad

3. a. his story was not believable   b. there is a physical feeling of fear   c. in the victim's place, looking at something from the victims point of view

Guess Meaning from Related Words (Page 8)

1. suspect / suspicious
   charity / charitable
   offend / offensive
   injure / injury
   coward / cowardice / cowardly
   assist / assistance

2.
Noun (person): suspect, coward
Noun (thing): charity, injury, cowardice, assistance
Verb: suspect, offend, injure, assist
Adjective: suspicious, charitable, offensive, cowardly
Adverb:

3.

Prefix/Suffix	Meaning	Word	Meaning
mis-	wrong	misread	interpret or read wrongly
in-	not	inaction	not acting
en-	give	endanger	to place in danger
-er	a person who	fighter	someone who fights

Reading Skills

Understanding the Historical Present (Page 9)

1. Reading 2
2. The historical present draws the reader in and gives a sense of immediacy.

Identifying Transition Words (Page 9)
1. Answers will vary.
2. for as long as I can remember
   a few days after . . .
   all these years later
   still

Discussion (Page 9): Answers will vary.

PART II
Read It (Page 10)
1. a study to investigate the effects of being a prison guard or prisoner
2. seventy-five male volunteers
3. prisoners and guards
4. Guards wore a plain khaki shirt, trousers, and reflecting sunglasses. Prisoners wore loose-fitting shirts, rubber sandals, and a hat. The purpose of the uniforms was to increase group identity and reduce individuality.
5. in the basement of a building at Stanford University
6. The guards' one rule was that they were not allowed to use physical punishment.
7. (Answers may vary.) The prisoners were arrested in a realistic and humiliating way; they stood naked and alone in the yard after being sprayed with something; they had to memorize the rules; they had limited toilet visits and limited time for reading or letter writing; they had daily work assignments.
8. (Answers may vary.) The guards became aggressive; the prisoners experienced anxiety and depression; the experiment was called off after only six days.

Vocabulary Work
Guess Meaning from Context (Page 12): Answers will vary.

Reading Skills
Identifying the Author's Purpose (Page 12)
1. The reading is a description. It gives details about the experiment and has a neutral tone.
2. Answers will vary.

CNN Video Activities: Work from Home Scam
Understand It (Page 191)

1. b.   2. d.   3. a.   4. a.   5. d.

VIDEO TRANSCRIPT—Chapter 1: Work from Home Scam
DVD Title 2   Running time: 01:35

Video Vocabulary
bogus   false
crackdown   strong actions taken to stop something; severe discipline
scam   a plan to make money by deception or fraud
teaser   gets attention with promises of something good that doesn't really exist

Video Script
Reporter: In an effort to stop bogus work-at-home businesses, Project Biz Opp Flop is the largest business opportunity fraud <u>crackdown</u> by the Federal Trade Commission and its partners.
Deborah Platt Majoras: Quite simply, they purport to offer the route to fulfilling the American dream. The reality is that these are <u>scams</u> . . .
Reporter: Going after good old-fashioned greed. Law enforcement agencies in over a dozen states have taken action against hundreds of operations that affected tens of thousands of consumers who have lost more than 100 million dollars.
Peter Keisler: The reality is once they write that check and send it in the mail, the money is in all likelihood gone for good.
Reporter: Some of the <u>bogus</u> work-at-home businesses: making refrigerator magnets and stuffing envelopes, which yielded losses of 50 to 100 dollars per consumer, to operating DVD vending machines and coin change machines that in some cases cost consumers their life savings—thirty to forty thousand dollars.
   The FTC says it looked far and wide for someone who got rich at one of these work-at-home opportunities and found no one. The FTC has set up a <u>teaser</u> Web site to educate consumers. Do a search for a work-at-home businesses and this one might pop up, but try to buy into the business and consumers will get warnings about work-at-home

scams. And some questions to ask before investing: Does the ad offer big money for little effort? Are you getting the disclosure documents promised? And can you verify information from current investors? If the answer is yes to the first and no to the others, the FTC says knock elsewhere for opportunity.

Julie Vallese, Washington, D.C.

CHAPTER 2 — CRIME AND PUNISHMENT: JUSTICE FOR ALL?
Pages 14–27

Summary Innocence, guilt, and the justice system are the topics of Chapter Two. Reading 1A discusses a case in which DNA testing exonerated a man who spent seventeen years in prison for sexual assaults he did not commit, and Reading 1B talks about the Innocence Project that helped him. Reading 2 discusses a man whose sentence was commuted after 44 years. In Part II, we learn how the state of Virginia is controlling its prison population, not by reducing crime, but by reducing sentences for those who are statistically less likely to be repeat offenders.

Audio The readings in this chapter can be heard on the *Hot Topics 3* Audio CD 1 Tracks 4-7 or Audio Tape 1 Side A.

Background In 1953, Watson and Crick unveiled their model of the DNA molecule that is responsible for every aspect of heredity, but it was more than thirty years later when Alec Jeffreys discovered a method of "DNA fingerprinting" to identify individuals based on DNA samples. With DNA fingerprinting available, police agencies soon began using DNA evidence in criminal cases. People who were convicted of crimes before the late 1980s or early 1990s were convicted without DNA evidence, so today the Innocence Project works to reverse wrongful convictions in cases where DNA evidence can definitively prove innocence.

Teaching Idea Conduct an experiment to test the reliability of eyewitnesses. First, arrange for a colleague at your school to interrupt class. He or she should enter the room and the two of you should have a brief discussion, preferably with some heated words at the end. Before leaving the room, your colleague should do something surprising such as throw an eraser to the floor angrily or snatch something of yours before leaving hurriedly. After reassuring your students that everything was planned, ask them to write down exactly what happened. Who entered the room? What was he or she wearing? What happened? What was said? Afterwards, have small groups compare answers and try to agree, then report out to the whole class. Would your students make good eyewitnesses? Invite your colleague back and encourage students to check their own reliability as eyewitnesses.

Internet Activity The Innocence Project's homepage at www.innocenceproject.org features a section called *Recent Developments* where students can read about real cases of wrongful conviction and exoneration. The articles describe the crimes that were committed, so if that is not appropriate reading material for your group, have them use a good search engine to find out how DNA fingerprinting works.

CNN Video Clip Summary Reporter Bill Tucker looks at DNA evidence, wrongful convictions, and the death penalty. In Illinois, the governor stayed all pending executions because of the number of reversed convictions based on DNA evidence, and that state has also instituted reforms to prevent future mistakes.

Video Script Go to page 96 in this Instructor's Manual for the "DNA Will Set You Free" video script and recommended video vocabulary for review.

Video Activity Go to page 192 in the student book for activities to accompany the CNN video clip.

ANSWER KEY—Chapter 2: CRIME AND PUNISHMENT: JUSTICE FOR ALL?

PREVIEW (Page 14): Answers will vary.

PART I

Predict (Page 15): (Answers may vary.)

1. Reading 1 because it has a headline and says (AP) for Associated Press

2. All of the readings have something to do with crime and prisoners being released from prison, but the first two readings are about innocent people, and the third is about someone who committed a crime.

Hot Topics 3 • Chapter 2

3. Reading 1A is about a man who was helped by the Innocence Project, and Reading 1B gives information about the Innocence Project.
4. DNA evidence showed that he was not guilty.
5. He served his prison term.
6. Answers will vary.

Reading Comprehension

Check Your Predictions (Page 18): Answers will vary.

Check the Facts (Page 19)

Reading 1A

1. False
2. True
3. True
4. False
5. True
6. True
7. False
8. False

Reading 1B

1. False
2. True
3. True
4. False

Reading 2

1. False
2. False
3. True
4. True
5. False
6. True
7. False
8. False
9. False

Analyze (Page 20): (Answers may vary.)

1. No, because DNA evidence would not have proved him innocent.
2. Murder, because the juries gave him the death sentence and he served for more than 25 years.

Vocabulary Work

Guess Meaning from Context (Page 20)

1. (Answers may vary.)
   DNA: This is biological evidence, so it's something from the body.
   raped: It happened to a woman and she survived, so it could be sexual assault.
   sentenced: This is followed by 75 years, so it means to assign a prison term.
   exonerated: Moon was released from prison, so it means proved innocent.
   testified: It's logical that this is what Moon said.
   assailant: The first woman identified Moon as her attacker, so assailant must be like attacker.
   compensation: It says up to $25,000, so it must be money.
   evidence: My world knowledge tells me that this is used to prove guilt or innocence.
   inmates: They are on the Innocence Project's waiting list, and the project works with people who have been convicted of crimes, so they must be convicted criminals.
2. Answers will vary.

Guess Meaning from Related Words (Page 21)

1. I know line; it means people standing in a line.
   This contains wrong; it means incorrect.
   Turn over; reverse.
   self + educate = educated by oneself
2. racial / race (racial is the adjective form)
   hatred / hate (hatred is the noun form)
3. identify / identified / identification
   photographic / photographs
   testified / testimony
   raped / rapist
   attack / attacker / attacked
   innocence / innocent
4.
   Noun (person): rapist, attacker
   Noun (thing): identification, photographs, testimony, attack, innocence
   Verb: identify / identified, testified, raped, attack / attacked
   Adjective: photographic, innocent
   Adverb:
5. unjust (not just)
   nonprofit (not for profit)
   injustice (lack of justice)
   postconviction (after conviction)
   misidentified (identified wrongly)
   retried (tried again)

Reading Skills

Understanding Appositives (Page 23)

1. district attorney from El Paso County
2. Innocence Project co-director
3. a 19-year-old black janitor
4. a literary prison magazine

Discussion (Page 24): Answers will vary.

PART II

Read It (Page 24)

1. Statistics about who is likely to commit a crime.
2. reduce the prison population
3. They studied criminals.

4. 71 represents the highest possible score. If the score is 38 or less, the defendant doesn't have to go to prison.
5. age; employment; marriage

Vocabulary Work

Guess Meaning from Context (Page 26): Answers will vary.

Reading Skills

Finding Referents (Page 26)

1. predictions
2. who
3. judges in Virginia
4. legislators
5. researchers
6. the criminologists
7. criminals

Video Activities: DNA Will Set You Free
Understand It (Page 192)

1. free
2. revolution
3. letters
4. cleared
5. death row
6. imperfect
7. videotaped
8. evidence

VIDEO TRANSCRIPT—Chapter 2: DNA WILL SET YOU FREE
DVD Title 3   Running time: 02:05

Video Vocabulary

high profile — well-known
reform — change; improvement
statute — a law made by a state or national government
unreliable — undependable, not working well
vulnerable — exposed, unprotected

Video Script

Reporter: DNA evidence set these men free. It also set 130 other prisoners free, prisoners who all, as it turned out, spent years in jails for crimes they were convicted of but did not commit, according to the crime scene DNA evidence.

Peter Neufeld: DNA testing has actually caused a revolution in the criminal justice system. Um . . . On the one hand, the debate on capital punishment has been dramatically transformed. It's no longer people arguing politics or philosophy. But they're wondering whether or not we can allow the ultimate punishment in a system that's so <u>unreliable</u> and so <u>vulnerable</u>.

Reporter: Neufeld currently has 200 pending cases and 4,000 letters asking for help. All of the case reversals so far involved cases before the early 1990's, after which DNA collection and testing became a common crime scene practice. And there have been some very <u>high profile</u> case reversals. The five men convicted in the rape and beating of New York Central Park jogger—free on the basis of DNA evidence. DNA evidence also cleared 13 prisoners on death row in Illinois of crimes they were waiting to die for, prompting the state's then governor to commute the death sentences of all 166 prisoners on death row.

Governor Ryan: There is no margin for error when it comes to putting a person to death.

Reporter: The recent spate of DNA cases are enough to raise the question, is the American justice system broken?

Locke Bowman: I wouldn't say that our system is broken. I would say that it is imperfect and that we have a time and an opportunity here to examine ways in which specific <u>reforms</u> should be enacted in order to begin to correct a problem.

Reporter: Reforms are being put into place. For example, the state of Illinois now has a <u>statute</u> requiring that all confessions be videotaped. And a study by the justice department of 19 labs in the mid-nineties found that 23 percent of suspects were being excluded from further suspicion on the basis of DNA evidence, making wrongful convictions less likely.

Bill Tucker, CNN New York.

CHAPTER 3 — Fertility Now: Babies by Design
Pages 28–42

Summary Chapter Three sizzles with potential controversy. Reading 1 introduces a couple who wants a baby and will pay thousands of dollars for eggs from a tall, blonde donor, and Reading 2 describes women in their 60's who have recently become mothers thanks to fertility treatments. Surrogate motherhood is the topic of Reading 3, and the reading in Part II focuses on a British couple who traveled to the U.S. for in-vitro fertilization since selecting an embryo to become a tissue donor for their older child is illegal where they live.

Audio The readings in this chapter can be heard on the *Hot Topics 3* Audio CD 1 Tracks 8-11 or Audio Tape 1 Side A.

Background In an ironic twist, people in the developed world who grew up with a focus on limiting fertility may find themselves desperate to promote fertility later in life. In the 1960s, the birth control pill made headlines, and abortion was legalized in the U.S. in the 1970s. These developments coincided with a greater number of women in higher education and in the workplace, and an older average age for first births. With conception more difficult for older couples, interest in fertility options runs high nowadays.

Teaching Note Hot topics such as the ones in Chapter 3 can lead to very interesting discussions if your students are comfortable talking about human reproduction. Provide a speaking opportunity for your students by conducting a class debate on one of the issues from the chapter that your group found interesting. Write a statement such as "There should be a legal age limit for fertility treatments," then divide the class in half and randomly assign "pro" to one half and "con" to the other. Give the groups sufficient time to prepare their own arguments and predict those of the opposing group. Then set up a debate format that includes time limits for opening statements, rebuttals, and closing arguments.

Internet Activity Find a good fertility website for your students to visit such as www.babycentre.co.uk or www.fertilitext.org. Have them explore the options for infertile couples, and then report back to the class or write a report describing what they thought was the most surprising information and the most helpful information. Use the reports as a starting point for class discussion.

Video Clip Summary The video clip discusses surrogacy in general, including technical aspects of the fertilization procedure, and the success story of a couple whose son was born with the help of a surrogate mother. The clip follows the group through their attempt to create a second child for the infertile couple, and includes scenes of Sam on the table for the implantation procedure, but is free of anything graphic.

Video Script Go to page 99 in this Instructor's Manual for the "A Surrogate's Story" video script and recommended video vocabulary for review.

Video Activity Go to page 193 in the student book for activities to accompany the CNN video clip.

ANSWER KEY—Chapter 3: Fertility Now: Babies by Design

PREVIEW (Page 28): Answers will vary.

PART I

Predict (Page 29)
A:
1. Readings 2 & 3; Reading 1
2. Readings 1, 2, & 3; Readings 1 & 2; Reading 1
3. Answers will vary.
4. Answers will vary.

Reading Comprehension

Check Your Predictions (Page 33): Answers will vary.

Check the Facts (Page 34)

Reading 1
1. They ran the ad in Reading 1 in March 1999. They are all Ivy League schools.
2. musical ability and beauty
3. $50,000
4. They said the couple was elitist.
5. They wanted the child to be as similar to themselves as possible.

6. Women have a limited number of eggs, and the egg donor must undergo surgery.

Reading 2

1. 263; around 240
2. 66
3. nine years
4. an anonymous sperm donor
5. 65
6. 50 years
7. Mrs. Mahapatra's niece

Reading 3

1. a woman who carries another woman's child
2. No, because they can be implanted with another woman's fertilized eggs.
3. her brother and sister-in-law
4. Aunt Jody (Answers may vary, but she calls her own children the baby's cousins.)
5. She is Hammond's mother.
6. They can avoid legal problems.
7. Laws and health problems can create problems for family relationships.

Vocabulary Work

Guess Meaning from Context (Page 35)

1. (Answers may vary.)
   candidates: a person or thing ready for something
   sperm: a male cell with a tail that can join with a female cell and make babies
   limited: within limits; restricted
   elitist: thinking that one is superior to other people
   surgery: the medical practice of treating injuries and disease by operating on the body
   donor: one who gives without charge
   trend: a general curve or pattern
   ethical: related to moral or correct behavior
   conceive: to become pregnant
   anonymous: not named; unknown
   fraternal: twins from two separate eggs (not identical twins)

2. In artificial insemination, a doctor injects semen into a woman's uterus.
   In this procedure, egg and sperm are combined in a laboratory.
   A surrogate mother is a woman who carries another woman's child.

3. (Answers may vary.)
   turn to: look for help from
   taken lightly: done easily without careful consideration
   give birth: have a baby

Guess Meaning from Related Words (Page 36)

1. under and go: go through something
   increase: more and more
   long and live: something that lives a long time
   long and wait: something that people waited for a long time

2. donate / donor
   elite / elitist
   surgeon / surgery / surgical
   semen / inseminated
   fertile / fertility / fertilized / fertilization

3.
Noun (person): donor, elitist, surgeon
Noun (thing): surgery, semen, fertility / fertilization
Verb: donate, inseminated, fertilized
Adjective: elite, surgical, fertile
Adverb:

4. *implanted:* placed inside the uterus
   nontraditional: not in a traditional way
   eggless: without eggs
   childless: without children
   unusual: not usual
   unlimited: not limited
   unable: not able
   unsuccessful: not successful

Analyze (Page 37)

1. **Adrianna Iliescu:** Artificial insemination
   Satyabhama Mahapatra: third-party egg donor
   Jody Williams: in-vitro fertilization
   Tina Cade: in-vitro fertilization

2. **Adrianna Iliescu:** genetic mother
   Satyabhama Mahapatra: birth mother
   Jody Williams: birth mother
   Jody's sister-in-law: caregiving mother
   Tina Cade: birth mother
   Camille Hammond: caregiving mother

Reading Skills

Understanding the Author's Purpose (Page 38)

1. Reading 1: instruct
   Reading 2: warn
   Reading 3: describe
2. (Answers may vary.)

Reading 1: Why are eggs so much more valuable? Men have an unlimited amount of sperm... (The author asks a question and then answers it.)

Reading 2: ... one has to wonder about children raised by elderly parents.

Reading 3: Some women become surrogates for money. Some do it to help friends and relatives. (The author describes kinds of surrogates.)

PART II

Read It (Page 39)

1. He had a rare blood condition.
2. to be a genetic match for Charlie
3. They did not get permission from the government in the UK to select an embryo.
4. The Hashmi boy's illness was hereditary; the Whitakers' was not. The Hashmi's child was going to be born anyway; the Whitakers would only implant an embryo that was a genetic match.
5. They think designing a child as a tissue donor for a sick sibling is undesirable, unnecessary, and that the current decision-making process is undemocratic.

Vocabulary Work

Guess Meaning from Context (Page 40): Answers will vary.

Reading Skills

Identifying Main Ideas and Evaluating Types of Supporting Details (Page 41): Answers will vary.

CNN Video Activities: A Surrogate's Story

Understand It (Page 193)

1. False
2. True
3. True
4. False
5. False
6. False
7. False
8. True
9. True
10. False

VIDEO TRANSCRIPT—Chapter 3: A Surrogate's Story

DVD Title 4   Running time: 03:22

Video Vocabulary

going for the gravy   something extra
ovary   the organ of a woman or a female animal that produces eggs
step   one action toward a goal
surrogate   a person who acts in place of another; a substitute
synchronize   to coordinate the schedule or timing of one or more activities
uterus   female organ where a baby develops; the womb

Video Script

Reporter: This is a story about the Guagenti family, and the extraordinary steps the couple took to become parents.

Pam: When I found out I couldn't have kids, I just, always in my head I knew I would, somehow. I would, I would.

Reporter: Pam was born without a uterus, but she has ovaries that produce eggs.

Doctor: This is a person who a decade ago would have been hopeless. There would have been no way for her to have a baby except by adoption.

Reporter: So Pam and husband Gary turned to Sam, a surrogate to have their child. Sam's husband Tristan agreed. They have two sons of their own.

Sam: I love being a mom; I have two beautiful sons of my own. Can't imagine, can't imagine someone ever telling me, 'Sorry, you're never going to have a baby—your own.'

Reporter: The couples entered into an agreement. Sam carried the Guagenti's baby for nine months. His name is Chase. Then, she handed him over.

Sam: I carried a baby; it wasn't my genetic anything. It was their baby, biologically, completely. And I just was an oven.

Pam: I can't explain what she did. I mean, she gave us our son, you know, and hopefully another son or daughter. That was the night we met.

Reporter: The Guagentis and the Woods were so successful the first time around, they decided to do it again. You have to go through the morning sickness, through the stretch marks. Anybody who's had a baby knows that's not easy. Why do you do it?

Sam: Um, everyone always asks that question. Um . . . I don't have really bad pregnancies. I actually like being pregnant.

Reporter: Dr. Art Wisot is a reproductive specialist.
Doctor Wisot: It's pretty rare for this to be so successful that they would get to the point that they have a baby and are now going for the gravy, which is the second baby.
Reporter: But it's a complex process. Both women must first take drugs to synchronize their cycles. Pam's is stimulated to produce eggs, while Sam's cycle is suppressed. So essentially, you are renting her womb, or she is acting as an incubator?
Doctor Wisot: That's exactly what she's doing. She's acting as an incubator for this pregnancy. And we want to be sure that that pregnancy is Pam and Gary's pregnancy.
Reporter: Pam and Gary's embryos were created here in this lab over a year and a half ago using Gary's sperm and Pam's eggs. They were just thawed out, and in a few moments they'll be transferred into Samantha.
Reporter: Gary and Pam are able to look at their embryos.
Pam: This is everything I want. It's right there. And not many people get to see their kids right there.

Nurse: Get undressed. You can leave your top on.
Reporter: Everyone is present for the procedure.
Doctor: We want her uterus to relax as much as possible. You'll see the catheter come up here and deposit the embryos right about there.
Reporter: Three embryos make the journey. The whole thing takes just minutes.
Doctor Wisot: Congratulations. Good luck.
Reporter: Two weeks later we check back. What are the results?
Pam: They were negative, which, surprisingly we weren't as upset as we thought we were going to be. I think we were just more prepared this time.
Sam: I mean, I knew I was in it for the long haul. I am in it for the long haul.
Reporter: What does that mean?
Sam: It means until we get a pregnancy.
Reporter: A disappointment this time, but they will try again next month. After all, Chase is proof it works.

Thelma Gutierrez, CNN Los Angeles.

CHAPTER 4 — Gambling: Wanna bet?
Pages 43–53

Summary Chapter 4 discusses several aspects of gambling. In Reading 1, we meet a man who makes his living playing online poker. Reading 2 gives information about problem gambling, and provides a test for determining if someone is a compulsive gambler. In Part II, a former gambler explains why people really gamble, and he says it's *not* for the money.

Audio The readings in this chapter can be heard on the *Hot Topics 3* Audio CD 1 Tracks 12–14 or Audio Tape 1 Side B.

Background It's a little hard to believe that Major League Baseball's all-time hit leader cannot be found in the National Baseball Hall of Fame in Cooperstown, New York. And what is keeping long-time player and manager of the Cincinnati Reds, Pete Rose, from attaining that honor? Although he still maintains his innocence, Rose was accused of betting on baseball games. It may be legal in many places, but it is not part of America's vision of wholesome family entertainment.

Teaching Note After reading Chapter 4, the students will have quite a bit of information about the problems associated with gambling. Have them apply this knowledge by discussing the case of Greg Lawrence in Reading 1. Is Lawrence a problem gambler? How can we tell? Why does Lawrence enjoy his "job"? How is it possible for him to beat the odds and make money from gambling? Will he have a hard time giving it up in the future?

Internet Activity Reading 2 mentions that eighteen states allow gambling on Indian reservations. If your students wonder why, have them research the subject on the Internet and write a short report. They may also be interested in the ways reservations use the money that is generated by casinos, and in the ways that states benefit from the tax dollars generated by casinos.

CNN Video Clip Summary The reporter speaks with Arnie Wexler, a recovering compulsive gambler who runs a hotline for people looking for help with their gambling problems. He describes a low point in his life when he contemplated suicide, and explains that because gambling is a behavioral problem, it is an invisible addiction, and one that is not covered by most insurance policies.

Video Script Go to page 102 in this Instructor's Manual for the "Gambling Addiction—Chasing the Big Win" video script and recommended video vocabulary for review.

Video Activity Go to page 194 in the student book for activities to accompany the CNN video clip.

ANSWER KEY—Chapter 4: *Gambling: Wanna bet?*

PREVIEW (Page 43)
1. poker—d; roulette—e; slot machine—a; Bingo—c; lottery—b
2. Answers will vary.
3. Answers will vary.

PART I

Predict (Page 44)
1. (Answers may vary.)
   The topic of Reading 1 is probably a man who plays poker for a living.
   The topic of Reading 2 is probably problems associated with gambling.
2. Reading 1 and Reading 2 probably come from textbooks. They have numbered lines and Reading 2 also contains a footnote.
3. Answers will vary.

Reading Comprehension

Check Your Predictions (Page 47): Answers will vary.

Check the Facts

Reading 1 (Page 47)
1. No, because most people are interested in it.
2. $40 an hour
3. 30 hours a week
4. He plays tennis.
5. Online poker is faster because no one talks during the game, and nobody can see you when you play online poker.
6. He does not have a good poker face, so he does better with online poker.
7. When your cards are bad, you have to stop.
8. $5,000 in both cases
9. He lost $1,500 in one day and it destroyed his confidence.
10. No, because he wants to get married and have children, and he doesn't want to tell his children that he's a professional gambler.

Reading 2 (Page 48)
1. a. one type of person who gambles
   b. people who gamble more than they can afford to spend
   c. a gambler who has a disease; The compulsive gambler cannot stop.
2. Answers will vary. Any of #1 to #13 on lines 18-30.

Analyze (Page 48)
1. He might have thought that gambling wasn't a respectable job.
2. He means that he doesn't feel compelled to play poker. It's not an addiction or disease for him.
3. Since bluffing in poker is a kind of lying, it's important that the other players not know if you have good cards or bad cards.

Vocabulary Work

Guess Meaning from Related Words (Page 48)
1. bet / bettor
2. legal / legally / illegally
3. gamble / gambler / gambling

Guess Meaning from Context (Page 48)
1. a. *bluff* lines 15 & 19 (Reading 1)—to make people think your hand is better than it really is
   b. *casino* line 18 (Reading 1)—a place where people gamble
   c. *hand* line 18 (Reading 1)—the cards that you are holding
   d. *poker face* lines 15 & 19 (Reading 1)—not smiling or frowning

Analyzing Words and Phrases (Page 49)

A. 1. & 2.
Verb: win, bet, gamble
Noun (person): winner, bettor, gambler
Noun (thing): win, bet, gambling / gamble

3. profession / professional
short-term / long-term
confidence / overconfident
know / knowledge

B. Phrase: *body language*, Lines 13-14 (Reading 1)
Meaning: a person's gestures and facial expressions
Phrase: *against the law*, Line 3 (Reading 2)
Meaning: an illegal activity

PART II
Read It (Page 50)

1. because the odds are in favor of the casinos
2. He would wait until one color had come up several times, then start betting on the other color, doubling his bet after each losing bet.
3. They confuse the short-term outcome with the long-term probability.
4. They enjoy the thrill of taking a risk.
5. They have in common a build-up, climax, and release of tension.

Vocabulary Work

Guess Meaning from Context (Page 51): Answers will vary.

Reading Skills

Identifying the Author's Opinion (Page 52)

1. He probably thinks that gambling is unwise. He says it would be "crazy" and "It makes no sense;" He talks about losing $225 at roulette; He mentions the "mistake" that most beginning gamblers make; He compares gambling games to drugs.
2. Before he started gambling, he thought he could definitely win. The system he worked out for roulette shows this. His opinion has changed. Now, he doesn't think people gamble for money, but rather for the thrill of taking a risk.
3. He probably thinks that gambling is unwise. He says it would be "crazy" and "It makes no sense;" He talks about losing $225 at roulette; He mentions the "mistake" that most beginning gamblers make; He compares gambling games to drugs.

CNN Video Activities: Gambling Addiction—Chasing the Big Win
Understand It (Page 194)

1. Arnie is a compulsive gambler.
2. Arnie now runs a hotline for compulsive gamblers.
3. Arnie wished he had enough guts to kill himself.
4. Compulsive gamblers can't control themselves.
5. An invisible addiction has no telltale physical signs.
6. The thrill of gambling and the idea that they will hit it big drives the compulsion to gamble.
7. Every day of his life Arnie chased the Big Win.
8. Insurance companies do not cover treatment for compulsive gamblers because it is viewed as a behavioral problem, something that most people should be able to control.

VIDEO TRANSCRIPT—Chapter 4: *Gambling Addiction—Chasing the Big Win*
DVD Title 5   Running time: 02:21

Video Vocabulary
guts   courage, determination
hotline   a telephone number people can call when they need help
telltale   an identifying sign
thrill   a feeling of strong excitement, fear, or pleasure

Video Script

Reporter: The attraction is irresistible. Bright lights, glitzy rooms, and lots of money for the taking, if you're lucky enough to win it. It seems like a fun time, but for many, gambling is a compulsion, an addiction that destroys lives. Arnie Wexler is a reformed compulsive gambler, who now runs a hotline for gamblers. He says gambling nearly destroyed him.

Arnie Wexler: I was running around at the time in my life wishing and praying I had enough guts to kill myself. I thought that if I killed myself and left my wife with 5,000 dollars worth of insurance and two kids in the house, it was the only way out of this mess.

Reporter: Clinical psychiatrist Doctor David Yamins says compulsive gambling is a real illness.

Doctor Yamins: The addiction to gambling is different in that it's purely a behavior. It's not an addiction to a chemical, to a substance, but it involves a similar process in that it's a compulsive behavior that the person has no control over.

Reporter: And because there is no chemical or substance, gambling is an invisible addiction. There are no telltale physical signs, no track marks, no smell of alcohol. Wexler says that's what makes the compulsive gambler so elusive.

Arnie Wexler: I'm going to tell you that I'm recovering 31 years and you don't know I just didn't come from buying a thousand lottery tickets, or calling my bookmaker before you walked in here or I just didn't come up from Atlantic City an hour ago.

Reporter: What drives the compulsion to gamble? Doctor Yamins says it's the thrill.

Doctor Yamins: They're holding onto the myth, the idea that they're going to hit it with one big turn of the wheel, or one big play of the slots, that they can correct all the troubles in their lives.

Reporter: Many compulsive gamblers do occasionally have large paydays. Wexler's had a few. But that only made things worse.

Arnie Wexler: I chased that big win every day of my life, figuring that I could do this again.

Reporter: Even though gambling is considered a legitimate medical diagnosis, it's not covered by most major insurance companies. That's because society views compulsive gambling as a behavioral problem, as something most people should be able to control. Experts say that policy is unlikely to change unless society views compulsive gambling as a true addiction.

Dr. Steve Salvatore, CNN, New York.

CHAPTER 5 — THE DISABLED: HANDICAPPED? NOT US!
Pages 54–66

Summary This chapter works to dispel myths about people with disabilities and highlight some of their achievements. Reading 1 is a list of common myths and stereotypes about the disabled along with the facts that refute them. Reading 2 concentrates on the deaf community, looking back at past prejudices and ahead to possible changes in their culture that some deaf people fear will come with technological advances. The reading in Part II is about one disabled person, Kyle Maynard, and his personal, academic, and athletic achievements and positive outlook on life.

Audio The readings in this chapter can be heard on the *Hot Topics 3* Audio CD 1 Tracks 15-17 or Audio Tape 1 Side B.

Background The first schools for the deaf opened in Europe in the 1700's. Louis Braille began attending a school for the blind in Paris in 1819. Since then, disabled people have continued to make progress in earning equal consideration in society and under the law. Modern day people with disabilities include author and speaker Helen Keller (she was blind and deaf), physicist Stephen Hawking (Lou Gehrig's disease), deaf baseball player Curtis John Pride, and even Rick Allen, the drummer for rock group Def Leppard who re-learned to play after an auto accident left him with only one arm. The Americans with Disabilities Act (ADA), which took effect in 1992 and prohibits any employer from discriminating against disabled workers, was a legal triumph for disabled people in the United States and has led to a huge increase in accessible workplaces and employment possibilities.

Teaching Note English morphology is often a challenge for learners, who may confuse one grammatical form of a word with another. Item #3 on page 60 instructs the students to work in pairs to complete a chart containing different forms of the vocabulary words in item #2 on page 60. After the pairs have checked to see that they have all the words in all the right columns, ask them to write sentences using the words in order to provide active language practice. For example, they might write *The opera singer has a lovely voice*, and *Only some Deaf people are able to use vocal communication*.

Internet Activity Invite the students to find out more about the famous people pictured on page 54. They can enter the names in a good search engine to find articles, then report back to the rest of the class. Assign each of the celebrities to one or more of the students in order to get reports on everyone who is pictured.

Video Clip Summary Reporter Frank Buckley visits a deaf football team in Riverside, California. The team is in the playoffs and won their league championship the year before. Coach Len Gonzales encourages the players to think about their abilities rather than their deafness, and the players themselves hope to earn respect for the fact that they can play football.

Video Script Go to page 107 in this Instructor's Manual for the "A Deaf Football Team" video script and recommended video vocabulary for review.

Video Activity Go to page 195 in the student book for activities to accompany the CNN video clip.

ANSWER KEY—Chapter 5: THE DISABLED: HANDICAPPED? NOT US!

PREVIEW (Answers on page 55.)

PART I

Predict (Page 55)

1. a. neither, b. Reading 1 c. Reading 2
   d. Reading 1 and Reading 2
2. Answers will vary.

Reading Comprehension

Check Your Predictions (Page 58): Answers will vary.

Check the Facts (Page 58)

Reading 1

1. False
2. True
3. False
4. True
5. False

Reading 2

1. The blind can communicate verbally; the Deaf cannot, so traditionally they've been more isolated from society.
2. Lip reading is a convenient way for deaf people to communicate with hearing people; ASL is the first language (main way of communicating) of most deaf people.
3. Long ago, the Deaf could not own property. Bell campaigned against sign language and believed deaf people should not marry each other.
4. Closed-captioned TV's and the Internet keep deaf people at home. They don't socialize in big groups as much.
5. surgery to improve the hearing of people with very limited hearing
6. They believe it is a rejection of deaf culture.
7. an operation that would change people from black to white

Analyze (Page 59): (Answers may vary.)

1. Any of the myths could have applied since they all separate disabled people from "normal" people. People who are different are easier to discriminate against.
2. People may still believe all of the myths. That is why the author wrote the article.

Vocabulary Work

Guess Meaning from Context (Page 59): (Answers may vary.)

Word	Reading	Type of clue	Meaning
assumption	1	c. logic (It is followed by an opinion, so it's like "think.")	to believe something is true without knowing
carry out	1	c. logic (It's like "do" since it is about activities.)	to do or perform some task
devices	1	c. logic (It comes after "high-tech".)	an electrical or mechanical machine
utensil	1	e. definitions or synonyms in the reading (device)	a tool or implement, especially for eating food
Velcro	1	c. logic (It comes before "strap," looks like a brand.)	a patented material for closing or attaching things
severe	1	c. logic ("Even those with . . ." It must be the worst kind.)	very strong
constant	1	c. logic (some kind of supervision)	happening all the time; continuous
adequate	1	c. logic (some kind of community services)	enough; sufficient
animatedly	2	b. knowledge of the Deaf (I have seen this.)	in a lively manner
unique	2	c. logic (It must be something like "special.")	singular; one of a kind
innovators	2	d. examples in the reading (Bell invented the telephone.)	person who makes or does something new
campaigned	2	c. logic (He was against sign language.)	an organized effort by people to reach a goal
distinct	2	b. knowledge of the Deaf (They have their own culture.)	separate; different
advances	2	c. logic (technological)	improvements
closed-captioned	2	c. logic (TV that deaf people can understand)	television with subtitles
shunned	2	a. knowledge of social attitudes	(how people treat "former friends") to reject

2. (Answers may vary.)
"Sign Language Barbie" dolls may signify that the mainstream culture recognizes and/or accepts the Deaf more than before. Closed-captioned television may mean the same thing, although the article also mentions its detrimental effects on the Deaf community.

Guess Meaning from Related Words (Page 60)

1. wheel + chair = a chair with wheels
   sign + language = a way of talking using signs (gestures)
   lip + read = to understand someone by watching their lips

2. **Reading 1**
   able / disability / disabled / nondisabled
   hero / heroic
   damage / damaging
   afford / affordable
   social / society

   Reading 2
   voice / vocal
   convenient / convenience
   reject / rejection
   cohere / cohesion
   bible / biblical
   active / activist
   dominate / dominant
   social / socialize

3. Noun (person): hero, activist
   Noun (thing): disability, damage, society, voice, convenience, rejection, cohesion, bible
   Verb: afford, socialize, reject, cohere, dominate
   Adjective: able / disabled / nondisabled, heroic, damaging, affordable, social, vocal, convenient, biblical, active, dominant
   Adverb:

4. *intermarry*—form a marriage between Deaf people
   nondisabled—not disabled

Reading Skills

Identifying Time Markers (Page 61)

In the future; Years ago; Today; In the age of . . . ; In biblical times; As recently as the last century; In the past; In recent years

PART II

Read It (Page 62)

1. He's an honor role student. He's one of the top high school wrestlers in Georgia. He has won two awards.
2. He feels like an average guy and doesn't want to be admired.
3. before he was born
4. They let him learn to do things for himself.
5. It was hard on him. Both his feet were broken.
6. No. He lost his first 35 matches.
7. They developed special wrestling moves that take advantage of Kyle's low center of gravity.
8. It's not what I *can* do; it's what I *will* do.
9. He's traveling across the country as a motivational speaker.
10. He is able to try to help people.

Vocabulary Work

Guess Meaning from Context (Page 64): Answers will vary.

Reading Skills

Understanding Introductory or Fronted Phrases (Page 65)

1. Kyle quickly taught himself to hold objects between his two highly sensitive bicep muscles by watching other toddlers hold crayons in their fingers.
2. The game was tough on Kyle despite his determination.
3. Kyle uses a problem that the world sees as a handicap as a gift.
4. He replies, "Not really" when he is asked if he ever thinks, "Why me?"

CNN Video Activities: A Deaf Football Team
Understand It (Page 195)

1. True
2. True
3. False
4. False
5. True
6. False
7. False

VIDEO TRANSCRIPT—Chapter 5: A DEAF FOOTBALL TEAM

DVD Title 6   Running time: 02:26

Video Vocabulary

beat   to defeat an opponent
cheerleader   a person who leads cheers at a sporting event
feel sorry   to have sympathy for
quarterback   in USA and Canada, the football player who tells the others what to do and starts the team's action
sign   to use finger motions to communicate with people who can't hear
snap   in football, delivering the ball to the quarterback
whistle   a small pipe or instrument that makes a whistle

Video Script

Reporter: Under the Friday night lights in Riverside, California, this team is making history. For the first time in the history of the California School for the Deaf in Riverside, the school's football team is playing as league champion. Maybe you didn't notice when the quarterback didn't call for the snap, or when the cheerleaders signed to the fans. If you didn't, these players and their coaches have succeeded, because they don't want you to see them as deaf football players, but as football players who are deaf.

Mark Korn: The deaf and hearing are . . . are the same, you know, we just can't hear, you know, we can play football.

Reporter: And play it well. This is what a perfectly executed play looks and sounds like to them. The Cubs of Riverside went into this playoff game with a 9 and 1 record.

Len Gonzales: You belong where you're at.

Reporter: Under head coach Len Gonzales.

Len Gonzales: When I arrived here, I told the players to stop . . . stop feeling sorry for themselves. "I can't beat hearing schools." You know, "They're too strong for us." He says, "No, you're equal, you know. You have equal opportunities. You have eyes. You know, the only thing you can't do is hear."

Reporter: They don't hear the whistle, they simply stop when the play is over. There's no cadence. Players go when the ball is snapped. Coaches communicate by signing. They insist on receiving no special treatment, but they do ask the referees to clearly use hand signals on the field. Referees oblige the deaf coaches. Opposing teams regularly underestimate the deaf players.

Gary Sidansky: I think at first they react like we're nothing. We're handicapped. We can't do anything. But after the game they realize that we can play football.

Reporter: Tackle William Albright, articulates what he and his teammates hope to gain this season. Read his lips.

William Albright: Respect.

Reporter: On this night they got it. Scoring more points in a playoff game than any in the school's history, 27. But in the end it wasn't enough. They lost. Still, their journey from boys who didn't believe in themselves to young men who made it to the playoffs is one for the history books.

Frank Buckley, CNN Riverside, California.

CHAPTER 6 — MARRIAGE: WHY MARRY JUST ONE?
Pages 67–78

Summary Is nothing sacred? Chapter 6 tells us that traditional marriages consisting of a married couple with children are now clearly a minority. In Reading 1 we learn that couples are choosing to live together rather than get married, and one researcher predicts a future full of single parents. Reading 2 introduces a Utah polygamist who is serving prison time for marrying five wives and fathering twenty-five children, and the reading in Part II discusses Internet brides, an update on the mail-order brides of earlier generations.

Audio The readings in this chapter can be heard on the *Hot Topics 3* Audio CD 1 Tracks 18-20 or Audio Tape 1 Side B.

Background One common note rings through the widely diverse views on marriage found in this chapter, and that is choice. Couples choosing to live together before marriage or choosing not to marry at all would have been unthinkable in the past, just as someone who chooses to have five wives, or to be married to someone with multiple wives is a shock to many of us now. Choosing to look outside one's country for a mate with the help of the Internet, or choosing to take a chance on such a match due to the economic pressure in one's homeland also represent newer options. Not everyone will agree that people *should* have all these choices when it comes to marriage, but everyone is sure to have an opinion!

Teaching Note A graphic organizer is a way for students to analyze the information found in a reading, and it may be especially appealing to the more visual learners in your group. Use a Venn diagram (two large, overlapping circles) to analyze the reading about mail-order brides in Part II. Label one circle "Picture Brides" and the other "Mail-Order Brides". In the center section where the circles overlap, have students write the similarities between the two, for example the fact that in both cases, men could find wives from faraway countries. Then write the differences in the appropriate circles so that it is easy to see what the two have in common and what is distinct about each.

Internet Activity Two websites with nearly identical URLs offer completely opposing points of view on polygamy. Students can find pro-polygamy information at www.polygamy.com, then read about allegations of mistreatment and child abuse at www.polygamy.org, which is sponsored by the non-profit group Tapestry Against Polygamy. Have a discussion about bias after the students read these two very different websites. Alternatively, have the students use a good Internet search engine to find out more about Margaret Mead's views on "modern marriage", or the reasons men and women choose to get involved in "mail-order marriages".

Video Clip Summary The video clip exposes a case of bigamy—well, it was almost bigamy. After his first wife's death, a Florida man married the woman he had been seeing secretly for 20 years, and with whom he had two children. People quickly realized that he had been living a double life.

Video Script Go to page 110 in this Instructor's Manual for the "Father's Double Life" video script and recommended video vocabulary for review.

Video Activity Go to page 196 in the student book for activities to accompany the CNN video clip.

ANSWER KEY—Chapter 6: MARRIAGE: WHY MARRY JUST ONE?

PREVIEW (Page 67): Answers will vary.

PART I
Predict (Page 68)
A. a. a human interest story, b. a news article
B. 1. a. Both
   b. Reading 1
   c. Reading 2
2. a Mormon polygamist who lives in Utah
3. Answers will vary.

Reading Comprehension

Check Your Predictions (Page 71): Answers will vary.

Check the Facts (Page 71)

Reading 1
A. a. 56%   e. 38%
   b. 75%   f. 55%
   c. 26%   g. 40%
   d. 45%

B.

1. Now it is instead of marriage rather than before marriage.
2. Relationships will be shorter, and in-vitro fertilization will be used.

Reading 2

1. Utah
2. five years
3. 25 years
4. polygamy is a tradition of Mormon culture
5. no
6. Green's children

Analyze (Page 72): (Answers may vary.)

Green's marriage is like the 26 percent of Americans who are married with children, except that Green has five wives instead of one. Green is unlike the couples who choose cohabitation over marriage.

Vocabulary Work

Guess Meaning from Context (Page 72): (Answers may vary.)

1. *proportion:* the relationship of one part of something to another part in size and shape
   cohabitation: living together
   prelude: something that comes before
   mobility: capability of going from one place to another
   in-vitro fertilization: the combining of an egg and sperm in a test tube
   concurrent: at the same time
   bigamy: having two wives
   remote: distant
   compound: a group of buildings
   give up: to stop doing something
   thrown out of: forced to leave
   pleading: requesting urgently
2. *Opinionated* is probably negative because it contrasts with *hardworking*, which is positive.
   Obnoxious is probably negative because it is in addition to *loud*, which is negative.
   Distressed is probably negative because it contrasts with *enthusiastic*, which is positive.
   Adored is probably positive because it contrasts with *badly*, which is negative.

Guess Meaning from Related Words (Page 73)

1.
   tradition / traditional
   increase / increasingly
   sex / sexual
   possible / possibility
   polygamy / polygamist
   prison / imprisonment

2.
Noun (person): polygamist
Noun (thing): tradition, increase, sex, possibility, polygamy, prison / imprisonment
Verb:
Adjective: traditional, sexual, possible
Adverb: increasingly

Reading Skills

Identifying Cohesive Words and Phrases (Page 74)

1. married for the first time
2. no referent
3. people
4. marriage
5. cohabitation instead of marriage
6. single parent families will be normal
7. count
8. polygamy
9. people (implied referent)
10. polygamy

PART II

Read It (Page 75)

1. Picture brides usually married men from the same ethnic groups as them. Mail order brides often come from different countries than picture brides did.
2. the Philippines, Thailand, Latin America, and the former Soviet Union
3. Australia, North America, Western Europe, and Japan
4. They use an Internet bride service.
5. subservient, obedient, devoted to husbands and families, uncorrupted by feminism, good Catholic girls
6. No, because many of the brides are white, and some of the men are not.
7. It's not harmless because many women get involved due to poverty and they can be abused.

Vocabulary Work

Guess Words from Context (Page 77): Answers will vary.

Reading Skills

Understanding Advanced Punctuation (Page 77)

1. "Picture bride" was a new term at that time. It had not normally been used before.
2. Usually one orders a product—a thing—but here, the men are ordering human beings.
3. Here, "traditional" refers to something that never really existed because it was just a stereotype. Usually it refers to things that have lasted a long time.
4. "Sell" usually means exchange an item for money. Here, it refers to advertising.

CNN Video Activities—Father's Double Life

Understand It (Page 196)

1. Jean Ann Cone was a woman from Tampa who enjoyed fundraising.
2. She died from carbon monoxide intoxication.
3. Douglas Cone was Jean Ann Cone's husband.
4. Donald Carlson was the alias or other name used by Douglas Cone.
5. Hillary Carlson was the woman with whom he had an affair.
6. Yes. They sat on the school board together.
7. After Jean Ann Cone died, he went to the Sumter County courthouse to apply for a marriage license.
8. Friends and family found out that something was wrong when Cone married Hillary at the courthouse.
9. Cone's eldest son knew about the double life.

VIDEO TRANSCRIPT—Chapter 6: Father's Double Life
DVD Title 7   Running time: 02:49

Video Vocabulary

alias a name used to hide one's identity, especially by criminals, a false name
autopsy a medical examination of a dead human body to determine what caused death
carbon monoxide an extremely poisonous gas with no color, taste, or smell, and occurring especially in the exhaust from gasoline engines
pass out lose consciousness
socialite a person who is well-known among fashionable, rich people
upscale expensive; high-class

Video Script

Reporter: Jean Ann Cone. Her friends call her a socialite with a conscience. Always raising money for causes. Active in the art museum. On the board of the exclusive prep school her three children attended.
Investigator 1: From, uh, all accounts, she was a wonderful lady.
Reporter: Married for more than 50 years to the wealthy, Douglas Cone, 75. Friends say he spent weekends at their upscale Tampa home and traveled during the week. He was away on business last March when, after a wine and cheese fundraiser meeting, Jean Ann pulled her Rolls into their garage, closed the door and, police say, she passed out. The keys still in the ignition, the car in drive, when she was found the next day.
Investigator 2: It was death by carbon monoxide intoxication.
Reporter: An autopsy put her blood alcohol level at twice the legal limit. Is there any indication that this was anything other than an accidental death?
Investigator 2: Absolutely not.
Reporter: About two months later, a shocking discovery.
Investigator 2: Mrs. Cone's husband was actually leading a double life.
Woman: Mr. Cone, can I give you a . . . ?
Reporter: For more than half his married life police say Douglas Cone, using the alias Donald Carlson, was also involved with Hillary Carlson, about 20 years his junior. Police say they had two children of their own. The eldest is pictured here. They attended the same school where Cone's three other children

had gone. The women sat on the school board together. And when he wasn't with his wife at their Tampa home, the Carlsons lived at this secluded, sprawling, sixty plus acre lakeside estate about 20 miles up the road. Jean Ann's grieving friends didn't have a clue until eight days after his wife Jean died until Cone came here to the Sumter County courthouse, about 50 miles north of Tampa, and applied for a marriage license. It's not clear why he chose to come here. A few days later, he and Hillary were married here at the courthouse. That's when the news started to unravel. The wedding notice was published, people started reading it and tongues started wagging. Court clerk, Gloria Hayward, performed the ceremony.

Gloria Hayward: As an observer, I'm just amazed that he could pull that off for that length of time, especially living in the same area.

Reporter: According to a source close to the Cones, his eldest son knew of the double life. As for Jean Ann, most friends doubt she knew anything, though as one admits, it's a secret she may have taken to the grave.

Susan Candiotti, CNN Tampa.

CHAPTER 7 — Prostitution: Looking for a good time?
Pages 79-90

Summary Sex for money, from a well-run brothel in Nevada to human trafficking in southeast Asia, is the topic of Chapter 7. In a letter to Ann Landers in Reading 1, a prostitute extols the benefits of the job. Reading 2 looks at the ways prostitutes in the U.S. are joining together to push for decriminalization, arguing that prostitution is only dangerous when it's illegal. The reading in Part II tells the story of a teenage girl who left her home in Cambodia to find work, but found herself a prisoner instead, forced into prostitution.

Audio The readings in this chapter can be heard on the *Hot Topics 3* Audio CD 2 Tracks 1-3 or Audio Tape 2 Side A.

Background The prostitutes discussed in this chapter include one who is happy with her job, and one who was literally locked up in a brothel as a sex slave, but these extremes really only hint at the breadth of the sex industry. Besides brothels and streetwalking, the sex industry encompasses escort services, phone sex services, strip clubs and peep shows, all forms of pornography, sex tourism, and human trafficking—often in children and teenagers. It is also important to remember that a large number of "sex workers" are male.

Teaching Note There are some excellent questions on page 90 for sparking a class discussion. To get the students more involved in the process, give each person an index card and ask them to write an additional discussion question of their own. If the group is small enough, all the cards can be collected and each student's question can be discussed by the class. Otherwise, divide the class into manageable groups.

Internet Activity Reading 2 hints that prostitution is not always a safe occupation when it says, "It's only a risk when it's illegal." Many would disagree that even legal prostitution is safe, and your students might want to know about some of the risks faced by prostitutes. If you and they feel comfortable, have your students research and report on one of the following topics violence against prostitutes (including rape and murder), drug abuse among prostitutes, mental illness (including post-traumatic stress disorder) among prostitutes, and human trafficking.

CNN Video Clip Summary The video clip looks at a case in a Maryland community in which the internal documents of an upscale brothel have been made public.

Video Script Go to page 113 in this Instructor's Manual for the "Little Black Book Revealed" video script and recommended video vocabulary for review.

Video Activity Go to page 197 in the student book for activities to accompany the CNN video clip.

ANSWER KEY—Chapter 7: Prostitution: Looking for a good time?

PREVIEW (Page 79): Answers will vary.

PART I
Predict (Page 80)
1. a. Reading 1 & Reading 2
   b. Reading 1 & Reading 2
2. a. She thinks that prostitution is a choice, not an economic necessity, and that it should be legalized.
   b. decriminalize it
   c. Yes. Norma Hotaling and Celia Williamson are both working to help women leave prostitution.
3. Answers will vary.

Reading Comprehension
Check Your Predictions (Page 83): Answers will vary.

Check the Facts (Page 84)
Reading 1

1. True
2. False
3. True
4. False
5. True (in most counties)
6. True
7. False

Reading 2
1. prostitution
2. form support groups; raise money; get involved in politics; publish a magazine; form online communities
3. decriminalization of prostitution
4. stopping violence; improving working conditions; making prostitution more socially acceptable
5. because prostitution is illegal
6. an international organization created to help prostitutes leave sex work
7. They are victims of violence and suffer from drug addiction and mental illness
8. domestic violence

Analyze (Page 84): (Answers may vary.)
1. The prostitute in Reading 1 and the advocates of prostitutes' rights in Reading 2 both think it is a legitimate profession, and they both, along with Ann Landers, favor legalization or decriminalization.
2. Magdalene works in a brothel, so she is not on the street, and has not experienced the violence, drug abuse, or mental illness described in Reading 2.

Vocabulary Work
Guess Meaning from Context (Page 84): (Answers may vary.)

1. *assessment*—opinion
   trade—exchange
   fascinating—interesting
   clients—customers
   pursue—work on
   starve—go without food
   options—choices
   rights—permission to do something guaranteed by law
   support groups—groups of people who help each other
   labor—work
   ultimate—final
   advocate—person who works for the rights of another
   degrading—to lower in the opinion of others or in self-respect
2. *my side of the story*—my opinion
   burns me up—makes me angry
   before her eyes—where she can see it
   make a living—earn money
   sick and tired—disgusted
3. *support groups*—groups of people who help each other
   drug addiction—dependence on drugs
   mental illness—psychological disorders
   domestic violence—violence at home, e.g. beating a spouse

Guess Meaning from Related Words (Page 85)
1. criminal / decriminalization
   legal / illegal / legalize
   exploit / exploitative
   public / publicly
2. **Noun (person):** criminal
   Noun (thing): decriminalization, public
   Verb: legalize, exploit
   Adjective: legal / illegal, exploitative
   Adverb: publicly
3. *messed up*—mess means disorder, so in a bad condition
   beaten up—beat means hit, so it means getting hit
   speak out—talk about something
   open doors—open + access to something, so it means creating exposure to something
   new wave—new + trend or movement, so it means a new style
   longtime—long + time, so lasting for a long time

Hot Topics 3 • Chapter 7

4. insignificant (not important) and decriminalization (make something not criminal)

Reading Skills
Understanding Appositives (Page 86)

1. Shelby Aesthetic, a landscaper and writer in Huntsville, Ala.
2. a social movement this one involving "sex workers" and their supporters
3. Norma Hotaling, a former prostitute and founder of SAGE
4. Celia Williamson, an assistant professor of social work at the University of Toledo in Ohio
5. a social worker who is chairwoman of the advisory board

PART II
Read It (Page 87)

1. sex trafficking and the case of Srey Rath
2. No, she was locked in a bar. She thought she would be getting a job as a dishwasher.
3. to a bar in Malaysia
4. She was arrested for illegal immigration, spent a year in prison, and was sold into prostitution again.
5. She escaped again.
6. She is earning money selling belts and key chains.
7. more scolding and shaming of countries with major sex trafficking problems
8. slavery in the 1860's (African slaves in the U.S.)

Vocabulary Work
Guess Meaning from Context (Page 88): Answers will vary.

CNN Video Activities—Little Black Book Revealed
Understand It (Page 197)

1. d 3. c 5. a
2. a 4. d

VIDEO TRANSCRIPT—Chapter 7: Little Black Book Revealed
DVD Title 8   Running time: 02:20

Video Vocabulary

black book   a book that lists telephone numbers of one's romantic or sexual contacts

fuss   a show of great concern over something unimportant

misdemeanor   minor legal offense usually punished by a fine, not prison

seize   to take by force or by law

spoof   a comic performance that makes fun of a more serious topic

sue   to file a lawsuit, to make a claim in court that one's legal rights have been violated by others, that they should be protected or restored, and that the others should pay for one's suffering and damages

Video Script

Reporter: Frederick, Maryland, a picturesque and historic city about 50 miles northwest of Washington. But a few years ago police surveillance cameras caught another side of the city, unfamiliar to most.

Donald Campbell: It's one of those things you sort of know it's there. It's sort of everywhere . . . the oldest profession I'm told.

Reporter: Details of that oldest profession were made public right here at Frederick City Hall, where city officials released thousands of pages of documents, video tapes, and pornographic materials, <u>seized</u> from what police say was a local brothel. The documents, including emails seized from Madam Angelika Potter's business reveal a thriving prostitution ring that catered to customers' requests for 250 dollars an hour. From Sam, a wish for a woman with a conservative office suit but with sexy high heals. From Thomas, price is no object. And Louis expresses an interest in flying Danielle to New York for two or three days. Potter also ran a porn website. In 2000 she pled guilty to a <u>misdemeanor</u> charge of running a house of prostitution and paid a 100 dollar fine. But that seemingly light punishment prompted some to suspect officials wanted the clientele kept secret. The local papers <u>sued</u>, years

Chapter 7 • Hot Topics 3   113

passed, and this week, Madam Potter's so-called <u>black</u> <u>book</u> was made public right outside the Mayor's door.

Mayor Dougherty: While it is a little uncomfortable to have this sort of thing in the landing outside my office, it's still important that people know that we, we are not trying to cover anything up.

Reporter: 8500 pages of emails and financial ledgers, the police tapes and even an explicit computer disc are available for anyone to see, but besides the media, only a handful of residents have turned out. Eric Kasner, who had this t-shirt made and wants to include material for a film <u>spoof</u>, says people are taking this scandal too seriously.

Eric Kasner: It's a big <u>fuss</u> over nothing.

Reporter: But others say those on the list are getting what they deserve.

Edie Ciufolo: If you don't want to be caught up in that kind of thing, then you shouldn't participate in that.

Reporter: For hundreds of unsuspecting clients, it's too late. They're now a public part of Frederick's history.

Elaine Quijano, CNN Frederick, Maryland.

CHAPTER 8 — Education: Is everyone cheating?
Pages 91–104

Summary This chapter examines the problem of cheating in high schools, colleges, and universities. The *Preview* section tells the story of a woman who cheated in high school, and whose conscience was still bothering her 47 years later. Reading 1 explains the reasons so many high school students cheat, while Reading 2 provides insights into cheating at colleges and universities, and what some schools are doing to fight cheating. The reading in Part II is a personal narrative from a university graduate who faced and resisted the temptation to cheat.

Audio The readings in this chapter can be heard on the *Hot Topics 3* Audio CD 2 Tracks 4-6 or Audio Tape 2 Side A.

Background For anyone who has ever taken a peek at a classmate's test, used a crib note, or "borrowed" a bit of someone else's writing without giving them credit, this chapter will reassure you that you are not alone. But cheating defeats the purpose of education. Cheaters get credit for doing assignments, but they don't extract the potential benefits of those assignments. Cheaters may also improve their grades on papers and exams, but teachers and professors never find out what those students have actually learned or not learned, so they don't have the chance to help them strengthen their weak points.

Teaching Note The *Reading Skills* section on page 100 asks the students to paraphrase topic sentences. Paraphrasing requires a lot of practice, and is a skill that is essential for avoiding plagiarism, one of the forms of cheating mentioned in the chapter. Give the students additional practice by having them paraphrase the quotations in the chapter, starting with the one in the *Preview* reading. They should begin by using attributive language, for example, "The grandmother says that . . . ," or "Niels explains that . . . ," and they should conserve the meaning of the quotation while changing the grammar and vocabulary as much as possible.

Internet Activity Send your students to the Internet to learn what plagiarism is and how to avoid it. Several universities offer good online writing resources, including the University of Wisconsin's Writing Center at http://www.wisc.edu/writing/. Click on the Writer's Handbook, which offers a section called *Citing References in Your Paper* that includes information about plagiarism. Alternatively, search for additional readings on cheating using the search terms "cheating" and "academic", or try http://teaching.berkeley.edu/bgd/prevent.html, which offers descriptions of cheating and advice for professors.

Video Clip Summary The reporter visits a high school where cheating is common, and talks to students and staff about the reasons students cheat, and whether or not there is anything wrong with cheating. One teacher explains how he can now use the Internet to detect plagiarism in student papers, and that he finds it in about a third of them.

Video Script Go to page 117 in this Instructor's Manual for the "System Failure: Cheating in School" video script and recommended video vocabulary for review.

Video Activity Go to page 198 in the student book for activities to accompany the CNN video clip.

ANSWER KEY—Chapter 8: Education: Is everyone cheating?

PREVIEW (Page 91)
PART I
Predict (Page 92)

1. The *Preview* reading probably comes from a newspaper because it opens with the name of a city and is arranged in columns. Reading 1 probably comes from a magazine because it has a title and headings, and because the content is human interest. Reading 2 probably comes from a newspaper because it opens with the name of a city—Boston.
2. a. Reading 1
   b. Readings 1 & 2
   c. all the readings
3. a. Reading 2
   b. all the readings
   c. the *Preview* reading and Reading 1
   d. all the readings
4. Answers will vary.

Reading Comprehension
Check Your Predictions (Page 96): Answers will vary.
Check the Facts
Reading 1 (Page 96)

1. True
2. False
3. True
4. True
5. True
6. False
7. True

Reading 2 (Page 97)

1. They can buy term papers and copy from articles and news reports.
2. Yes, because standards are changing.
3. 41 percent believe that plagiarism is common; 30 percent say cheating during exams or tests happens quite often; 60 percent admit asking their friends for help when they're supposed to work alone; 27 percent say that falsifying laboratory data happens often or very often; 45 percent said that falsifying data did not count as cheating.
4. to combat cheating
5. • Duke University has an honor code.
   • The University of Maryland gives cheaters grades of XF to indicate failure because of cheating.
   • Cornell University requires freshmen and teaching assistants to take courses to teach them what cheating is and how to avoid it.
   • Wellesley College allows students to take exams when and where they want, but if they are caught cheating, the punishment can be severe.
6. Yes, because schools with honor codes have only half the cheating of schools without them.

Analyze (Page 97): (Answers may vary.)

1. Both are against cheating, and both say that students need to be taught not to cheat and be punished for cheating.
2. Parents probably have less influence over their children once the children are at a college or university, so that solution from Reading 1 might not work. On the other hand, teachers and professors can be alert to cheating and not use multiple choice tests at a college or university.

Vocabulary Work
Guess Meaning from Context (Page 98):
(Answers may vary.)

1. *vast:* great
   surveys: a set of questions designed to measure opinions
   inconsistent: not in agreement with
   integrity: strong morals, honesty
   multiple-choice: having many choices for answers, as on a test
   rigorous: having strict or high standards
   tolerate: accept
   struggle: use much mental effort
   temptations: attractions, especially to something wrong, harmful, or evil
   resist: not to do something that you want to
   plagiarism: stealing another's writing and calling it your own
   standards: expectations
   strive: try; make an effort
   combat: fight against
2. **Reading 1**
   saving face: avoiding embarrassment or shame
   point the finger: accuse someone
   moral compass: sense of right and wrong; rules to live by
   top-down / bottom-up: from parents to children; from children to parents
   cut corners: not do something completely

Reading 2

with the click of a mouse: fast and easy because it's done with a computer
get away with: do without getting caught or punished
"teeth:" strength because they carry serious consequences
make a difference: cause change
a carrot and a stick: a reward and a punishment

Guess Meaning from Related Words (Page 99)

1. embarrass / embarrassment
   survive / survival
   compete / competition
   academic / academically
   rigor / rigorously
   false / falsifying
   honor / honorable
   accept / acceptable
   cheat / cheating

2.
   Noun (person):
   Noun (thing): embarrassment, survival, competition, rigor, honor, cheating
   Verb: embarrass, survive, compete, falsifying, honor, accept, cheat
   Adjective: academic, false, honorable, acceptable
   Adverb: academically, rigorously

3. illegitimate (not legitimate); immoral (not moral); dishonest (not honest)

Reading Skills

Finding Main Ideas in Topic Sentences (Page 100)

Reading 1 (Paraphrases may vary.)

Paragraph	Sentence number	Main idea
1	3	What is the reason high school students cheat even though they believe it is wrong?
2	2-3	Adults should teach children right from wrong.
3	2-3	One reason students cheat is that schools and teachers make it easy for them to cheat.
4	1	Schools must prohibit and prevent all cheating.

Reading 2 (Paraphrases may vary.)

Paragraph	Sentence number	Main idea
1	1	Cheating is a problem for many college students.
2	1-2	Many college students aren't sure what cheating is, in part because rules and expectations are changing.
3	1	Colleges and universities are making more of an effort to detect cheating at the same time college students are less worried about the consequences of cheating.
4	1	Honor codes are increasing in popularity nationwide.
5	1	Honor codes carry both rewards and punishments.
6	1	Although some think that honor codes are ineffective, schools with honor codes have only half as much cheating as other schools.

PART II

Read It (Page 101)

1. He worked at a university research institute.
2. no
3. the answer keys for his economics course
4. It was his most difficult course that semester.
5. Nobody would see him. There were many copies. The assignments were becoming more difficult.
6. He thought about the possible consequences and the honor code he'd signed and decided not to take an answer key.
7. He's proud of his diploma, and wonders if he would be less proud of it if he had cheated.

Vocabulary Work

Guess Meaning from Context (Page 102):
Answers will vary.

Reading Skills

Summarizing a Narrative (Page 103): Answers will vary.

Video Activities: System Failure: Cheating in School
Understand It (Page 198)

1. survive
2. cutting corners
3. rampant
4. three quarters
5. plagiarized
6. submit
7. pressure
8. honor

VIDEO TRANSCRIPT—Chapter 8: System Failure: Cheating in School

DVD Title 9   Running time: 03:04

Video Vocabulary

average Joe   average person
cut corners   the easiest or cheapest way to do something, usually with a bad result
jaded   tired from doing something too much
no big deal   something not important
outrage   great anger, caused by such an act
rampant   uncontrollable and widespread
shortcut   a faster way to do something

Video Script

Reporter: To Alice Newhall, cheating is <u>no big deal</u>.
Alice Newhall: Cheating is a <u>shortcut</u>, and it's . . . it's a pretty efficient one in a lot of cases.
Reporter: Alice is a 17-year-old senior at George Mason High School in northern Virginia. She's typical of what a survey shows is a growing number of kids who see cheating as a way to survive high school. Do you not have any moral <u>outrage</u> about cheating?
Alice: Not really. It's just . . . it's not the biggest deal in high school.
Teacher: Our secretary, Alice.
Alice Newhall: You know, what's important is getting ahead. You know, the far . . . the better grades you have, you know, the better school you get into, is . . . you know, the better you're going to do in life. And if you've learned to <u>cut corners</u> to do that, you know, you're going to be saving yourself time and energy. And in the real world, you know, that's what's going to be going on is, you know, the better you do, that's what shows. It's not, you know, how moral you were in getting there.
Reporter: High school cheating is <u>rampant</u>. A national survey of 4500 students found that three quarters of them engaged in serious cheating. More than half have plagiarized work off the Internet. If you have a credit card and a modem, it's simple.
Teacher: . . . on disk, I just put it into the machine.
Reporter: Schools have begun using the kids' weapons against them. George Mason is one of thousands of high schools fighting web plagiarism with a new service called Turnitin.com. Teachers submit students' papers to the company, which then searches the Web for matching prose.
Teacher: Between 24 and 48 hours, a report will come back and it's color-coded.
Reporter: This paper is code red, 97 percent plagiarized. Turnitin says about a third of the papers submitted have some sort of plagiarism.
Donald McCabe: Students today find it so much easier to rationalize their cheating.
Reporter: Donald McCabe, whose survey of high school students found that 50 percent don't even consider Internet plagiarism cheating, says students feel driven by the tremendous pressure to excel and compete for colleges.
Donald McCabe: For one reason or another, they convince themselves that, you know, a tenth of a point on their GPA is going to make a dramatic difference on their futures and they feel compelled to cheat.
Reporter: Of course not all students cheat. Mike Denny, also a senior at George Mason, thinks it's simply wrong. Do you think that honor is lacking in the average high school student?
Mike Denny: I think honor is . . . honor's lacking in a large part of society. And I think it's . . . you often see the, the liars and the people who take the easy way get much higher in life than, you know, your <u>average</u> honest <u>Joe</u> on the street.

Chapter 8 • Hot Topics 3   117

Reporter: Mike also blames a high school culture where grades and test scores are more important than integrity.
Mike Denny: By now many of us are so <u>jaded</u>, we feel like oh, our whole life has been taught for one test. It's pretty sad that things such as who you are and standing by your word and whatnot. That's something that we haven't really been taught.
Reporter: Maybe American high schools are teaching their students the wrong lesson.

Kathy Slobogin, CNN, Falls Church, VA.

CHAPTER 9 — Gender: Are women weak? Are men necessary?
Pages 105–118

Summary It seems to be a never-ending battle. In this round, women are barred from combat jobs in the military, but the author of Reading 1 cites two different studies showing women to be as physically capable as men with the proper training. The author of Reading 2 supports suggestions by Harvard University's president that the small number of women scientists may have a biological basis. The reading in Part II gives a short lesson in genetics, and explains that men may not be entirely necessary, at least for reproduction.

Audio The readings in this chapter can be heard on the *Hot Topics 3* Audio CD 2 Tracks 7-9 or Audio Tape 2 Side B.

Background While the term "sex" refers to our biology, "gender" refers to a large number of traits we think of as feminine or masculine. As you might expect, that set of traits varies with geography and over time, so our gender roles are based on a given culture at a given point in history. But is there more? Scientists are looking at ways in which the male and female brain differ in an attempt to explain observed differences in how men and women behave and the prevalence of certain neurological diseases such as autism in one sex or the other. Brain chemistry may also be able to explain sexual preference and gender identity—feeling male or female.

Teaching Note Readings 1 and 2 are a rich source of interesting adjectives, something that student writers need to collect in order to convey precise meanings. Help your students compile a list of adjectives from the readings including words like *political, patriarchal, religious, capable, controversial,* and *emotional.* After the students have time to work with their dictionaries, ask pairs or small groups to discuss whether they associate each adjective more strongly with males, females, or neither. There are no right or wrong answers, but it will give the students a chance to think about the meanings of the words as well as the content of the chapter.

Internet Activity Use the Internet to explore the topic of gender differences in communication. You are likely to find articles by the well-known language researcher Deborah Tannen, and look for a recent article by Paolo Rossetti, who has found that gender differences in communication extend to our emails: http://iteslj.org/Articles/Rossetti-GenderDif.html Alternatively, have students research gender differences in response to pain.

CNN Video Clip Summary The video clip shows some of the debate that was sparked by the comments of Lawrence Summers, President of Harvard University, which were covered in Reading 2. On one side are people who say that genetic differences account for the relatively small number of female scientists. On the other are people who see just another case of unfounded gender bias.

Video Script Go to page 120 in this Instructor's Manual for the "Debating Gender Differences" video script and recommended video vocabulary for review.

Video Activity Go to page 199 in the student book for activities to accompany the CNN video clip.

ANSWER KEY—Chapter 9: Gender: Are women weak? Are men necessary?

PREVIEW (Page 105): Answers will vary.

PART I

Predict (Page 106)

1. a. & b. both readings
2. It defends him.
3. negative (old-fashioned concepts that fill the closed minds, etc.)
4. Answers will vary.

Reading Comprehension

Check Your Predictions (Page 109): Answers will vary.

Check the Facts (Page 110)

Reading 1

1. False
2. False
3. False
4. True (according to Reading 1. Reading 2 says that women have small amounts of testosterone.)
5. False
6. False
7. True
8. False

Reading 2

A.
1. why there are not more women at the top levels of science
2. prejudice in the hiring of women in university departments and possibly genetics
3. Professor Nancy Hopkins because she was offended by Summers' comments
4. He does not agree because he doesn't think it's offensive to consider a hypothesis, whether it turns out to be right or wrong. He thinks it's part of the free inquiry that should take place at universities.
5. The comments are not ridiculous because scientists are discovering differences between male and female brains.
6. Men score better in tests of spatial and mathematical reasoning, and boys are more likely to be autistic.
7. No. He says that people have varying degrees of intelligence, musical talent, and mathematical abilities.

B. Fewer women than men are naturally good at science.

Analyze (Page 111): (Answers may vary.)

1. They are unconnected because Reading 1 is about physical strength and Reading 2 is about scientific (mental) abilities.
2. Yes, because they deny women certain jobs without a good reason.

Vocabulary Work

Guess Meaning from Context (Page 111)

glaring: obvious
combat: a violent struggle
media: the combination of television, radio, news magazines, and newspapers
concludes: to form an opinion, a judgement
tough: strong
regimen: routine
civilian: someone who is not a member of the military or police forces, an ordinary citizen
endurance: the ability to do something for a long period of time
contrary: opposed or opposite in opinion
faculty: the teaching staff at a school
debate: disagreement
bias: prejudice
hypothesis: theory
taboo: forbidden
traits: characteristics
innate: natural part of a person

Guess Meaning from Related Words (Page 111)

1. *open mind:* without prejudice
   closed mind: prejudiced
   brotherhood of the sword: the military
   get into hot water: get into trouble
   off the record: just between the people present
2. under + go = experience
   carry + out = do
3. rigor / rigors / rigorous
   aggressive / aggression
   edgy / edginess
   generalize / generalizations
   behavior / behavioral
   doubt / undoubtedly
   gene / genetics

4.
Noun (person):
Noun (thing): rigor / rigors, aggression, edginess, generalizations, behavior, doubt, gene / genetics
Verb: generalize
Adjective: rigorous, aggressive, edgy, behavioral
Adverb: undoubtedly

5. *disproven:* proven to be untrue
discrepancy: difference, inconsistency
disabilities: something that takes away normal ability, especially as a result of an accident or disease
hyperactive: overly active
included: to make something a part of something else
involved: participating, taking part in
into: in
inborn: natural part of a person
innate: natural part of a person

Reading Skills

Identifying Main Ideas and Supporting Details (Page 113)

1. that women should not be excluded from any military job
2. The author uses citations from two scientific studies that showed women to be capable of the same degree of physical strength as men. Statistics from the studies are given.
3. that people should not reject hypotheses showing innate differences in male and female brains
4. There is a quotation from Pinker expressing this idea, and the examples of male/female differences in spatial ability and math, and the higher number of male children with autism.

PART II

Read It (Page 114)

1. genetic and technological
2. XX produces a female and XY produces a male.
3. It has been losing genes.
4. The Y chromosome will eventually disappear, ending sexual reproduction.
5. No, because some say that the Y chromosome has found new ways of rebuilding itself.
6. sperm
7. an egg dividing to produce an embryo with no sperm at all

Vocabulary Work

Guess Meaning from Context (Page 116):
Answers will vary.

Reading Skills

Understanding Organization (Page 117)

1. technological
2. the Y chromosome will disappear
3. create sperm in a laboratory
4. asexual reproduction
5. The Y chromosome has found new ways of rebuilding itself.

CNN Video Activities: Debating Gender Differences

Understand It (Page 199)

1. Katherine Spillar   5. Katherine Spillar
2. Nancy Pfotenhauer   6. Nancy Pfotenhauer
3. Nancy Pfotenhauer   7. Katherine Spillar
4. Katherine Spillar   8. Nancy Pfotenhauer

VIDEO TRANSCRIPT—Chapter 9: Debating Gender Differences
DVD Title 10   Running time: 02:07

Video Vocabulary
bias prejudice
innate part of someone from birth, natural
off-the-record referring to something that should not be heard by the public
spatial of or about space or area

Video Script
Crowd: No! We vote no!
Reporter: What a debate it has become, moving from the campus of Harvard, to the headlines, to the airwaves.
TV Anchor: By Harvard President—
Reporter: Outrage from women's liberal groups—

Katherine Spillar: Well, the heart of the matter is the bias that President Summers exhibited himself in his comments.

Reporter: Support from conservatives—

Nancy Pfotenhauer: So this poor guy basically told the truth in an off-the-record meeting, and now he's being painted as someone who is anti-women.

Reporter: Two women, two very different views. So we asked them first: Are there innate differences between the sexes?

Nancy Pfotenhauer: In the field of neurobiology it's pretty well established that men have a superior spatial ability on average. Women have superior verbal reasoning skills on average.

Katherine Spillar: Well the research is in and it's conclusive. Women are every bit an equal to a man in any of these fields.

Reporter: Why then do fewer women than men become scientists and engineers? Bias says one.

Katherine Spillar: What is clear is that when women face discrimination in the workplace and in education of course their opportunities are stunted.

Reporter: Career choice says the other.

Nancy Pfotenhauer: The women are going to law school because they are likely to be better than the male lawyers they're up against, and the men are going to science and math because they are likely to be better than their competition.

Reporter: One says women too often complain about discrimination

Nancy Pfotenhauer: I think that you are basically setting someone up to have a victim mentality.

Reporter: The other says women too often are discriminated against.

Katherine Spillar: This is stealing from girls their chances of achieving their full potential, and that's wrong.

Reporter: Both however agree on this: society benefits from the debate sparked by one speech, by one Ivy League president. Because if a goal is eventually seeing more women in science and engineering, both women say we must first identify the problem, and then figure out what to do about it.

Kelly Wallace, CNN New York.

CHAPTER 10 — IMMIGRATION: IS IT TIME TO SHUT THE DOOR?
Pages 119–132

Summary Chapter 10 takes a look at immigration issues in Europe, Mexico, and the United States. Reading 1 describes the surprising case of Denmark, where conservative new laws are preventing immigrants, and even some Danes, from living there. The topic of Reading 2 is a controversial government publication that could help Mexicans enter the U.S. illegally. The reading in Part II describes the general state of confusion over immigration in Europe, where some people fear the loss of jobs and national identity, and others argue that labor shortages and a shortage of younger workers mean that Europe needs immigration, especially managed immigration.

Audio The readings in this chapter can be heard on the *Hot Topics 3* Audio CD 2 Tracks 10-12 or Audio Tape 2 Side B.

Background The immigration issues discussed in this chapter hint at the global population picture. The total world population is rapidly increasing, but most of that growth is taking place in certain areas. Africa, India, and China will see a large percentage of the increase in world population in coming years. Latin America and the Middle East are also continuing to grow. Meanwhile, the developed countries in Europe, East Asia, and North America are seeing their birth rates drop and their populations age.

Teaching Note The *Reading Skills* section on page 126 calls attention to pronouns and other cohesive elements. Give the students additional practice with this critical skill by having them identify the pronouns and their referents in Part II. You could assign different sections of the reading to groups of students and ask them to tell the class where the pronouns are and what their referents are.

Internet Activity Use the *Search* feature at www.npr.org (National Public Radio) to find radio reports and interviews that your students can read about and listen to. Use the search term "immigration" to find a list of archived programs on the topic. Clicking on the program title brings up a summary and a link to the page where the story or interview can be heard.

Video Clip Summary The reporter talks to the principal of a school in the Kansas City area that is striving to meet the needs of students who speak 18 languages. Some people speak in favor of immigration to states like Missouri, but a group called the Federation for American Immigration Reform is concerned about the cost of services for immigrants and the loss of their local culture.

Video Script Go to page 124 in this Instructor's Manual for the "Immigration in Middle America" video script and recommended video vocabulary for review.

Video Activity Go to page 200 in the student book for activities to accompany the CNN video clip.

ANSWER KEY—Chapter 10: *IMMIGRATION: IS IT TIME TO SHUT THE DOOR?*

PREVIEW (Page 119): Answers will vary.

PART I

Predict (Page 120)

1. Reading 1 is from Copenhagen, Denmark. Reading 2 is from Mexico City.
2. Readings 1 & 2
3. In Reading 1, immigrants to Denmark and Danes married to foreigners are angry. In Reading 2, some U.S. lawmakers are angry.
4. Reading 2 uses quotations from government officials. Reading 1 talks about people who don't want to immigrate.
5. Answers will vary.

Reading Comprehension

Check Your Predictions (Page 123): Answers will vary.

Check the Facts

Reading 1 (Page 123)

1. True	4. True	6. False
2. False	5. Not sure	7. True
3. Not sure	(probably not)	8. True

Reading 2 (Page 124)

1. the Mexican government
2. illegal immigrants
3. drowning and dehydration
4. Avoid calling attention to themselves. Stay away from loud parties and leave a bar if a fight starts.

Analyze (Page 124)

a. Some people in Mexico want to immigrate to the U.S.
b. The Danes moving to Sweden are immigrating legally.
c. The Mexican people are looking for work.
d. The Mexican group is getting help from their government.
e. The Danes are getting help from a foreign government.

Vocabulary Work

Guess Meaning from Context (Page 124)

1. *exile:* forced to live outside one's home country
   ironically: showing the opposite of what one would expect
   commute: to travel to and from one's work or school regularly
   bans: to block, to forbid
   spouse: a husband or wife
   journey: a trip, especially a long one
   minimize: the least amount of something
   drowning: to die by breathing in water or other liquid
   dehydration: a lack of water, thirst
   retain: keep
   documents: passport and visa
   border police: police who patrol the U.S.—Mexican border
2. *marriage of convenience:* marrying someone so they can stay in the country
   indigenous: native-born
3. *making good on:* fulfilling, doing what was promised
   call attention to: draw attention, be obvious
4. *absurd:* stupid is possible; helpful and good are very unlikely
   furious: confused and angry are possible; amused and understanding are very unlikely

Guess Meaning from Related Words (Page 125)

1. *neighboring:* (neighbor) nearby
   native-born: (native + born) born in that place
   arranged: (arrange) an arranged marriage is arranged by families, not the couple themselves
   forced: (force) a forced marriage happens without someone's consent
   booklet: (book) a small book

Hot Topics 3 • Chapter 10

2.
Reading 1
Denmark / Dane / Danish
expel / expulsion
immigrant / immigration

Reading 2
legal / illegal / illegally
immigrant / immigration / migrant

3.
Noun (person): Dane, immigrant / migrant
Noun (thing): Denmark, expulsion, immigration
Verb: expel
Adjective: Danish, legal / illegal
Adverb: illegally

4. *anti-immigration:* against immigration
   non-Danish: not Danish
   misunderstood: understood wrongly

Reading Skills

Understanding Cohesive Elements (Page 126)

1. models of social awareness
2. politicians
3. Denmark's
4. the whole previous sentence
5. a non-Danish spouse
6. no referent
7. Marriages Across Borders
8. couples
9. the whole previous sentence
10. no referent

PART II

Read It (Page 127)

1. the concerns of their citizens, their country's economic problems, and the humanitarian needs of immigrants
2. those looking for asylum and those trying to escape poverty or war
3. that asylum seekers are too expensive for the EU's social welfare systems, that migrants may take their jobs, and the weakening of local cultures
4. They are against immigration because citizens fear a loss of national identity.
5. People-smugglers mistreat and sometimes cause the deaths of immigrants. Immigrants are mistreated in sweatshops. Women and children are sometimes forced into prostitution.
6. They have labor shortages in certain areas, such as IT in Germany or manual labor in Spain. Immigrants are also needed to fund retirement programs.

Vocabulary Work

Guess Words from Context (Page 129): Answers will vary.

Reading Skills

Understanding Organization (Page 130)

Europe is struggling to create a balanced immigration policy.

<u>Arguments against immigration</u>
economic burden
migrants may take jobs from natives
local cultures may be weakened
loss of national identity

<u>Arguments in favor of immigration</u>
shortage of skilled workers
shortage of manual labor
shortage of funds for retirement programs

CNN Video Activities: Immigration in Middle America

Understand It (Page 200)

1. languages
2. exploding
3. immigrants
4. illegal
5. identity
6. taxes
7. annually
8. Vietnamese
9. closed
10. taking care

VIDEO TRANSCRIPT—Chapter 10: IMMIGRATION IN MIDDLE AMERICA
DVD Title 11   Running time: 05:16

Video Vocabulary
battlefield a place where battles are fought
overrun to spread over in large numbers, usually causing harm
unfounded false, not factual

Video Script

Reporter: On a cold morning in Missouri, children pour into Garfield Elementary School, from every corner of the Earth.

Children: . . . to the flag, of the United States of America.

Reporter: This public school is in the middle of one of the state's largest immigrant communities, students here speak 18 different languages, and principal Gwendolyn Squires must communicate with them all.

Gwendolyn Squires: I have a little saying that on my way to work each day it's like I'm driving to another country. As you know often when those kids arrive here, they come here with nothing.

Reporter: No school records, no medical records.

Gwendolyn Squires: No, no, I don't think half of Kansas City knows what exists here on the northeast area of the city, at all.

Reporter: She may be right. The immigrant population in middle America is exploding—in Missouri alone up 81 percent in the 1990s. The number of Latinos has nearly doubled—pushed by the arrival of workers like Eric Ruiz.

Eric Ruiz: (in Spanish)

Reporter: I like it here, he says, because there is more work, and opportunity.

Teacher: So what are the four weather words that you came up with?

Children: Cloudy, sunny . . .

Reporter: So, not far from Garfield School, adults crowd into English language classes at an immigrant community center. And Program Director David Holsclaw thinks this is wonderful.

David Holsclaw: For hundreds of years, people have come here with a suitcase and they've made this the richest, freest country in world history, I think. And that's still happening.

Reporter: Immigrants still account for only about 3 percent of Missouri's population, so it's not like they're overrunning the state. But there are more than 35 million foreign-born people living in this country. And right now I'm going to see some people who think that is a pretty big problem. Hi, how you doing? I'm Tom. Good to meet you.

Joyce Mucci: Nice to meet you.

Reporter: We contacted Joyce Mucci and her friends through the Federation for American Immigration Reform, which suggests the federal government lets too many legal immigrants in, and does not keep enough illegals out.

Joyce Mucci: I think there's a great sense among Americans and I'm not the only one—that there's a great fear we are going to lose our identity as Americans.

Reporter: Their concerns are cultural. Their concerns are economic.

Charlene Bredemeier: I as a taxpayer, federal, state level. I'm going to have to pay more money for all this 'cause they're going to need more teachers, more help . . .

Frances Semler: Too bad that things bottom out at the dollar, but that's the reality in which we live.

Reporter: And their concerns are not unfounded. 800,000 legal immigrants now arrive annually, four times as many as forty years ago, and when illegal aliens are tossed into the mix, nobody can say reliably even how many there are.

Woman: I think we need to take a look at overall policy and get a handle on it. Maybe even stop it for a while until we can count everybody.

Reporter: Immigrants have brought undeniable benefits to Missouri over the years. The Vietnamese community, started three decades ago, has produced strong churches, businesses, and families. Visit with Nhuoun and Doan Tran for even a few minutes, and you cannot doubt their patriotism.

Nhuoun Tran: This is a good land, as the promised land in the Bible.

Doan Tran: So when we came over here. We tried to prove we are good people.

Reporter: But some children of the original immigrants now wonder if keeping America's doors so wide open is wise. Should our immigration policy be more open or more closed?

Girl: More closed.

Reporter: Really?

Girl: Yes. It has to be taken care of at the very first step.

Gwendolyn Squires: So what we have are like sheltered classrooms.

Reporter: Back at Garfield Elementary School, Gwendolyn Squires has heard all the arguments, and her answer is simple: Look at Saib.

Reporter: He arrived from Somalia three days ago. He speaks no English . . . never has been to school. Taking care of such children and their families she believes is what America is all about.

Squires: This is the <u>battlefield</u>.

Reporter: What are you battling?

Squires: I am battling whatever the children are battling, whatever they bring to us.

Reporter: America has always been an immigrant nation, but with 15,000 legal immigrants arriving every week, the descendents of some of those who came long ago are asking, how many more can we invite to American shores?

CHAPTER 11 — BUSINESS: GLOBALIZATION OR CULTURAL IMPERIALISM?
Pages 133–147

Summary Chapter 11 focuses on concerns about cultural dominance. Reading 1 is about the effect of English on other languages, which some countries' language academies are trying to stop even as the first academic conference on "Spanglish" is embracing that blend of languages. Reading 2 expresses concerns from people in the British music industry over the dominance of American music on the pop charts, but also points out the success of some British groups overseas. The reading in Part II is an essay on cultural imperialism, which the author believes is neither inevitable nor evil.

Audio The readings in this chapter can be heard on the *Hot Topics 3* Audio CD 3 Tracks 1-3 or Audio Tape 3 Side A.

Background The recent protests at the G8 (Group of Eight) summit meetings are a dramatic illustration of the tension between the two sides of the globalization issue. On the one hand are heads of state and industry who see international trade and relations as a desirable and inevitable part of the modern world. On the other hand, behind protective walls of police and chain link fences, are the protestors who insist that globalization benefits developed countries at the cost of all others. And as the chapter points out, this globalization is not only economic, but also cultural.

Teaching Note Have a class discussion about the pros and cons of globalization. Discuss the students' feelings about the foreign businesses they see in their countries, and whether or not they patronize those businesses. Ask for their views on multinational corporations and outsourcing. Do they help or hurt the countries where they do business? Include questions about the globalization of entertainment, including music and movies. Why is American entertainment so popular? Does it diminish the popularity of local entertainment or result in a loss of cultural identity?

Internet Activity The International Forum on Globalization offers a section called *News Room* with links to dozens of recent news stories related to globalization at http://www.ifg.org/news.htm. Choose an article that will interest your students, then ask them to read it using the vocabulary technique found in Part II, *Vocabulary Work: Guess Meaning from Context* section. Have the students ignore words from the reading that they don't really need for understanding the article, guess at the meanings of others when possible, and list some that they need to look up in a dictionary.

CNN Video Clip Summary Fred Katayama reports that many American brands and companies have undergone foreign buyouts. These buyouts are typically accompanied by the loss of American jobs, but some think that the buyouts eventually stimulate the economy and so replace those lost jobs.

Video Script Go to page 127 in this Instructor's Manual for the "Made in the USA" video script and recommended video vocabulary for review.

Video Activity Go to page 201 in the student book for activities to accompany the CNN video clip.

ANSWER KEY—Chapter 11: BUSINESS: GLOBALIZATION OR CULTURAL IMPERIALISM?

PREVIEW (Page 133): Answers will vary.

PART I

Predict (Page 134)

1. a. Readings 1 & 2
   b. Reading 2
   c. Reading 2
   d. Readings 1 & 2
2. Answers will vary.

Reading Comprehension

Check Your Predictions (Page 137): Answers will vary.

Check the Facts

Reading 1 (Page 137)

1. True
2. True
3. False
4. True
5. False
6. True
7. False
8. True

Reading 2 (Page 138)

1. Not Sure
2. False
3. Not Sure
4. False
5. True
6. True
7. True

Analyze (Page 138): (Answers may vary.)

1. The language academy in France is somewhat effective, but the one in Spain is less effective.
2.
   - The writer probably disagrees with **Mills** because the writer does not object to music being successful outside its country of origin, while Mills mentions "cultural imperialism".
   - The writer probably disagrees with **Wenham** because the writer does not object to music being successful outside its country of origin, while Wenham fears that American music will dominate everything.
   - The writer probably agrees with **White**, because the writer thinks that British musical acts can be successful, and White gives examples of that success in the U.K.
   - The writer probably agrees with **Redmond**, because the writer thinks that British musical acts can be successful, and Redmond gives examples of that success in the U.S.

3. Answers may vary. Sample response: The authors would probably agree with each other. They recognize that language and music may be being dominated, but it's not necessarily bad.

Vocabulary Work

Guess Meaning from Context (Page 138)

1. *deplore:* dislike strongly
   slogan: a saying or phrase that expresses a group's message
   key: very important
   aspect: part
   phenomenon: event, situation
   top: leading, at the top
   singles: recordings of single songs
   chart: list of best-selling recordings
   fondly: with warm feelings
   reversed: in a backwards direction
   homogeneous: uniform
   hegemony: dominance
   mergers: forming a larger company from smaller companies
   nurturing: to train, educate
   album: a recording that is a collection of songs
   export: something shipped from one country to another for sale

2.
Reading 1

leaps and bounds: quickly
pinned down: defined, limited
losing the battle: not succeeding

Reading 2

a shot in the arm: an influx of something beneficial
sour grapes: resentment

3. Johann Wolfgang von Goethe was a German poet and playwright.
4. *hybrid:* A hybrid plant is a combination of two or more plants. A hybrid language is a combination of languages.
   irrigation: Irrigation brings water to a dry landscape and improves it. Stavans says that Spanglish is the result of one language being added to another language.
   fertilizing: Just as fertilizer makes soil richer, languages can make each other richer.

Guess Meaning from Related Words (Page 140)

1. *intermixed:* (mix) mixed together
   recall: (call) remember
2. odd / oddity
   attend / attendee
   pure / purity
   dominate / dominance
   market / marketable
3.
   Noun (person): attendee
   Noun (thing): oddity, purity, dominance, market
   Verb: attend, dominate, market
   Adjective: odd, pure, marketable
   Adverb:
4. *multinationals:* companies located in multiple countries
   megastar: huge star

Reading Skills

Understanding Transition Words and Phrases (Page 141)

- *Meanwhile* links what is happening with Spanglish in the U.S. with the situation in Europe at the same time.
- *At any rate* connects the ideas that precede it with the fact that neither side can do much about it.
- *As a result* links a cause—multinationals not caring about nurturing local talent—with its effect—a situation where only American artists are at the top of the charts.
- *For their part* introduces the ideas of spokesmen from major record companies, and contrasts those ideas with the opinions in the previous paragraph.
- *Moreover* is used to add a point from Adam White to the point he made previously.
- *Still* contrasts the opinion of large corporations that it's all sour grapes with the statistic about the percentage of sales of British bands in the U.S. market.

PART II

Read It (Page 141)

1. They don't like it. They think it is invasive and a form of control.
2. France
3. No, the author says it's hypocrisy since they had no complaints when their culture was the dominant one.
4. The Midwest worries about the domination of New York and Los Angeles, and Miami worries about Hispanic domination.
5. Whichever culture is technologically superior will eventually dominate the others.
6. The power of multinational corporations and advertising

Vocabulary Work

Guess Meaning from Context (Page 144): Answers will vary.

Reading Skills

Evaluating Different Types of Supporting Details (Page 145): Answers will vary.

CNN Video Activities: Made in the USA

Understand It (Page 201)

1. False
2. True
3. True
4. False
5. True

VIDEO TRANSCRIPT—Chapter 11: MADE IN THE USA
DVD Title 12   Running time: 02:23

Video Vocabulary

axe (from the slang *to get the axe*) to get fired from a job
buyout the purchase of a controlling interest in a business
eliminate to remove or get rid of
icon one who is greatly admired
pump to supply a lot of something
transfer to move from one place, vehicle, etc. to another
xenophobia fear of foreigners; dislike of strangers

Video Script

Emcee: He's America's new singing sensation, our new RCA recording artist, here he is, a big reception for Elvis Presley!

Reporter: A true American <u>icon</u>. Elvis's label RCA is in German hands today. At another seemingly American hotel chain, the Holiday Inn, the profit-keepers are now British. The studio that put out E.T. lived up to its name. Universal has switched parent companies from U.S. to Japanese to Canadian to French. From the Seattle Mariners to Skippy's peanut butter, many of America's corporate icons have been sold abroad. Foreign <u>buyouts</u> of U.S. firms have more than doubled in the last five years with, surprise, Canada and Britain accounting for nearly half of the deals. They bring their <u>axes</u> with them.

Robert Scott: When foreign firms take over U.S. firms, typically they <u>eliminate</u> jobs in the U.S., administrative jobs and back-office jobs and <u>transfer</u> that work to their home country, so we lose those jobs forever.

Reporter: Chrysler's new German owner Daimler is working to cut 20 percent of Chrysler's workers over three years. This year Chrysler went back into the black after losing money for six straight quarters. Acquisitions aside, European and Japanese auto-makers build so many vehicles in the United States today that the industry has replaced nearly all of the jobs lost since 1978. Foreign companies <u>pump</u> in money and that boosts business.

David Richardson: All this new technology and new equipment and new ideas begins to take off in a kind of dynamic way and over a course of five to eight to ten years the growth rates are much stronger in these plants as far as the data show so that people who have lost their jobs may perhaps be able to come back to them.

Reporter: Partly as a result, America's <u>xenophobic</u> reaction to corporate Japan's buying binge in the eighties has disappeared. And if you don't know what 'xenophobia' means, you can look it up in your American Heritage Dictionary. Now, despite its name, this dictionary is now published by Vivendi of France, the very country that loves to decry what it calls American cultural imperialism.

Fred Katayama, CNN Financial News, New York.

CHAPTER 12 — SEX EDUCATION: HOW MUCH DO WE NEED TO KNOW?
Pages 148–161

Summary The topic of sex education is under consideration in Chapter 12. Reading 1 describes the elements of a good sex education program, and Reading 2 compares two types of programs that American schools are offering. The reading in Part II and the CNN video clip highlight the research of Alfred Kinsey, who is considered by many to be the father of sex education.

Audio The readings in this chapter can be heard on the *Hot Topics 3* Audio CD 3 Tracks 4–6 or Audio Tape 3 Side A.

Background Despite concerns that educating teenagers about sexuality would encourage them to have sex, sex education or "family life" courses have been part of the American educational system since the 1950s. Concerns over HIV-AIDS in the 1980s increased public support, as has research finding that sex education reduces teen pregnancy rates and raises the age at which teenagers first have sex. But not everyone is convinced. In 2002, U.S. President George W. Bush provided $135 million in federal funding for abstinence-only sex education programs to help American teenagers "face a choice between self-restraint and self-destruction," money which some states have decided to decline in order to offer more comprehensive sex education programs.

Teaching Note The *Analyze* section on page 153 asks students to use the information in Reading 1 to evaluate the abstinence-only programs described in Reading 2. For further practice with applying information from a reading, do the same sort of evaluation for the abstinence-plus programs in Reading 2.

Internet Activity The Sexuality and Information Council of the United States runs an informative website with recent news releases on the topic of sex education, which they are decidedly in favor of: http://www.siecus.org/. To read more from supporters of abstinence-only sex education, try: http://www.bestfriendsfoundation.org/.

Video Clip Summary The CNN clip is set against the opening of a movie based on the life of Alfred Kinsey, whose research methods have been criticized, but who is given credit for starting the "sexual revolution." The clip opens with brief images of sexy photographs from underwear or swimwear advertisements.

Video Script Go to page 131 in this Instructor's Manual for the "Kinsey Controversy" video script and recommended video vocabulary for review.

Video Activity Go to page 202 in the student book for activities to accompany the CNN video clip.

ANSWER KEY—Chapter 12: SEX EDUCATION: HOW MUCH DO WE NEED TO KNOW?

PREVIEW (Page 148): Answers will vary.

PART I

Predict (Page 149)

1. a. Readings 1 & 2
   b. Reading 2
   c. Reading 2
   d. Readings 1 & 2
2. Answers will vary.

Reading Comprehension

Check Your Predictions (Page 152): Answers will vary.

Check the Facts (Page 153)

Reading 1

1. abortion, birth control, STDs, sexual identity, avoiding risks
2. negotiation, toleration, finding information
3. Health messages may be in contrast to TV, advertisements, movies, and music.

Reading 2

1. abstinence-plus education and abstinence-only education
2. abstinence-plus education
3. abstinence-only education
4. The European rate is less than half the American rate.
5. In Europe, teens can easily obtain contraceptives.
6. 15 percent believe that abstinence-only education is best.
7. Yes, because abstinence-only education will alienate young people and not give them access to information they need to protect themselves.
8. not giving young people the information they need to protect themselves

Analyze (Page 153): (Answers may vary.)

The abstinence-only programs do focus on reducing one specific risky behavior: having sex. But they meet none of the other criteria on the list.

Vocabulary Work

Guess Meaning from Context (Page 154)

1. *acquire:* get
   intimacy: emotional and sexual closeness
   negotiating: talking in order to reach an agreement
   reliable: dependable
   coercion: using manipulation or force to get one's way
   abortion: ending a pregnancy
   imply: to suggest only indirectly
   mature: adult, fully grown
   lesbian and gay: homosexual
   promote: to advance in rank
   intercourse: sexual intercourse
   principle: a standard, such as a guide to behavior
   STDs: sexually transmitted diseases such as syphilis and HIV-AIDS
   condoms: a covering for the male sex organ worn during sex to prevent disease or pregnancy
   abstinence: abstaining from sex, not having sexual intercourse
   prominence: popularity
   sin: an act against religious beliefs
2. *one size fits all:* The same thing works for everyone.
   flies in the face of reality: Is contrary to reality.
3. *Plus* refers to the fact that the program gives additional information.

Guess Meaning from Related Words (Page 155)

1.

Reading 1

inform / information
sex / sexual
exploit / exploitation
able / enable
different / differentiate / difference
reduce / reducing / reduction

Reading 2

monogamy / monogamous
abstain / abstinence
alienate / alienating

2. **Noun (person):**
   Noun (thing): information, sex, exploitation, difference, reduction, monogamy, abstinence
   Verb: inform, exploit, enable, differentiate, reduce / reducing, abstain, alienate / alienating
   Adjective: sexual, able, different, monogamous
   Adverb:

3. *unintended:* not intended
   unrealistic: not realistic
   unfortunately: sadly
   intimacy: emotional and sexual closeness
   information / informed: knowledge, having knowledge
   inaccurate: not accurate
   influence: affect
   include: to make something a part of something else
   intercourse: sexual intercourse
   contraception: preventing conception
   contraceptives: methods of contraception such as condoms or contraceptive medications
   contradictory: opposing

Reading Skills

Understanding Transition Words (Page 156)

- *Of course* emphasizes the idea that educators have their own beliefs.
- *In short* restates the previous idea about what sex education is.
- *Despite* contrasts the government's idea with reality.
- *As much as* contrasts the fact that teenagers are having sex with the fact that we might not like it.
- *While* contrasts the fact that European teenagers are as sexually active as American teenagers but their rate of teen pregnancies is much lower.
- *Furthermore* adds specific information about STDs.

PART II

Read It (Page 157)

1. They thought it was something married people did, but only husbands enjoyed. Nobody talked about sex.
2. He was a biologist.
3. He and his wife began by informally advising university students about sex.
4. He asked students to complete a questionnaire. He conducted interviews.
5. The results did not correspond to the myth that men only had sex with their wives.
6. They were even more upset.
7. Kinsey lost government financial support for his research.
8. Some criticize his methodology, but everyone admits that he is largely responsible for the freedom to discuss sex that exists now.

Vocabulary Work

Guess Meaning from Context (Page 159): Answers will vary.

Reading Skills

Understanding Introductory Phrases (Page 160)

1. Kinsey, who was trained as a biologist, taught at Indiana University.
2. In 1938, Kinsey, who was upset at how little young people knew about sex, asked for permission to offer a "marriage course."
3. Kinsey promised his volunteers total confidentiality to persuade people to share their deepest secrets.
4. Kinsey's work is still controversial decades after his death.

CNN Video Activities: Kinsey Controversy
Understand It (Page 202)

1. controversial
2. disputed
3. revolution
4. casual
5. average
6. fraud
7. culture
8. talk

VIDEO TRANSCRIPT—Chapter 12: KINSEY CONTROVERSY
DVD Title 13   Running time: 02:33

Video Vocabulary

blame   to say someone is responsible for something bad
cheat   to deceive
cooked books   to enter false numbers in a company's accounting records
credit   to give admiration for something well done or for a person's good qualities
disputed   to question the truth of
questionable   doubtful, uncertain
throttle   on a machine, the valve that controls fuel, air, etc.

Video Script

Reporter: Sex sells. Sex appeals. Sex is everywhere, and one person often given credit or blame for spurring the sexual revolution is Alfred Kinsey. Now a controversial new movie explores the life of this radical researcher.

Teacher Actor: Why offer a marriage course? Because society has interfered with what should be a normal biological development.

Reporter: The film looks at how in the 1940s and 50s Kinsey shocked the nation by interviewing people about sex and concluding that half of all married men cheated on their wives, half of all women had pre-marital sex, and more than a third of men had a homosexual experience. His findings are still disputed, especially by conservatives.

Robert Knight: Kinsey may have died in 1956, but his cold dead hand is still on the throttle of the sexual revolution and is still harming lives.

Reporter: Robert Knight runs the Culture and Family Institute for Concerned Women of America.

Knight: Look at how society has promoted casual sex and what the results have been. The results have been heartbreak, more disease, broken marriages . . . you name it.

Reporter: Kinsey's methods, the film admits, were questionable.

Teacher Actor: I saw this coming.

Student Actor: What are we to you, Prof? We're just lab rats? Is this just another part of the project?

Reporter: He was criticized for having sex with his own assistants and for relying on a disproportionate number of interviews with prison inmates, homosexuals, and child molesters to develop his picture of average sexual practices.

Daniel Flynn: Kinsey's work has never been duplicated before; it's never been duplicated after—and that's because his work was a fraud, based on faulty numbers and cooked books.

Reporter: But the makers of the film say all his work cannot just be thrown aside.

Bill Condon: People have tried to malign him and destroy his reputation in order to somehow prove that the science was wrong and then somehow make the last 50 years disappear.

Neeson: Sex is controversial. And always will be.

Linney: Well he changed American culture completely.

Reporter: After all, they argue, Alfred Kinsey certainly got one thing right: America was ready to talk about sex, and that conversation continues.

Tom Foreman, CNN Washington.

CHAPTER 13 — Cults: Path to God or somewhere else?
Pages 162–177

Summary The strange world of cults is revealed in Chapter 12. Reading 1A explains the differences between cults and mainstream religions, while Reading 1B says that brainwashing does not happen in cults because, contrary to popular notions, it is not really possible. Reading 2 tells the story of the Heaven's Gate cult, which used the Internet to recruit members, then convinced them to take part in a group suicide. The "cargo cults" of the South Seas are the topic of the Reading in Part II.

Audio The readings in this chapter can be heard on the *Hot Topics 3* Audio CD 3 Tracks 7-10 or Audio Tape 3 Side B.

Background The definition of a cult is somewhat foggy, ranging from Sun Myung Moon's revision of Christianity, and possible evasion of tax laws, to the Jonestown mass suicide in which more than 900 people died. Somewhere between you'll find the siege of the Branch Davidians' compound in Waco, Texas, celebrities such as Madonna studying the Kabballah, and traditional belief systems such as voodoo. It is definitely hard to pin down, but perhaps we can draw a line between those belief systems that do or do not harm the participants or others.

Teaching Note On page 171, the students will fill a chart with useful vocabulary terms. Give them a chance to use some of these words actively by asking them to write a short summary of what happened to the Heaven's Gate members along with their personal reaction to the story. Ask them to use at least eight of the vocabulary words correctly. (The CNN video clip is on the same topic.)

Internet Activity To find many sorts of general articles on cults, follow the Yahoo directory to http://dir.yahoo.com/Society_and_Culture/Religion_and_Spirituality/Cults/. Alternatively, if your students don't find it utterly distasteful, they can find out more about the cults and cultists mentioned in the chapter or in the *Background* section above.

Video Clip Summary Anne McDermott reports on the group suicide of the members of the Heaven's Gate cult. The clip gives background information about the cult, and there is a statement from actress Nichelle Nichols, whose brother was one of the cult members. Images of the covered bodies inside the house and being removed from the house are disturbing.

Video Script Go to page 135 in this Instructor's Manual for the "One Cult's Trip: To heaven?" video script and recommended video vocabulary for review.

Video Activity Go to page 203 in the student book for activities to accompany the CNN video clip.

ANSWER KEY—Chapter 13: Cults: Path to God or somewhere else?

PREVIEW
1. Answers are on page 163. (Other answers will vary.)

PART I

Predict (Page 163)
1. a. Reading 2
   b. Reading 1A
   c. Reading 1B
2. a. none of them
   b. all of them
3. Answers will vary.

Reading Comprehension
Check Your Predictions (Page 167): Answers will vary.
Check the Facts
Reading 1A (Page 167)
1. Not Sure
2. Not Sure
3. False
4. True
5. True

Reading 1B (Page 168)

1. He's a professor of psychology at Stanford.
2. He does not, because government agencies have not been able to develop brainwashing techniques and because cult recruitment programs are relatively ineffective.
3. Cults offer simple solutions to the problems we face daily.
4. the CIA and the former KGB
5. drugs and electroshock
6. no
7. 90 percent of people persuaded to attend an overnight program had no further involvement. Only 8 percent joined the cult for more than one week.

Reading 2 (Page 168)

1. to leave their earthly bodies and join a spacecraft
2. Marshall Applewhite and Bonnie Lu Nettles
3. that they were space aliens in contact with aliens from a heavenly kingdom
4. to recruit members
5. Some worried that cultists had found an effective new way to spread their messages.
6. No, because there are simply too many websites.
7. It refers to a castaway who puts a plea for help in a bottle and throws it into the ocean hoping that someone will find it and help the castaway.

Analyze (Page 168): (Answers may vary.)

1. Religious people would say that cult leaders invent their belief system whereas the mainstream religion's beliefs come from a divine source. Nonreligious people might say that there are not a lot of differences since the list of points in Reading 1A applies to some extent to any religion.
2. Heaven's Gate encouraged excessive devotion to an idea, and the members certainly sacrificed their own welfare when they committed suicide.
3. The public thinks that cults exercise mind control over their members, but Zimbardo says there is no such thing.

Vocabulary Work

Guess Meaning from Context (Page 169)

1. *heretical*: in opposition to established church doctrine
   rituals: ceremonies that mark serious or sacred events
   exploit: to treat unfairly, take advantage of
   sacrifice: loss, or giving up of something valuable, for a purpose
   welfare: one's general condition
   connotation: association
   salvation: being saved
   regimentation: control, orderliness
   illusion: something imagined
   suicide: the taking of one's own life
   lethal: deadly
   cocktail: mixed drink
   phenobarbital: a sedative drug
   astrology: belief in the influence of stars, planets, sun, moon, etc. on human affairs and events
2. The KGB was a police organization in the former Soviet Union, and the CIA is the Central Intelligence Agency in the United States.

Guess Meaning from Related Words (Page 170)

1. *brainwash*: control someone's mind
   everyday: common, ordinary
   electroshock: a shock using electrical current
   turnover: change in personnel
   drown out: cover, make less noticeable
   spokesperson: representative who speaks for a group
2.

Reading 1A

suspect / suspicion
accept / acceptance
oppose / opposition
abuse / abusive
manipulate / manipulative
excess / excessive
dedicate / dedication
persuade / persuasion

Reading 1B

intense / intensely
increase / increasingly
relative / relatively

Reading 2

earth / earthly
dead / deadly
cult / cultist

3.

Noun (person): suspect, relative, cultist

Noun (thing): suspicion, acceptance, opposition, abuse, excess, dedication, persuasion, increase, earth, cult

Verb: suspect, accept, oppose, abuse, manipulate, dedicate, persuade, increase

Adjective: abusive, manipulative, excessive, intense, relative, earthly, dead / deadly

Adverb: intensely, increasingly, relatively

4. *astrology:* belief in the influence of stars, planets, sun, moon, etc. on human affairs and events
infrequently: not frequently
ineffective: not effective
unethically: not ethically
unusual: not usual
unlimited: not limited
unsuccessful: not successful
uneducated: not educated
unreasonable: not reasonable

Reading Skills

Understanding Appositives (Page 172)

- Philip Zimbardo, professor of psychology at Stanford . . .
- Hale-Bopp, an unusually bright comet
- Bonnie Lu Nettles, who died in 1985
- post office worker and Internet addict Yvonne McCurdy Hill
- Karen Coyle, a spokesperson for Computer Users for Social Responsibility

PART II

Read It (Page 172)

1. They began in the mid-1800s, but became more common during and after WWII on islands in the South Pacific.
2. WW II brought soldiers and large amounts of cargo to the South Pacific islands.
3. The soldiers left and no new cargo arrived. The tribes started cults in efforts to make the cargo reappear.
4. They believed that a mighty god would come from the air and the sea.
5. The islanders' belief in the legend was strengthened.
6. They tried to make the god John Frum come down from the volcano through rituals.

Vocabulary Work

Guess Words from Context (Page 174): Answers will vary.

Reading Skills

Identifying Cohesive Elements (Page 175)

1. goods or cargo
2. the soldiers
3. foreigners / goods or cargo
4. headphones
5. the John Frum cult
6. John Frum
7. islanders / John Frum

Understanding Elision (Page 176)

1. they
2. they were
3. who are
4. of the elders

CNN Video Activities: One Cult's Trip: To heaven?

Understand It (Page 203)

1. The Heaven's Gate founders were Do (Marshall Applewhite) and Ti.
2. Members were forbidden alcohol, tobacco, and sex.
3. They thought they would get to heaven in a spaceship.
4. She acted in Star Trek.
5. Some of the cult members wrote a screenplay.
6. Three years after the interview the followers of Heaven's Gate took their lives.
7. Thirty-nine members died.
8. Yes, the leader of Heaven's Gate also committed suicide.

Hot Topics 3 • Chapter 13

VIDEO TRANSCRIPT—Chapter 13: *One Cult's Trip: To heaven?*
DVD Title 14   Running time: 02:50

Video Vocabulary

odor a smell or scent, usually an unpleasant one
restrictions rules that limit something
screenplay the script for a movie
shed to get rid of something unwanted

Video Script

Reporter: The bodies have been removed. The autopsies are under way, and the families were being notified even as investigators were removing files and computers, any kind of evidence they think will help them figure out why 39 people killed themselves here. Robert Brunk was the first deputy on the scene and knew immediately it would be bad.

Robert Brunk: When I opened up the door, I noticed an <u>odor</u> that in my past experience has been associated with death.

Reporter: Later he was joined by his partner, Laura Gacek.

Laura Gacek: One of the most bizarre things you'd ever expect to see.

Reporter: The dead were all members of a cult called Heaven's Gate, and this was the leader of Heaven's Gate.

Do: I'm Do.

Reporter: Do, born Marshall Applewhite, co-founded the Heaven's Gate cult back in the seventies with this woman, who was called Ti. She died more than a decade ago. Applewhite made this informational tape in 1992, and in it, he said members were forbidden alcohol, tobacco, sex. In fact, according to the medical examiner, some of the dead men had been castrated, though apparently, the operations were not recent. And there were other <u>restrictions</u> placed on cult members.

Woman: We have not had contact with him in over 20 years, because part of their belief was to cut off ties with family and friends.

Reporter: But Applewhite, or Do, said Heaven's Gate was not necessarily boring.

Do: If we hadn't had a lot of fun, we would have lost our marbles even more than we thought we had already lost our marbles.

Reporter: Their goal was clear: to <u>shed</u> their human containers, their bodies, to go to heaven on a spaceship. In an odd footnote, one of the dead has been identified as the brother of actress Nichelle Nichols, the actress who played Lieutenant Uhura in the Star Trek television series, much of it set on a spaceship.

Nichelle Nichols: My brother was a highly intelligent and a beautifully gentle man. He made his choices, and we respect those choices.

Reporter: Spaceships and other elements of science fiction were featured in a <u>screenplay</u> written by some of the members of the cult. An established screenwriter, who was not a cult member, was asked to polish the work.

Screenwriter: The script opens with a series of vignettes, about 25, 30 vignettes of visitations, abductions, of this higher source that they believed in monitoring the Earth.

Reporter: Meanwhile a man who belonged to Heaven's Gate in 1994 talked about the upcoming transformation in a television interview.

Man: We just have no way of knowing when it's going to happen, but we do feel it's going to be soon, whether it's in months or a couple of years.

Reporter: It would be 3 years after that interview, when 39 members of Heaven's Gate took their own lives. Among the dead, their leader Do.

Anne McDermott, CNN Los Angeles.

CHAPTER 14 — Strange Brains: Unlocking the Secrets

Pages 178–190

Summary Chapter 14 examines our heads, and finds some unusual things! Reading 1 describes the neurological condition called "synesthesia," in which people's senses combine to produce colors that have certain smells or music that has an appearance. Reading 2 reports on research showing that temporal lobe epilepsy may lead to religious visions. The reading in Part II and the CNN video clip are both on the topic of Munchausen Syndrome by Proxy, in which a parent or caregiver's pathological need for attention endangers the health and safety of children.

Audio The readings in this chapter can be heard on the *Hot Topics 3* Audio CD 3 Tracks 11–13 or Audio Tape 3 Side B.

Background Sean Penn, starring as a heroic single father with autism in the popular movie *I Am Sam*, represents a shift in our thinking about mental illness. Penn's character is a highly functioning individual with a mental problem who is not shut away from society, but instead works and lives with people of all ability levels. When he faces problems, he finds support that allows him to continue to be the devoted father that he is. What has changed? Mental illnesses are coming out into the open as topics that can be discussed, not as secrets to be ashamed of.

Teaching Note Let your class explore the idea that we are all born synesthetes. Find an evocative piece of music without lyrics, perhaps classical music. Provide the students with art supplies such as modeling clay, pastels, colored markers, or even pencils. Encourage the students to relax and have fun as they listen to the piece of music and draw, paint, or sculpt anything that comes into their minds. Afterwards, have the students share their art with their classmates and explain what they experienced when they heard the music.

Internet Activity The Mayo Clinic provides an online glossary of terms related to mental illness at this site: http://www.mayoclinic.com. The definitions are clear and easy to read. Invite the students to skim the list to find out about other mental disorders they have heard about or are interested in.

CNN Video Clip Summary Reporter Don Knapp looks at two cases of Munchausen Syndrome by Proxy, in which caregivers intentionally make children ill. An attorney explains why someone might do this, and a psychologist says that the syndrome is not as rare as one might think.

Video Script Go to page 139 in this Instructor's Manual for the "Mother's Dangerous Love" video script and recommended video vocabulary for review.

Video Activity Go to page 204 in the student book for activities to accompany the CNN video clip.

ANSWER KEY—Chapter 14: Strange Brains: Unlocking the Secrets

PREVIEW (Page 178): Answers will vary.

PART I

Predict (Page 179)

1. a. Vladimir Nabokov was a famous Russian writer.
   b. Richard Cytowic has researched and written about synesthesia.
   c. Vilayanur Ramachandran is a researcher at the University of California.
   d. Rudi Affolter is an atheist with temporal lobe epilepsy who had a vision which convinced him he had gone to hell.
   e. Gregory Holmes is an American neurologist who studied the life of Ellen G. White.
   f. Ellen G. White was the founder of the Seventh-Day Adventist movement.
   g. Daniel Giang is a neurologist and a member of the Seventh-Day Adventist church.

Reading Comprehension

Check Your Predictions (Page 182): Answers will vary.

Check the Facts

Reading 1 (Page 182)

1. Synesthesia is an automatic physical experience in which one sense sets off a perception in a different sense or senses.
2. four

3. women
4. visions
5. no

Reading 2 (Page 183)

1. in the brain
2. No, he is an atheist.
3. He had a vision which convinced him he had gone to hell.
4. He measured his patients' galvanic skin response when they were shown religious images.
5. because she developed traits associated with epilepsy after a blow to the head
6. No, because the visions began many years after the head injury, and her visions lasted a long time.

Analyze (Page 183): (Answers may vary.)

1. Temporal lobe epilepsy probably has a more negative effect because it causes seizures. Many people could easily live with synesthesia, and it doesn't pose any health threats.
2. In Reading 1, Cytowic's belief that we are all born synesthetes is unproven, while the fact that synesthetic perceptions are constant over time is proven. In Reading 2, Holmes' theory that Ellen G. White had temporal lobe epilepsy is controversial, while the fact that epileptics have a strong physical reaction to religious images is proven.

Vocabulary Work

Guess Meaning from Context (Page 183)

neurologist: brain doctor
automatic: working by itself
sets off: triggers
phenomenon: event, situation
consistent: stays the same
atheist: a person who does not believe in God
galvanic skin response: the response that a lie detector measures
circuits: electrical networks
neural: having to do with the brain
prone: tending to
founder: a creator of something
thriving: successful
blow: a hard hit
traits: characteristics
paranoia: a psychological disorder, often with delusions of persecution
seizures: a physical attack from a sickness or disease

Guess Meaning from Related Words (Page 184)

1. *mind's eye:* one's imagination
   lie detector: a machine to determine whether someone is lying
2. imagine / unimaginable
   volunteer / voluntary
   synesthesia / synesthetic / synesthete
   perceive / perception
   religious / religiosity
   humor / humorlessness
3.
Noun (person): mind's eye, lie detector, volunteer, synesthete
Noun (thing): synesthesia, perception, religiosity, humor / humorlessness
Verb: imagine, perceive
Adjective: unimaginable, synesthetic, religious, voluntary
Adverb:

4. *disorder:* a sickness or disturbance (not healthy)
   unimaginable: not imaginable

Reading Skills

Identifying Main Ideas and Supporting Details (Page 185)

1. Both articles instruct or explain. They give information without opinions.

2.

	Main Ideas	Types of Supporting Details
Reading 1	Synesthesia is an automatic physical experience in which one sense sets off a perception in a different sense or senses.	examples related to how one might perceive the color purple
	Synesthesia has a different impact on different people	statistics, example of Nabokov and quote from him, more examples of synesthetic experiences
	Synesthetic perceptions are consistent over time.	research citation and example
	Cytowic believes that we are all born synesthetes.	logic
Reading 2	Science is discovering that there are differences in the brains of very religious people and others.	example of Rudi Affolter, description of research, quotation from Dr. Ramachadran
	Scientists now believe famous religious figures in the past could also have suffered from temporal lobe epilepsy.	example of Ellen G. White
	Dr. Daniel Giang disagrees.	logic
	Science now believes the condition provides a powerful insight into revealing how the brain may influence religious experience.	This is the conclusion based on previous information in the article.

Differentiating Fact from Opinion (Page 185)

1. Cytowic believes that we are all born synesthetes.
2. (in text)
3. the second to last paragraph of Reading 2 (Dr. Daniel Giang disagrees . . .)
4. a. The statement shows the writer believes there is a scientific basis for religiosity.
   b. The writer thinks science can help explain those religious figures.
   c. Again, the writer believes there is a scientific basis for religiosity.

PART II

Read It (Page 186)

1.
- Both cared for children with complex medical problems.
- Both spent most of their time taking their girls to doctors.
- Both received high praise from the First Lady for their devotion.
- Both had a psychiatric ailment called Munchausen syndrome by proxy.

2. They manufacture their children's illnesses because of their own needs for attention and sympathy.

3. They might suffocate the child then rush her to the hospital. They might place blood in the child's urine. They might scrub the child's skin with oven cleaner to cause a rash.
4. 9 percent
5. to get attention and feel special; to have a relationship with doctors

Vocabulary Work

Guess Meaning from Context (Page 188): Answers will vary.

Reading Skills

Understanding Transition Words (Page 189)

- *First, second, third* connect the things that Bush and Eldridge had in common.
- *Yet* contrasts the praise they received with the terrible things they did because of their illness.
- *For instance* connects the examples of tests and surgeries that Jennifer underwent with the general statement that precedes them.
- *Since* connects the reason (It may take many years for doctors to realize the truth) to the effect (9 percent of the children die).

Identifying Cohesive Elements (Page 189)

1. around twenty years ago
2. the parent with MSBP / the child the parent has made sick / the origin of the problem
3. the caretakers
4. the child she has suffocated / the staff at the hospital
5. the caretaker
6. the abused child
7. no referent

CNN Video Activities: Mother's Dangerous Love
Understand It (Page 204)

1. d
2. f
3. a
4. e
5. c
6. b

VIDEO TRANSCRIPT—Chapter 14: Mother's Dangerous Love
DVD Title 15 Running time: 01:58

Video Vocabulary

lapse   to fall gradually
poster child   a person who represents an idea or cause
suspicion   the state of being suspected

Video Script

Reporter: Yvonne Eldridge stopped on her way into court to brush her disabled husband's hair. Caring for foster children while caring for an ill husband won Eldridge national acclaim in 1988 when Nancy Reagan named her Mother of the Year. But now Eldridge faces charges of deliberately harming two of the children she cared for. Prosecutors claim Munchausen Syndrome by Proxy, a psychological disorder, motivated her to sicken the children to win attention.

Kelly Hargreaves: The child would be doing fine, eating fine, suffering no respiratory problems and then, an hour after Yvonne would visit, all of a sudden this child would lapse into some serious condition.

Reporter: Attorney Kelly Hargreaves helped California take away Eldridge's foster care license in 1993. The state claimed three children died and four others became ill while in Eldridge's care. Eldridge was never charged with the deaths.

Kelly Hargreaves: She loved being in emergency rooms; she loved being at the, at the doctor's office; she liked those midnight rides to the hospital; she liked calling 911.

Reporter: About the current charges, Eldridge's attorney says she did the best job she could taking care of sick kids.

In Florida, the mother of a poster child for national healthcare reform faces charges of abusing her daughter. Police say Kathy Bush deliberately sickened nine-year-old Jennifer, who's been to the hospital 200 times, and undergone 40 surgeries. A state attorney said Friday that when Jennifer gets out of the hospital this time, she will not go home, but to a children's shelter. Kathy Bush told the court she's innocent.

Schreier: Most of the harm that comes to these children comes at the hands of doctors in hospitals under the noses of the caretakers.

Reporter: Psychiatrist Herbert Schreier says Munchausen's may be bizarre, but it's not rare. Estimates range from hundreds to thousands of cases over the past decade, often forcing doctors to balance between support for the patient, and suspicion of the parent.

Don Knapp, CNN, San Francisco.